# THE SIXTH GUN

BOOK 1: COLD DEAD FINGERS

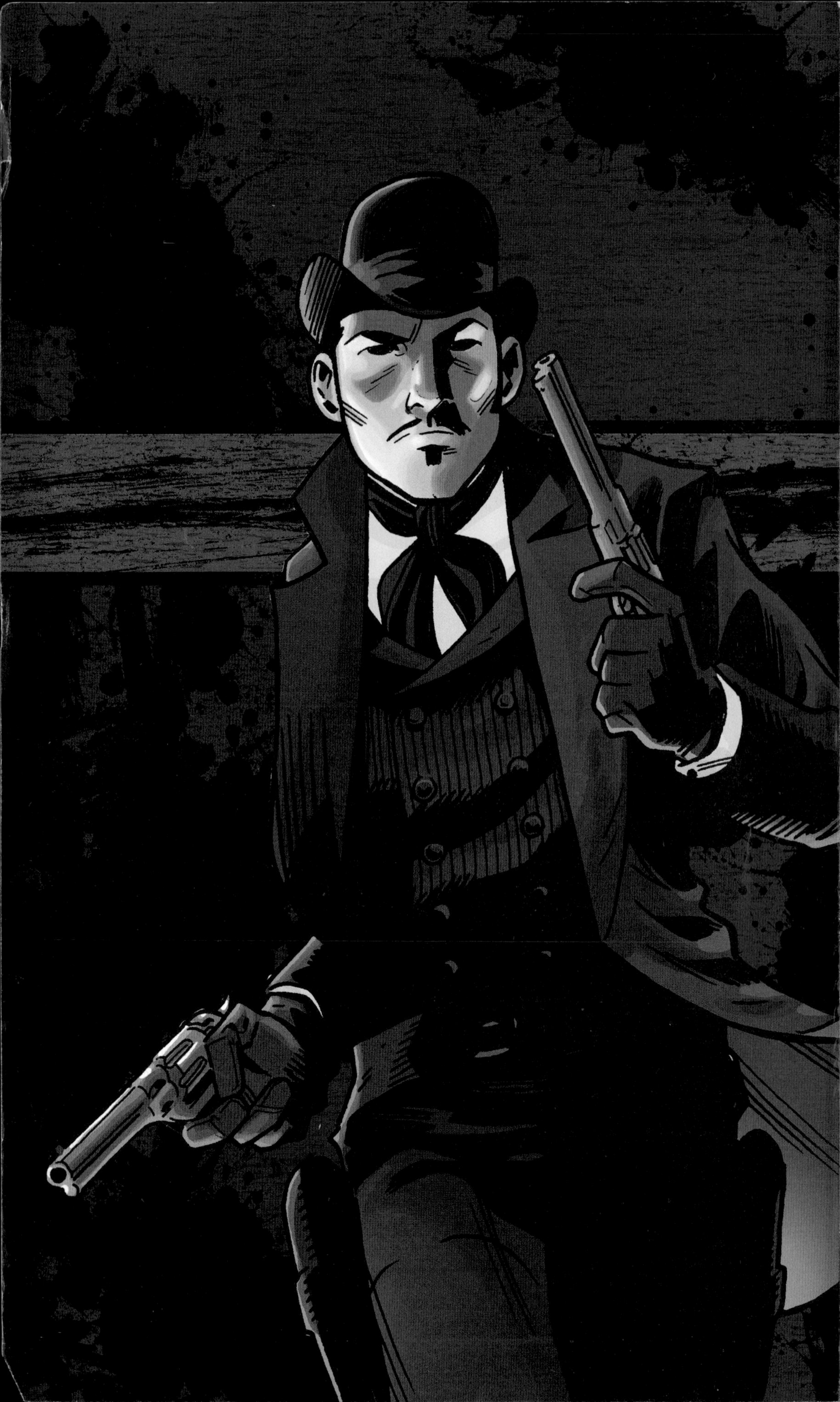

# THE SIXTH GUN

## BOOK 1: COLD DEAD FINGERS

WRITTEN BY

**CULLEN BUNN**

ILLUSTRATED & LETTERED BY

**BRIAN HURTT**

CHAPTER SIX COLORS BY

**BILL CRABTREE**

ORIGINAL SERIES EDITED BY

**JAMES LUCAS JONES** **CHARLIE CHU**

DESIGN BY

**KEITH WOOD**

COLLECTION EDITED BY

**CHARLIE CHU**

# THE SIXTH GUN™
## BY CULLEN BUNN & BRIAN HURTT

### PUBLISHED BY ONI PRESS, INC.

**JOE NOZEMACK** *publisher*

**JAMES LUCAS JONES** *editor in chief*

**CORY CASONI** *marketing director*

**KEITH WOOD** *art director*

**GEORGE ROHAC** *operations director*

**JILL BEATON** *associate editor*

**CHARLIE CHU** *associate editor*

**DOUGLAS E. SHERWOOD** *production assistant*

This volume collects issues #1-6 of the Oni Press series
*The Sixth Gun.*

ONI PRESS, INC.
1305 SE MARTIN LUTHER KING JR. BLVD.
SUITE A
PORTLAND, OR 97214
USA

onipress.com
Become our fan on Facebook: facebook.com/onipress
Follow us on Twitter: @onipress
onipress.tumblr.com

cullenbunn.com • @cullenbunn
theburttlocker.blogspot.com • @briburtt
@crabtree_bill

First edition: January 2011
ISBN: 978-1-934964-60-6

10 9 8 7 6 5 4 3

Printed in U.S.A.

# CHAPTER
# ONE

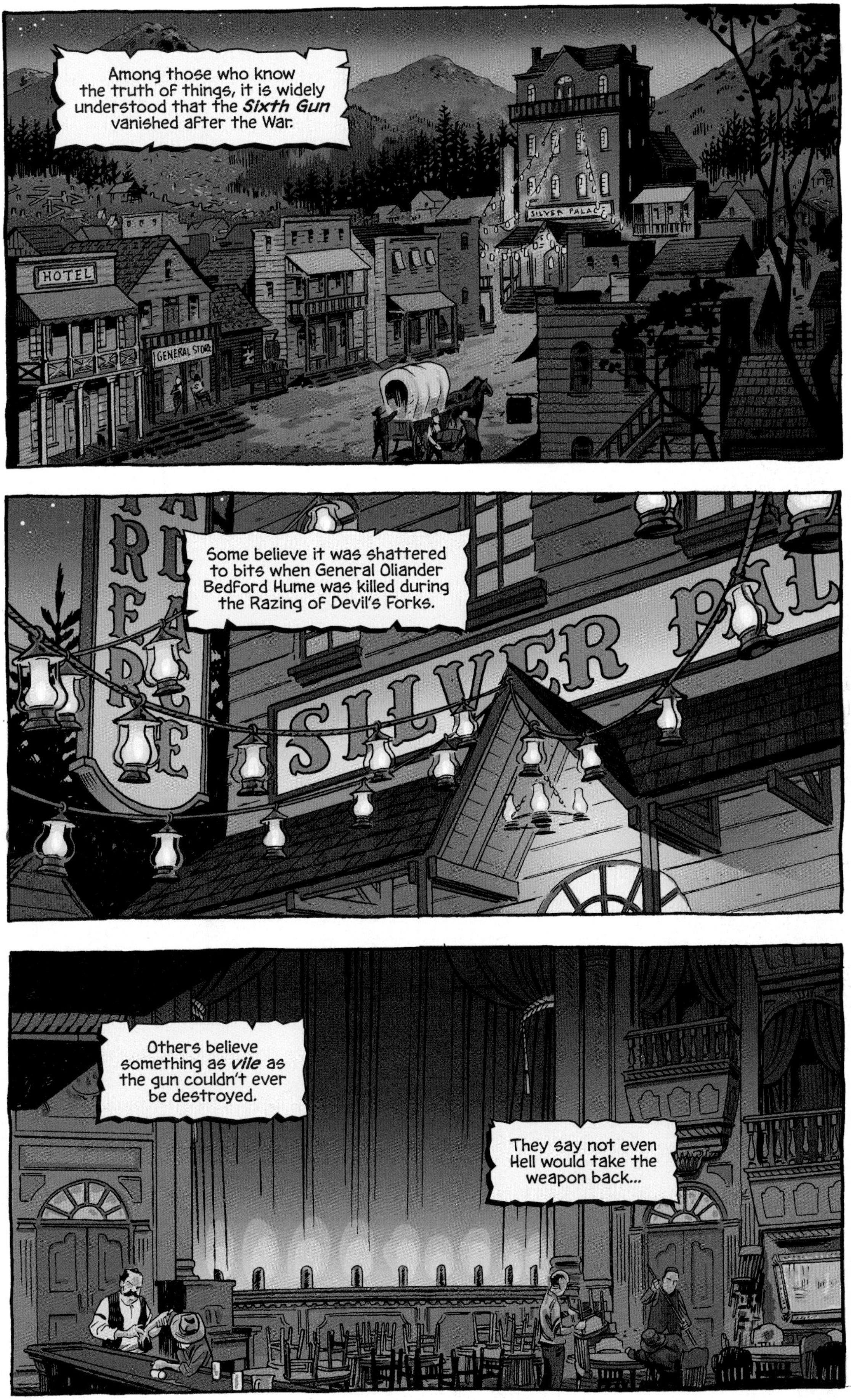
Among those who know the truth of things, it is widely understood that the *Sixth Gun* vanished after the War.
HOTEL
GENERAL STORE
SILVER PALACE
Some believe it was shattered to bits when General Oliander Bedford Hume was killed during the Razing of Devil's Forks.
SILVER PAL
Others believe something as *vile* as the gun couldn't ever be destroyed.
They say not even Hell would take the weapon back...

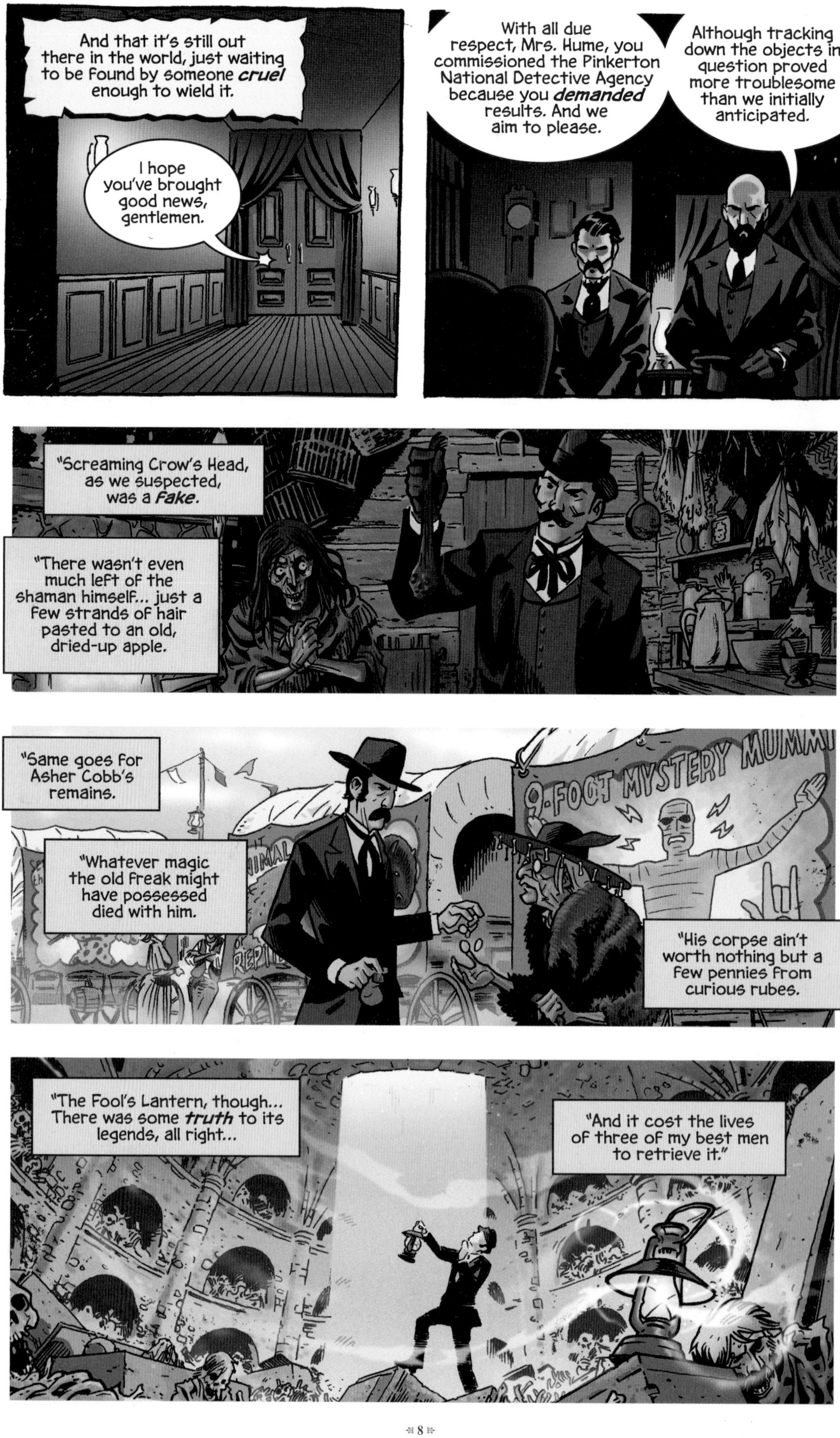
And that it's still out there in the world, just waiting to be found by someone *cruel* enough to wield it.
I hope you've brought good news, gentlemen.
With all due respect, Mrs. Hume, you commissioned the Pinkerton National Detective Agency because you *demanded* results. And we aim to please.
Although tracking down the objects in question proved more troublesome than we initially anticipated.
"Screaming Crow's Head, as we suspected, was a *fake*.
"There wasn't even much left of the shaman himself... just a few strands of hair pasted to an old, dried-up apple.
"Same goes for Asher Cobb's remains.
9-FOOT MYSTERY MUMM
"Whatever magic the old freak might have possessed died with him.
"His corpse ain't worth nothing but a few pennies from curious rubes.
"The Fool's Lantern, though... There was some *truth* to its legends, all right...
"And it cost the lives of three of my best men to retrieve it."

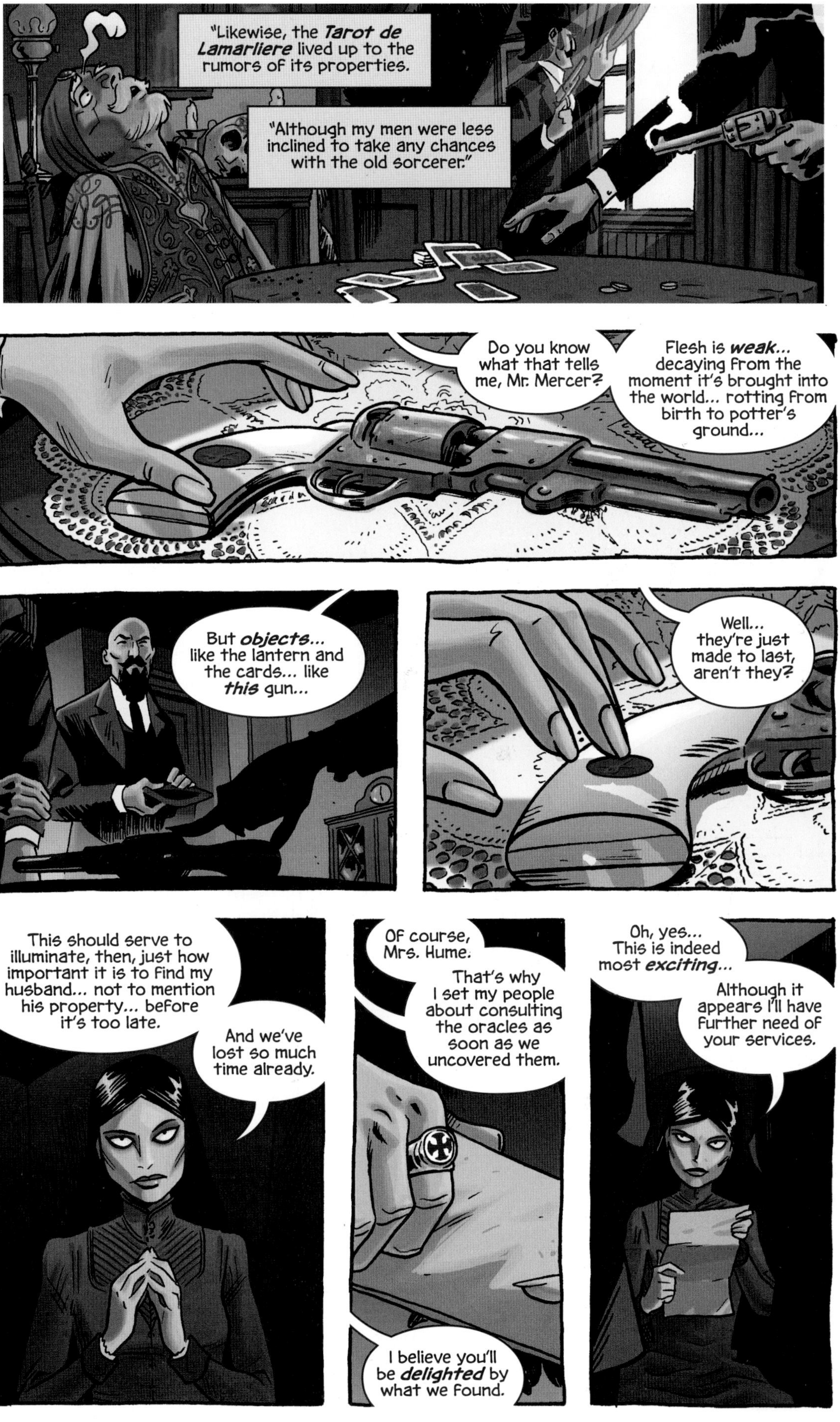
"Likewise, the Tarot de Lamarliere lived up to the rumors of its properties.
"Although my men were less inclined to take any chances with the old sorcerer."
Do you know what that tells me, Mr. Mercer?
Flesh is weak... decaying from the moment it's brought into the world... rotting from birth to potter's ground...
But objects... like the lantern and the cards... like this gun...
Well... they're just made to last, aren't they?
This should serve to illuminate, then, just how important it is to find my husband... not to mention his property... before it's too late.
And we've lost so much time already.
Of course, Mrs. Hume.
That's why I set my people about consulting the oracles as soon as we uncovered them.
I believe you'll be delighted by what we found.
Oh, yes... This is indeed most exciting...
Although it appears I'll have further need of your services.

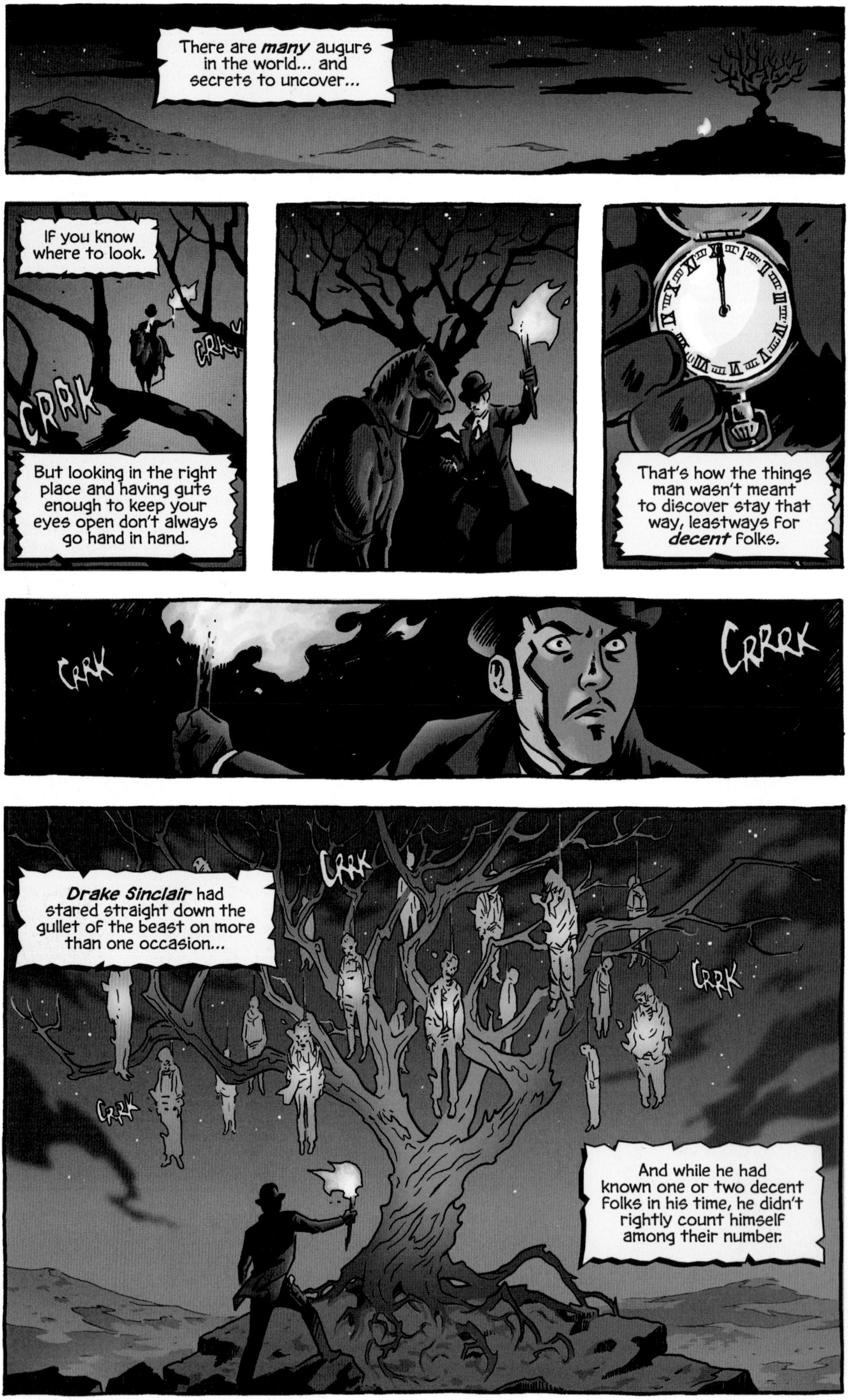
There are *many* augurs in the world... and secrets to uncover...
If you know where to look.
CRRK
CRRK
But looking in the right place and having guts enough to keep your eyes open don't always go hand in hand.
That's how the things man wasn't meant to discover stay that way, leastways for *decent* folks.
CRRK
CRRRK
Drake Sinclair had stared straight down the gullet of the beast on more than one occasion...
CRRK
CRRK
CRRK
And while he had known one or two decent folks in his time, he didn't rightly count himself among their number.

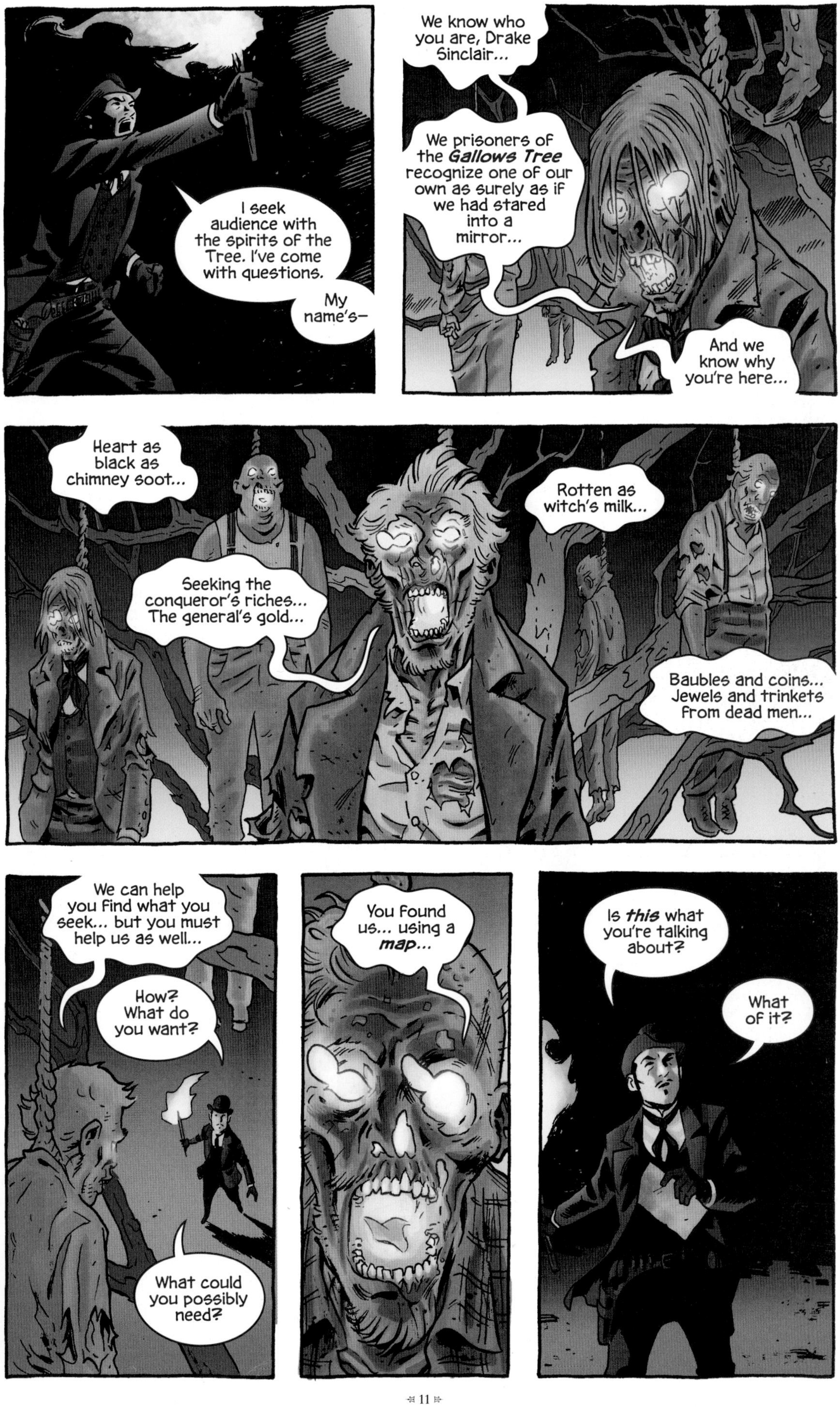
I seek audience with the spirits of the Tree. I've come with questions.
My name's—
We know who you are, Drake Sinclair...
We prisoners of the *Gallows Tree* recognize one of our own as surely as if we had stared into a mirror...
And we know why you're here...
Heart as black as chimney soot...
Seeking the conqueror's riches... The general's gold...
Rotten as witch's milk...
Baubles and coins... Jewels and trinkets from dead men...
We can help you find what you seek... but you must help us as well...
How? What do you want?
What could you possibly need?
You found us... using a *map*...
Is *this* what you're talking about?
What of it?

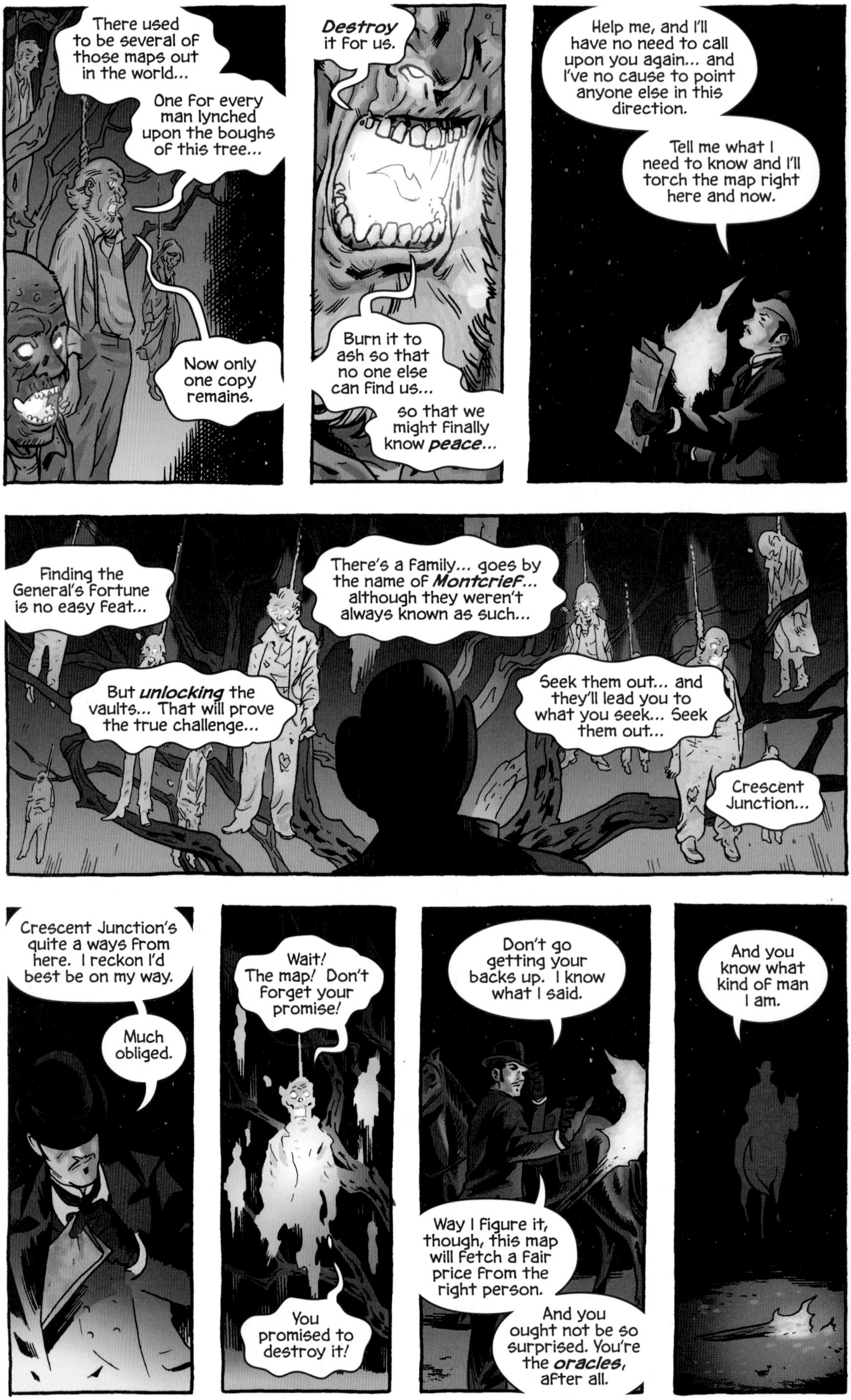

There used to be several of those maps out in the world...
One for every man lynched upon the boughs of this tree...
Now only one copy remains.
Destroy it for us.
Burn it to ash so that no one else can find us...
so that we might finally know peace...
Help me, and I'll have no need to call upon you again... and I've no cause to point anyone else in this direction.
Tell me what I need to know and I'll torch the map right here and now.
Finding the General's Fortune is no easy feat...
But unlocking the vaults... That will prove the true challenge...
There's a family... goes by the name of Montcrief... although they weren't always known as such...
Seek them out... and they'll lead you to what you seek... Seek them out...
Crescent Junction...
Crescent Junction's quite a ways from here. I reckon I'd best be on my way.
Much obliged.
Wait! The map! Don't forget your promise!
You promised to destroy it!
Don't go getting your backs up. I know what I said.
Way I figure it, though, this map will fetch a fair price from the right person.
And you ought not be so surprised. You're the oracles, after all.
And you know what kind of man I am.

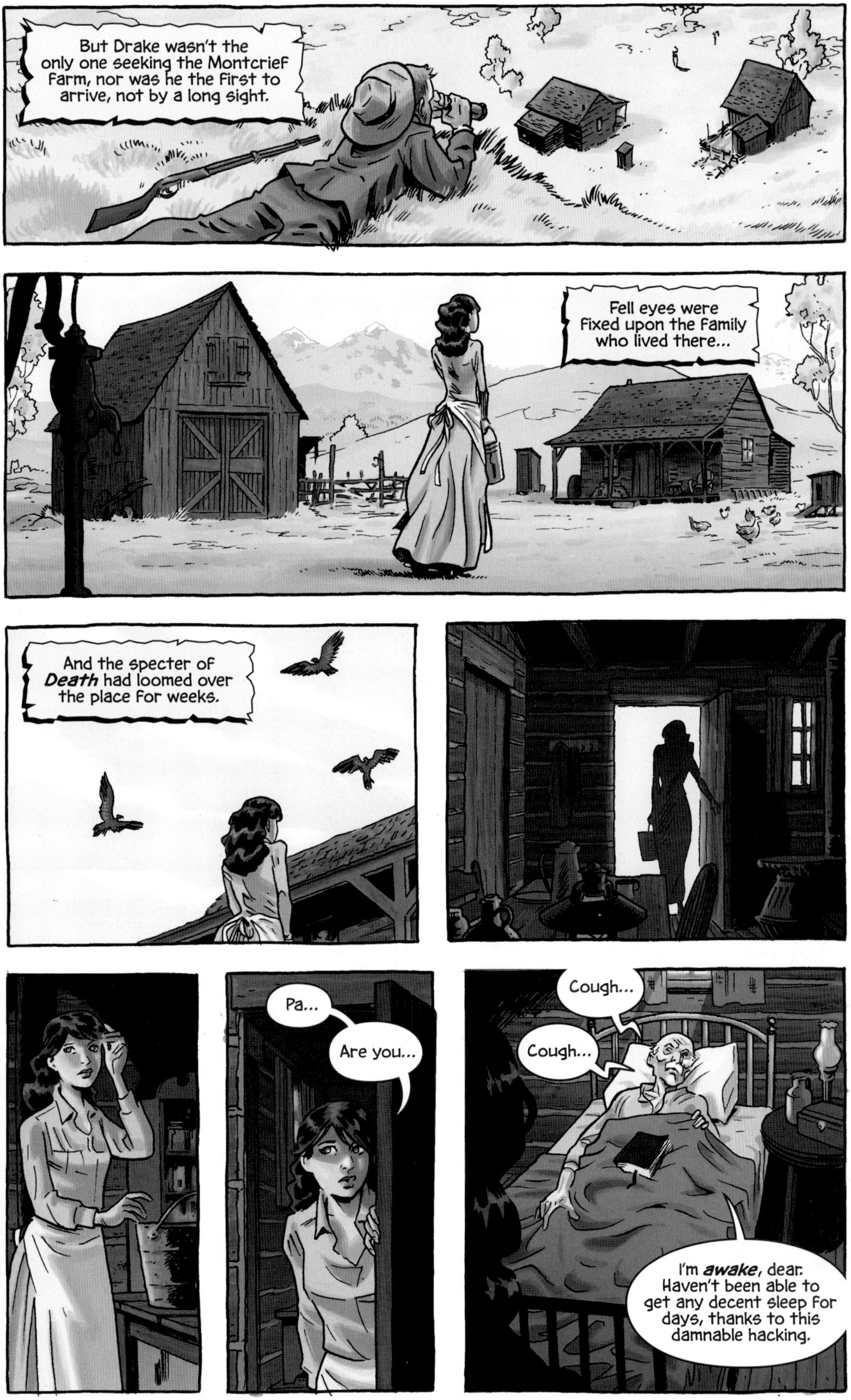
But Drake wasn't the only one seeking the Montcrief farm, nor was he the first to arrive, not by a long sight.
Fell eyes were fixed upon the family who lived there...
And the specter of *Death* had loomed over the place for weeks.
Pa...
Are you...
Cough...
Cough...
I'm ***awake***, dear. Haven't been able to get any decent sleep for days, thanks to this damnable hacking.

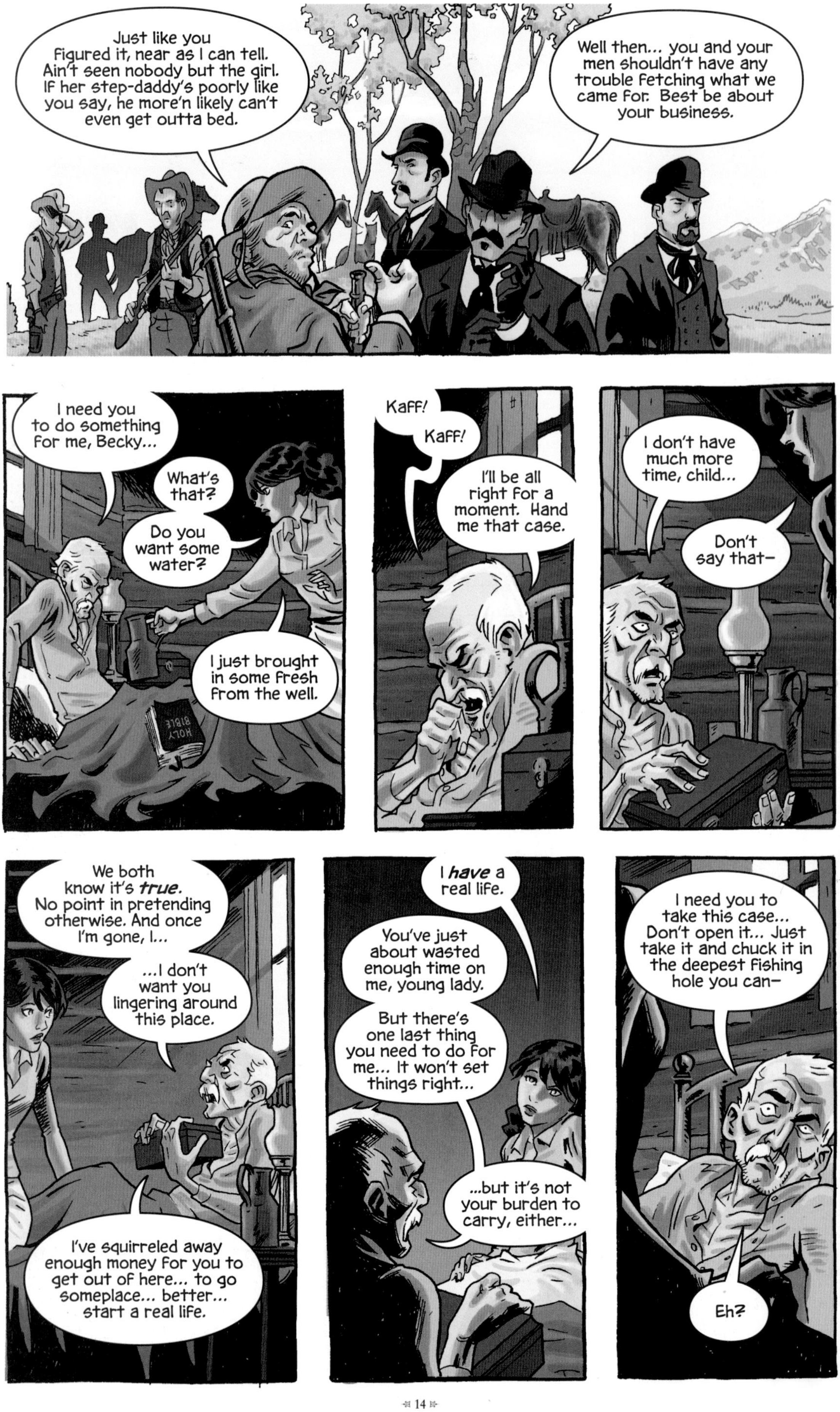
Just like you figured it, near as I can tell. Ain't seen nobody but the girl. If her step-daddy's poorly like you say, he more'n likely can't even get outta bed.
Well then... you and your men shouldn't have any trouble fetching what we came for. Best be about your business.
I need you to do something for me, Becky...
What's that?
Do you want some water?
I just brought in some fresh from the well.
HOLY BIBLE
Kaff!
Kaff!
I'll be all right for a moment. Hand me that case.
I don't have much more time, child...
Don't say that–
We both know it's *true.* No point in pretending otherwise. And once I'm gone, I...
...I don't want you lingering around this place.
I've squirreled away enough money for you to get out of here... to go someplace... better... start a real life.
I *have* a real life.
You've just about wasted enough time on me, young lady.
But there's one last thing you need to do for me... It won't set things right...
...but it's not your burden to carry, either...
I need you to take this case... Don't open it... Just take it and chuck it in the deepest fishing hole you can–
Eh?

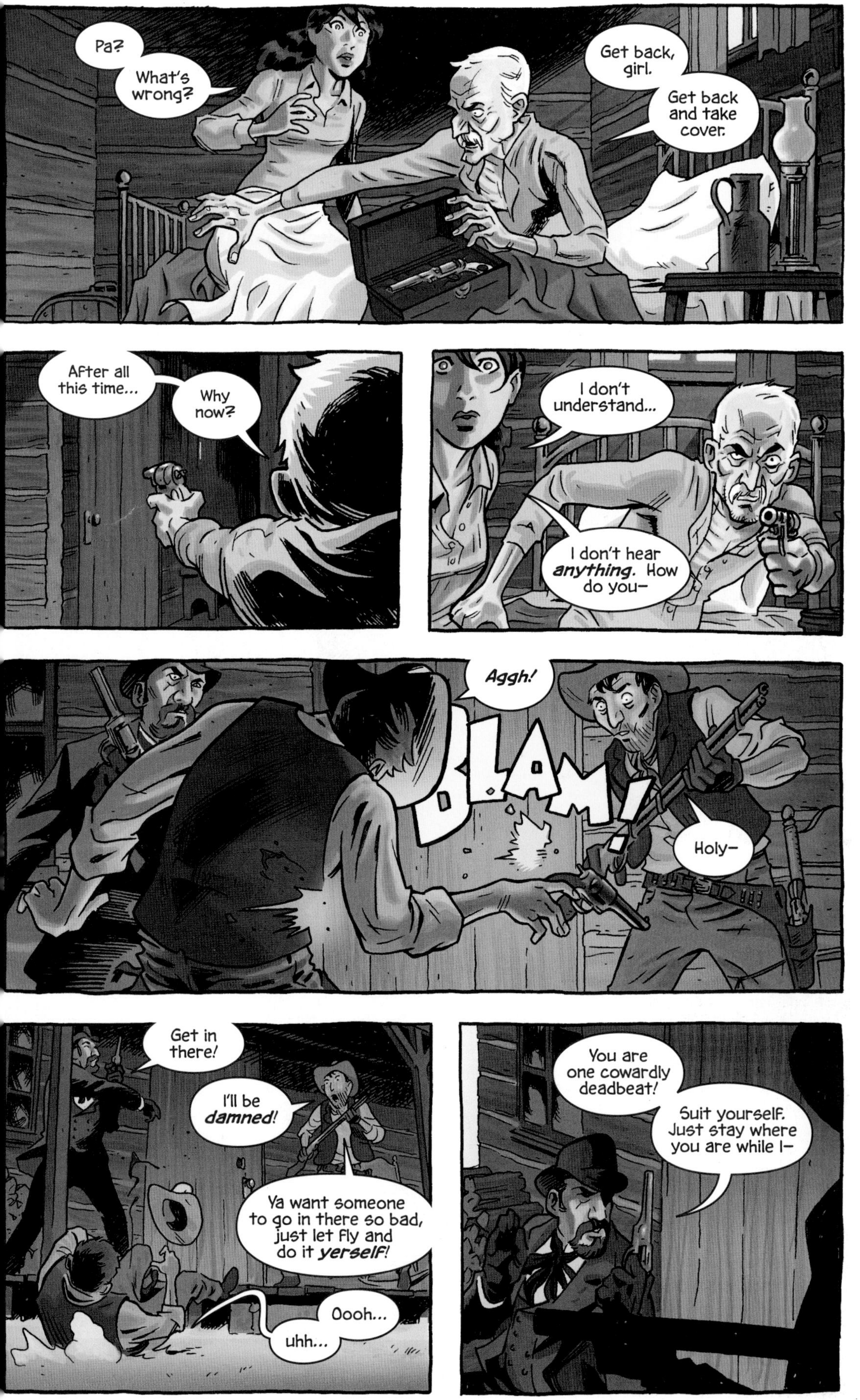
Pa?
What's wrong?
Get back, girl.
Get back and take cover.
After all this time...
Why now?
I don't understand...
I don't hear *anything*. How do you–
Aggh!
BLAM!
Holy–
Get in there!
I'll be *damned*!
Ya want someone to go in there so bad, just let fly and do it *yerself*!
Oooh...
uhh...
You are one cowardly deadbeat!
Suit yourself. Just stay where you are while I–

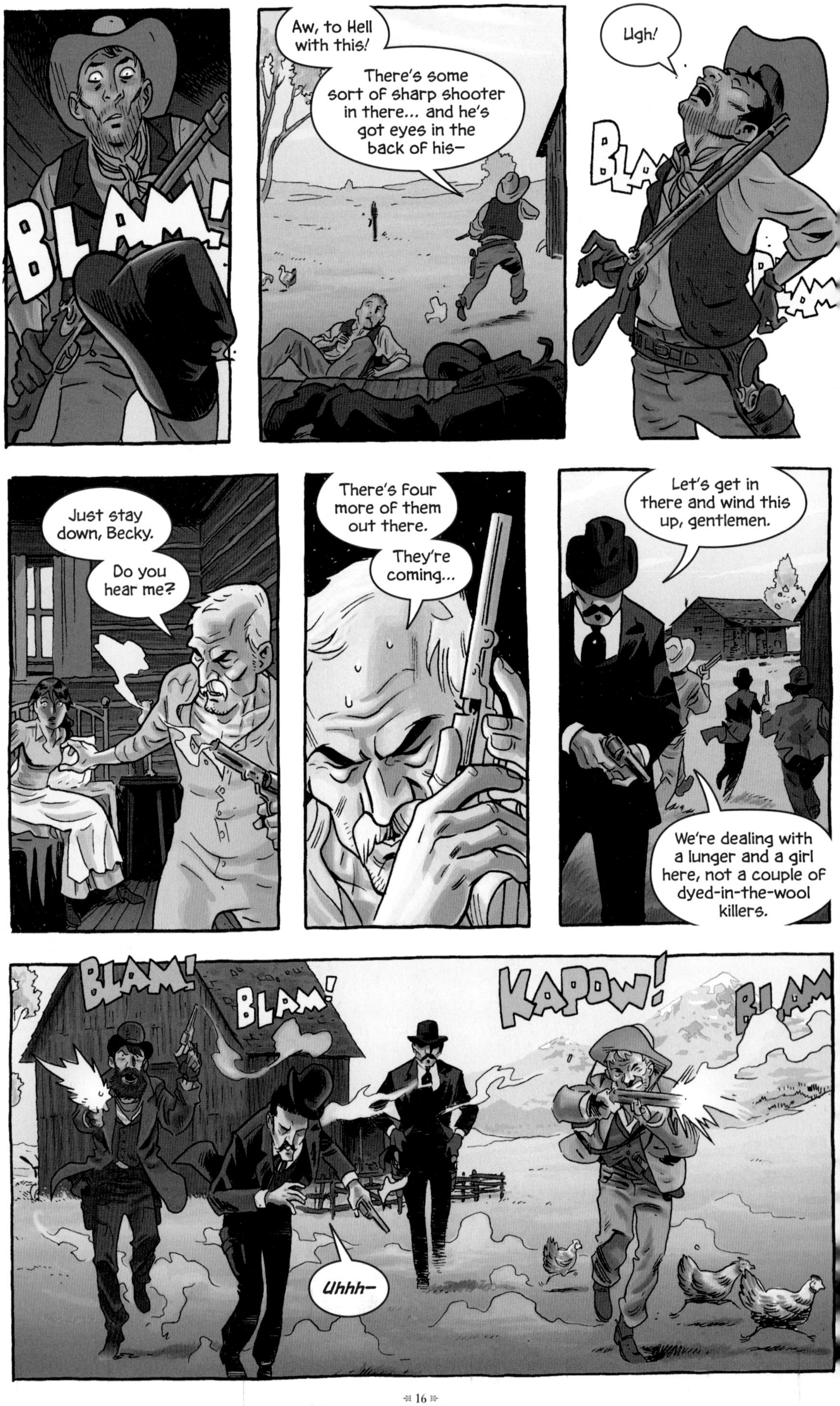
BLAM!
Aw, to Hell with this!
There's some sort of sharp shooter in there... and he's got eyes in the back of his–
Ugh!
BLAM
BLAM
Just stay down, Becky.
Do you hear me?
There's four more of them out there.
They're coming...
Let's get in there and wind this up, gentlemen.
We're dealing with a lunger and a girl here, not a couple of dyed-in-the-wool killers.
BLAM!
BLAM!
KAPOW!
Uhhh–

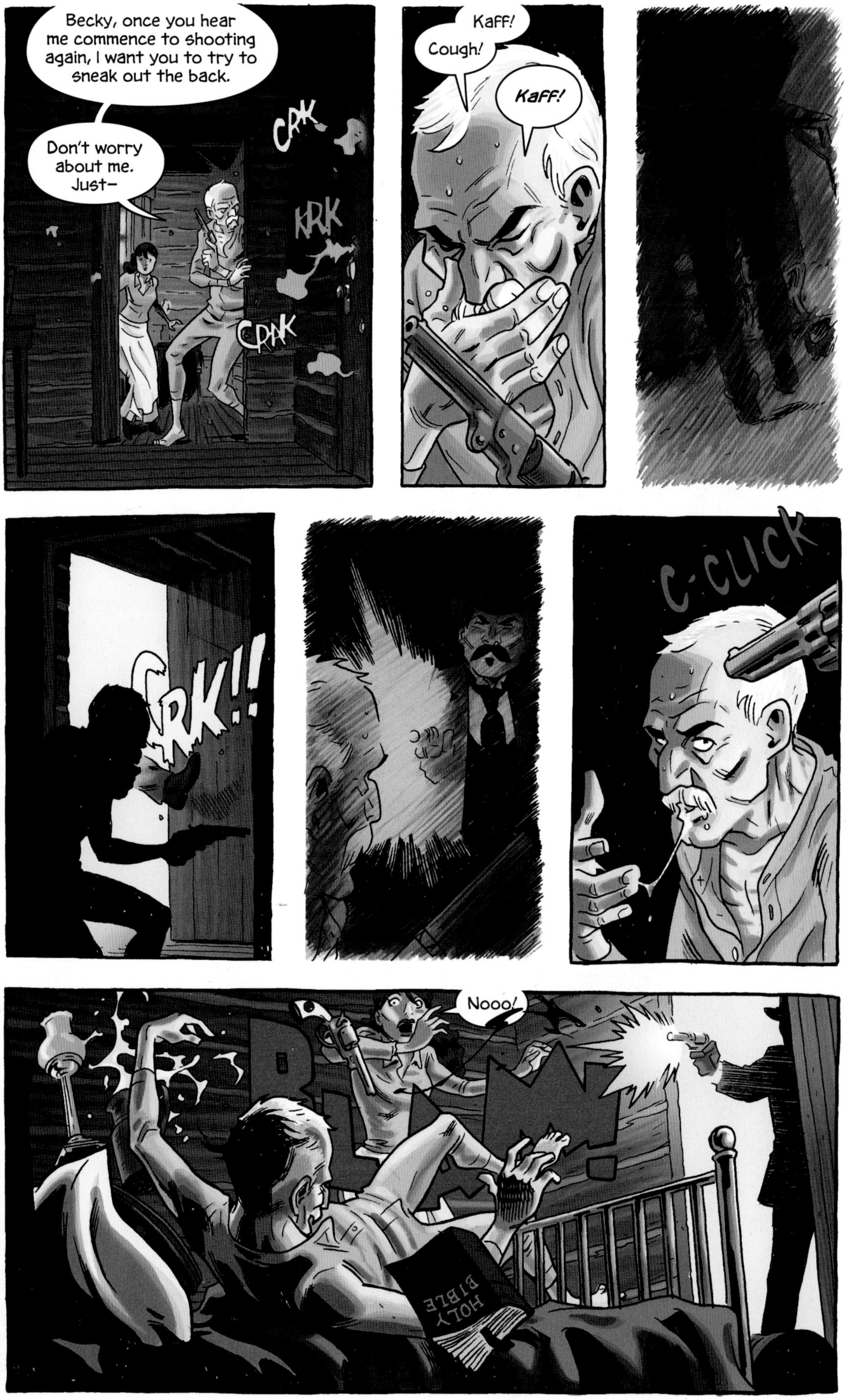
Becky, once you hear me commence to shooting again, I want you to try to sneak out the back.
Don't worry about me. Just—
CRK
KRK
CRAK
Kaff!
Cough!
Kaff!
CRK!!
C-CLICK
Nooo!
HOLY BIBLE

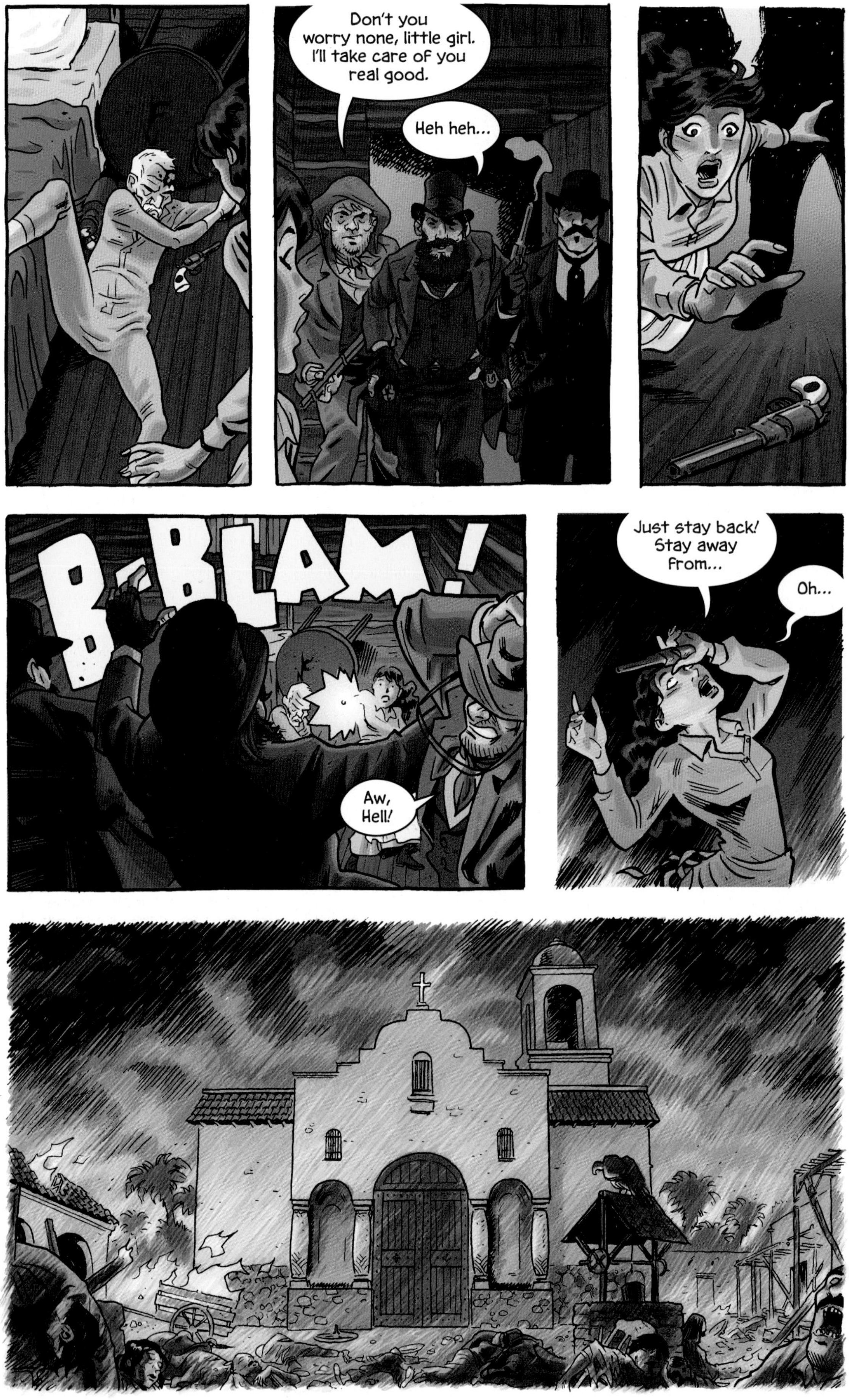
Don't you worry none, little girl. I'll take care of you real good.
Heh heh...
B-BLAM!
Aw, Hell!
Just stay back! Stay away from...
Oh...

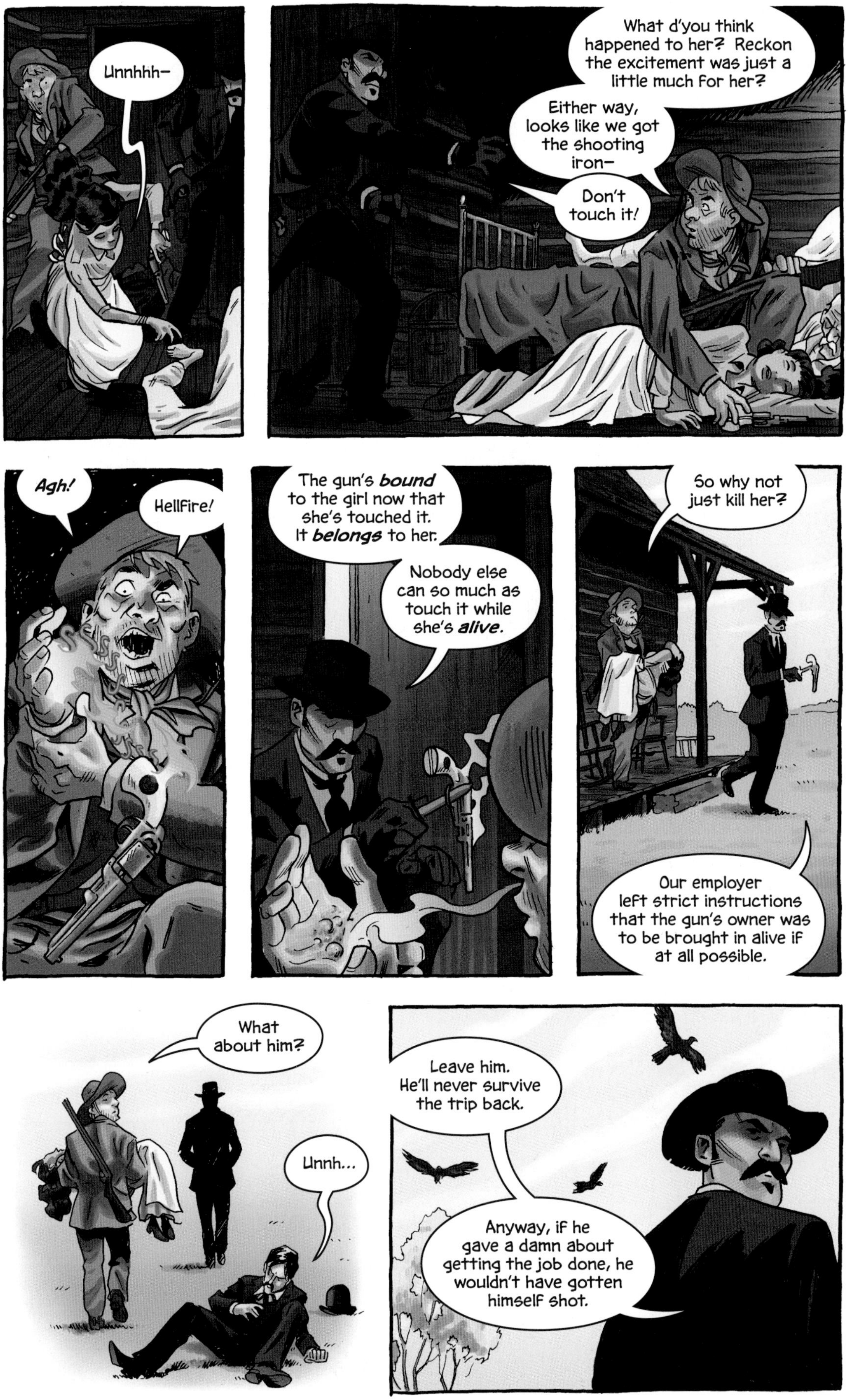
Unnhhh-
What d'you think happened to her? Reckon the excitement was just a little much for her?
Either way, looks like we got the shooting iron-
Don't touch it!
Agh!
Hellfire!
The gun's **bound** to the girl now that she's touched it. It **belongs** to her.
Nobody else can so much as touch it while she's **alive.**
So why not just kill her?
Our employer left strict instructions that the gun's owner was to be brought in alive if at all possible.
What about him?
Unnh...
Leave him. He'll never survive the trip back.
Anyway, if he gave a damn about getting the job done, he wouldn't have gotten himself shot.

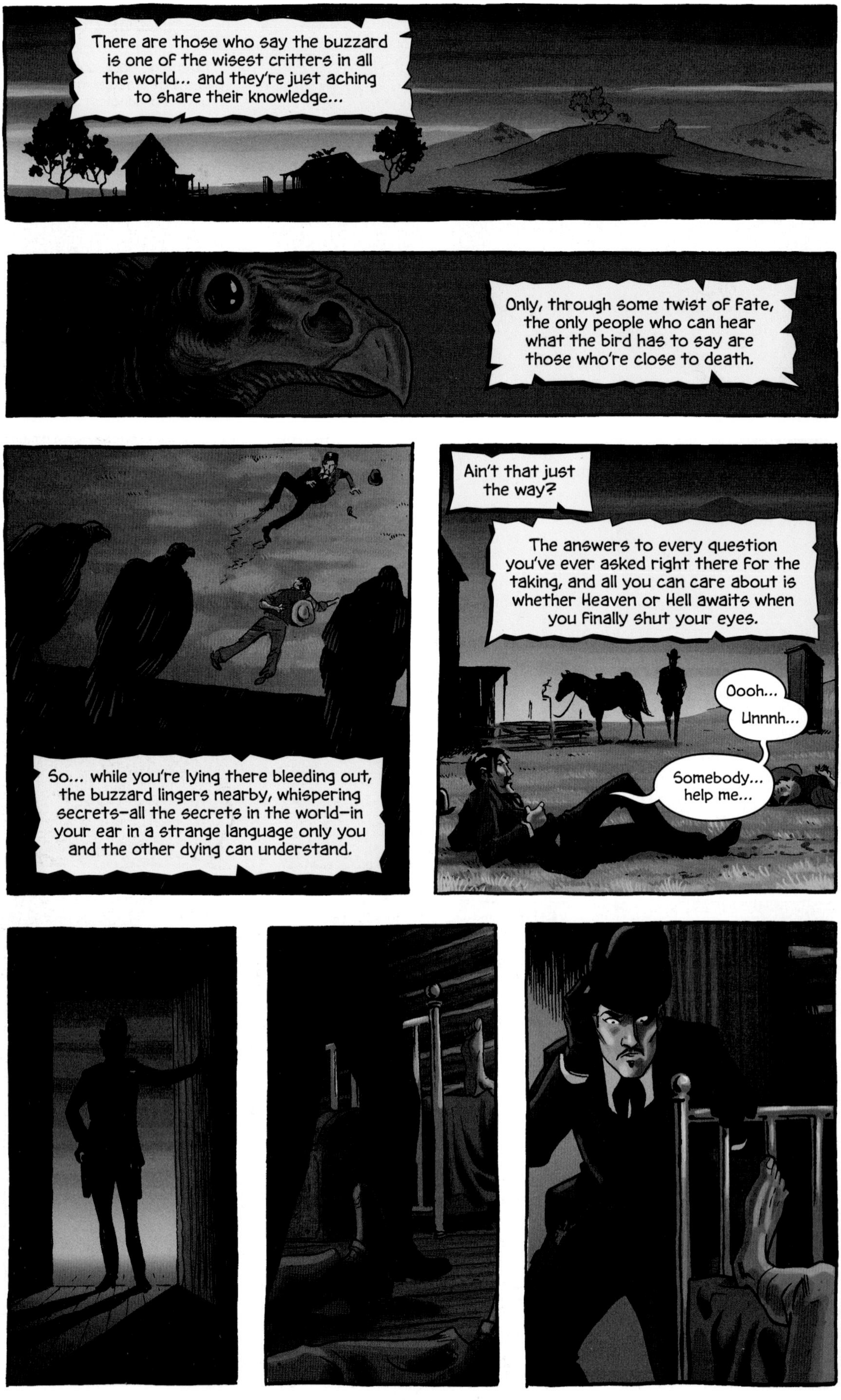
There are those who say the buzzard is one of the wisest critters in all the world... and they're just aching to share their knowledge...
Only, through some twist of fate, the only people who can hear what the bird has to say are those who're close to death.
So... while you're lying there bleeding out, the buzzard lingers nearby, whispering secrets—all the secrets in the world—in your ear in a strange language only you and the other dying can understand.
Ain't that just the way?
The answers to every question you've ever asked right there for the taking, and all you can care about is whether Heaven or Hell awaits when you finally shut your eyes.
Oooh...
Unnnh...
Somebody... help me...

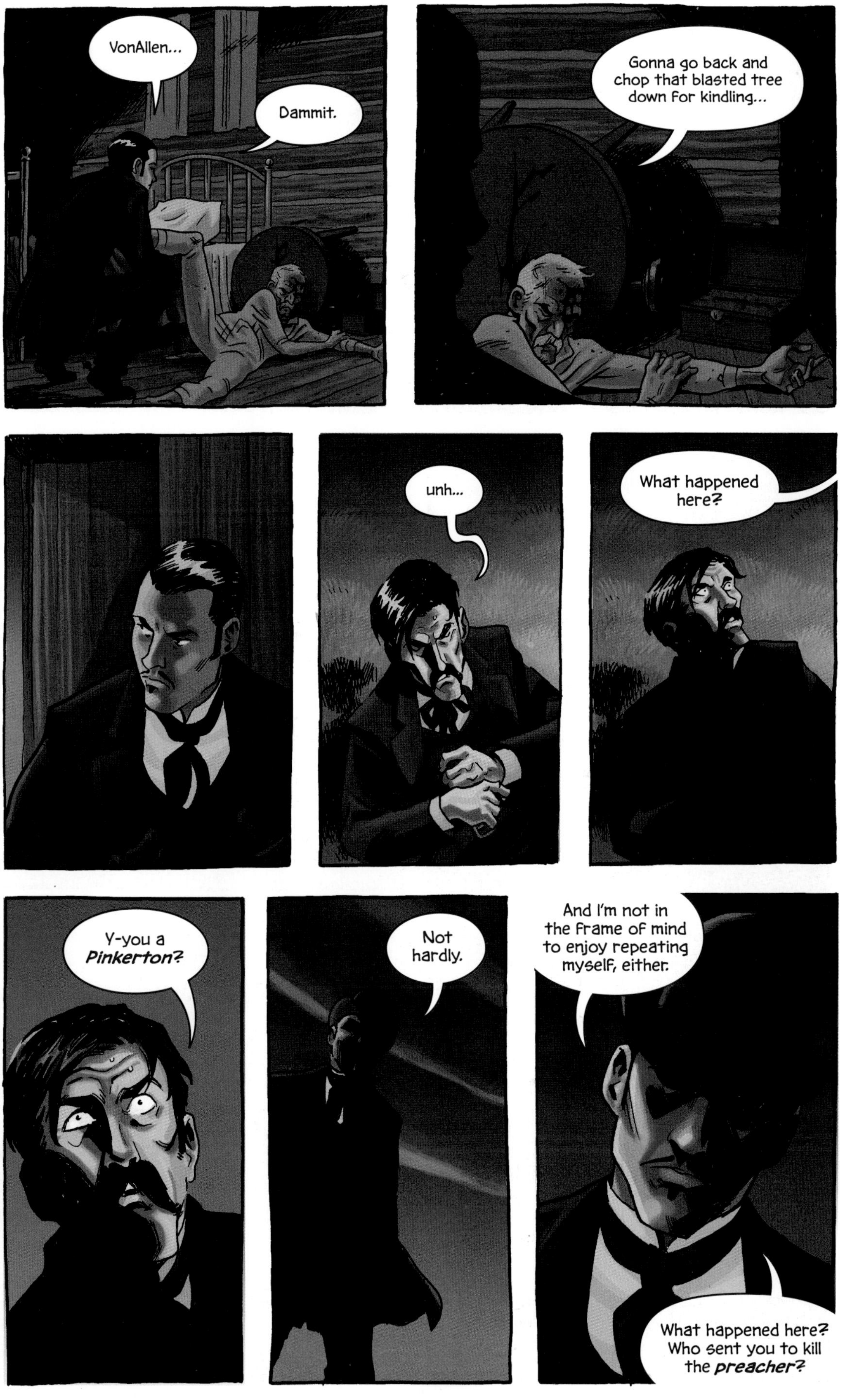
VonAllen...
Dammit.
Gonna go back and chop that blasted tree down for kindling...
unh...
What happened here?
Y-you a *Pinkerton?*
Not hardly.
And I'm not in the frame of mind to enjoy repeating myself, either.
What happened here? Who sent you to kill the *preacher?*

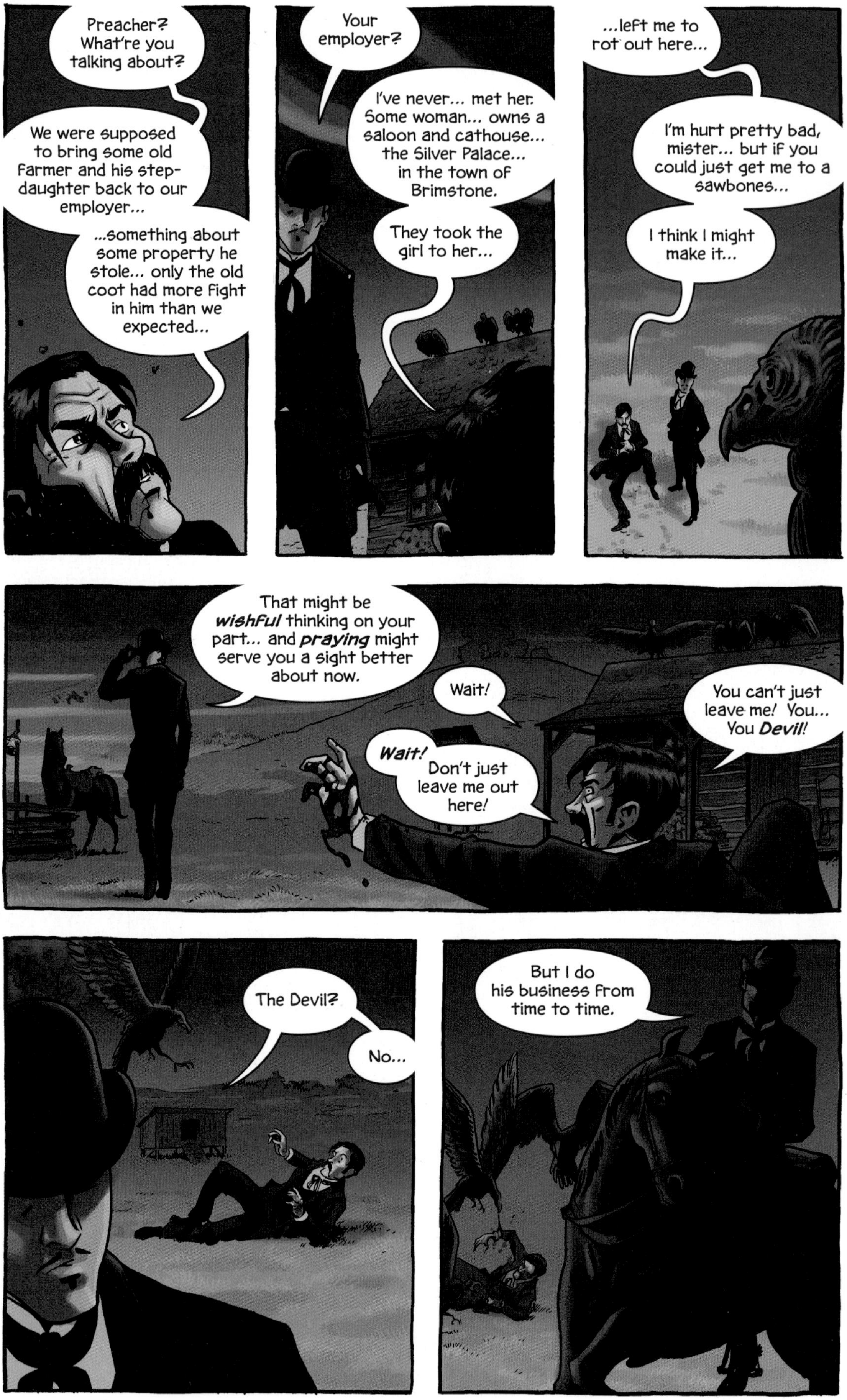
Preacher? What're you talking about?
We were supposed to bring some old farmer and his step-daughter back to our employer...
...something about some property he stole... only the old coot had more fight in him than we expected...
Your employer?
I've never... met her. Some woman... owns a saloon and cathouse... the Silver Palace... in the town of Brimstone.
They took the girl to her...
...left me to rot out here...
I'm hurt pretty bad, mister... but if you could just get me to a sawbones...
I think I might make it...
That might be *wishful* thinking on your part... and *praying* might serve you a sight better about now.
Wait!
*Wait!* Don't just leave me out here!
You can't just leave me! You... You *Devil*!
The Devil?
No...
But I do his business from time to time.

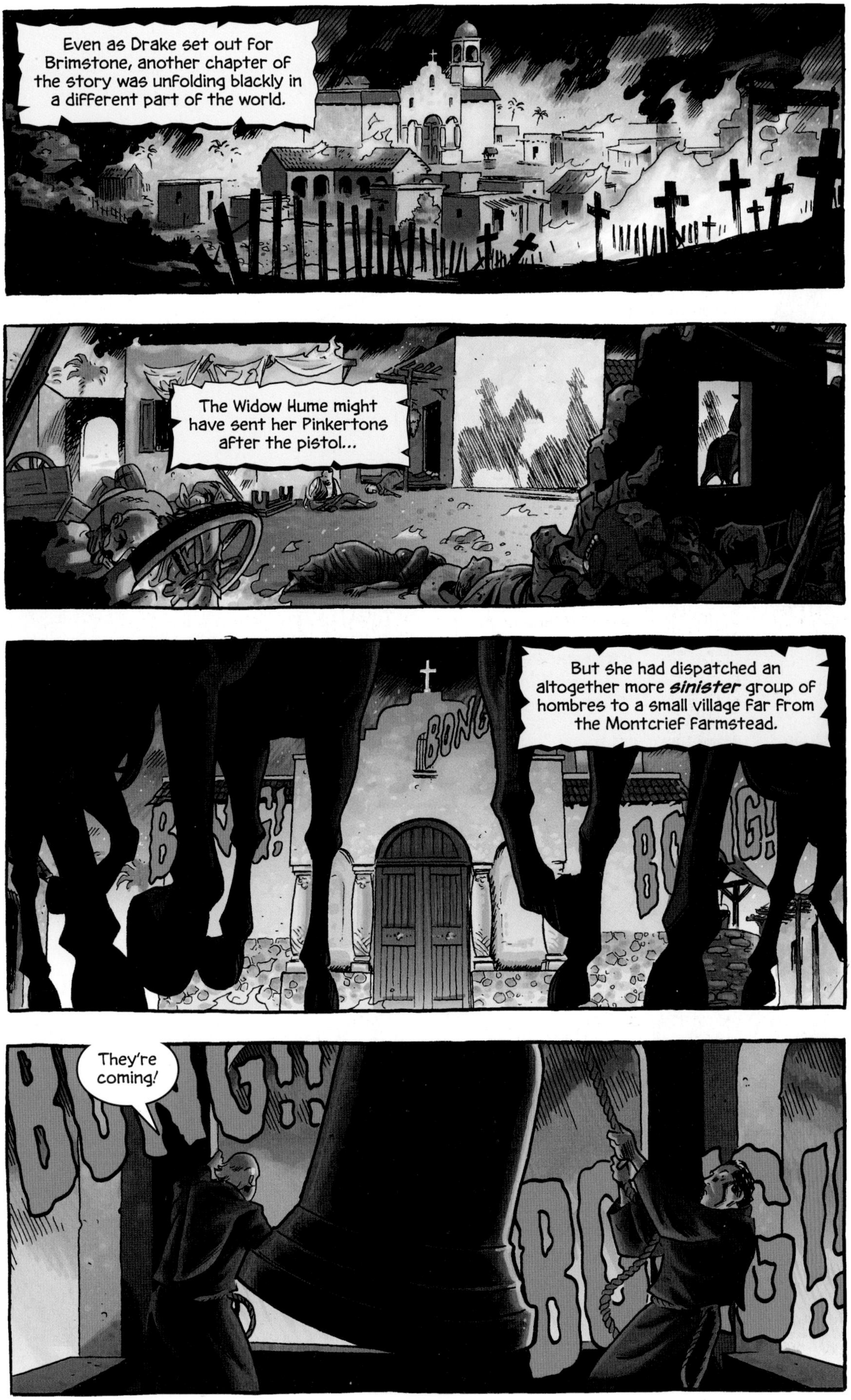

Even as Drake set out for Brimstone, another chapter of the story was unfolding blackly in a different part of the world.
The Widow Hume might have sent her Pinkertons after the pistol...
But she had dispatched an altogether more *sinister* group of hombres to a small village far from the Montcrief farmstead.
They're coming!

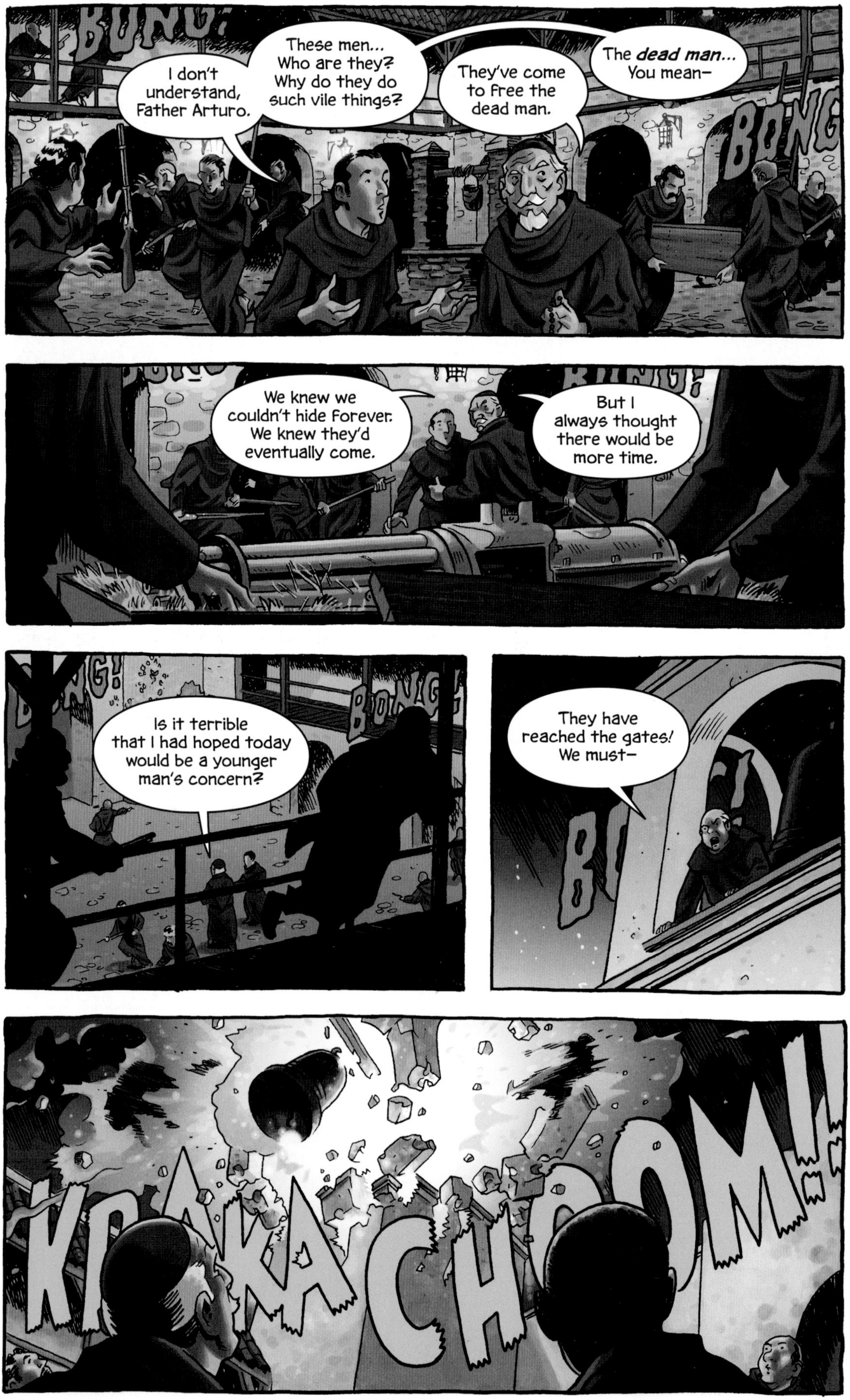
BONG!
I don't understand, Father Arturo.
These men... Who are they? Why do they do such vile things?
They've come to free the dead man.
The *dead man*... You mean–
BONG
We knew we couldn't hide forever. We knew they'd eventually come.
But I always thought there would be more time.
Is it terrible that I had hoped today would be a younger man's concern?
They have reached the gates! We must–
KRAKACHOOM!!

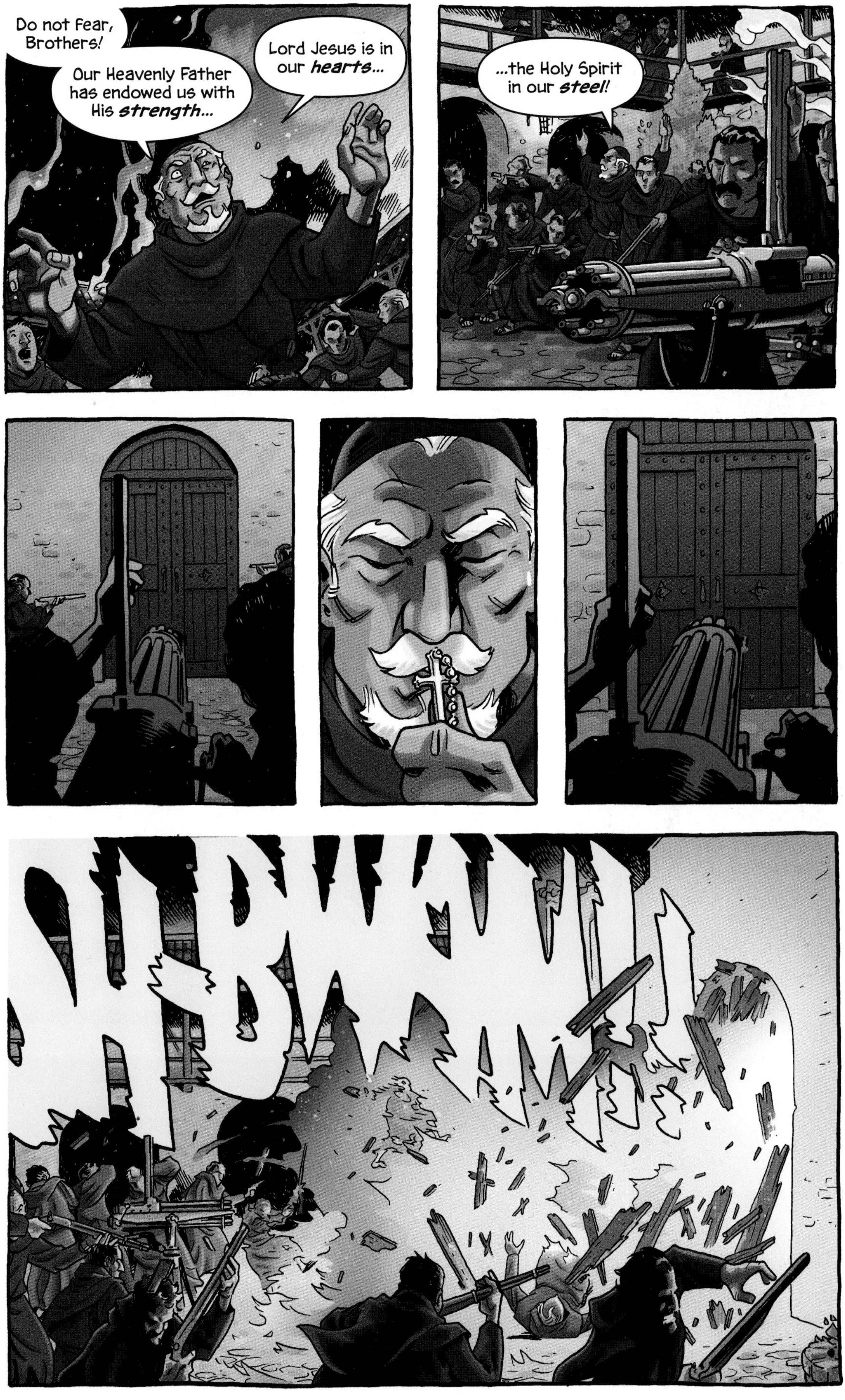
Do not fear, Brothers!
Our Heavenly Father has endowed us with His strength...
Lord Jesus is in our hearts...
...the Holy Spirit in our steel!

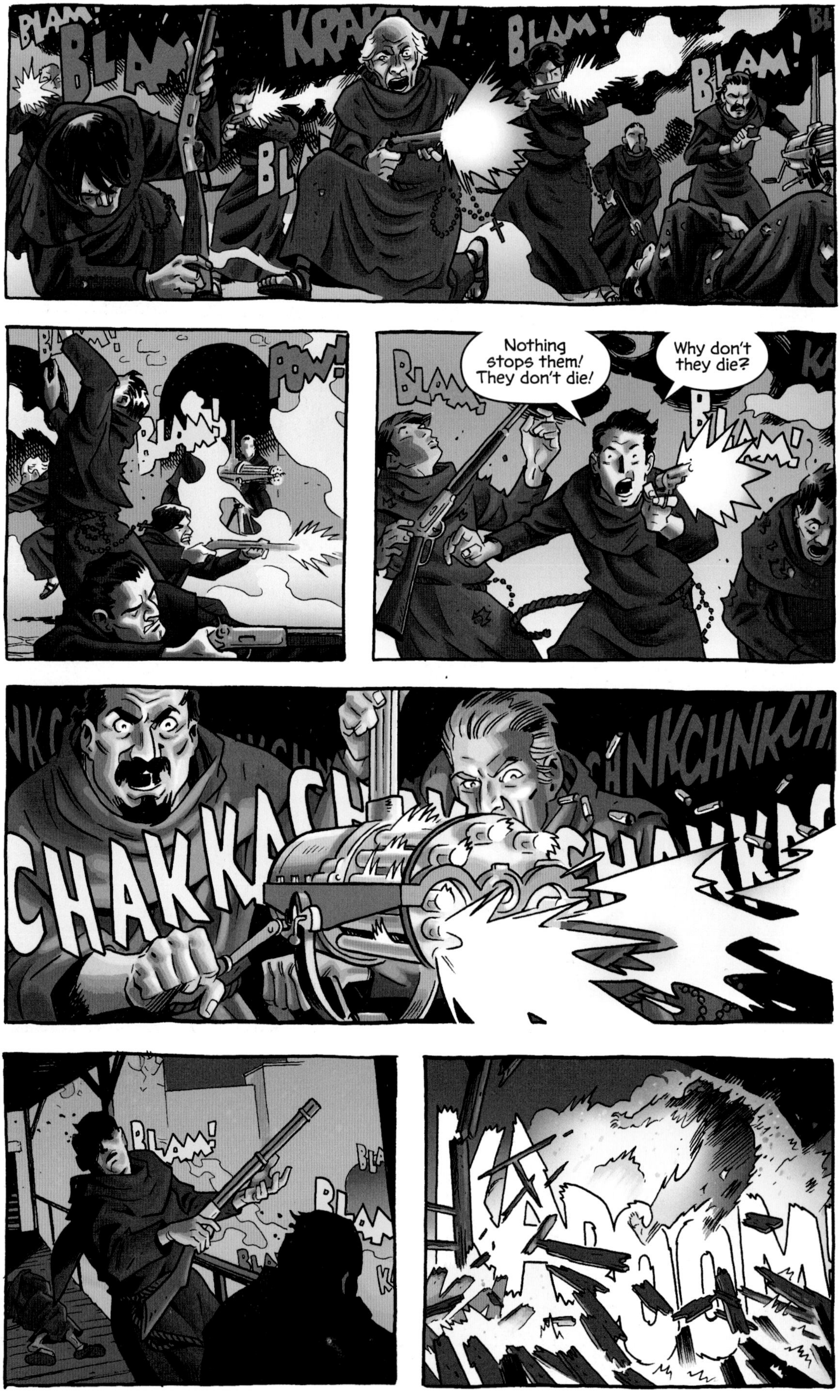
BLAM!
BLAM!
KRAKOW!
BLAM!
BLAM!
BLAM!
POW!
BLAM!
Nothing stops them! They don't die!
Why don't they die?
BLAM!
BLAM!
CHNKCHNKCH
CHAKKA
BLAM!

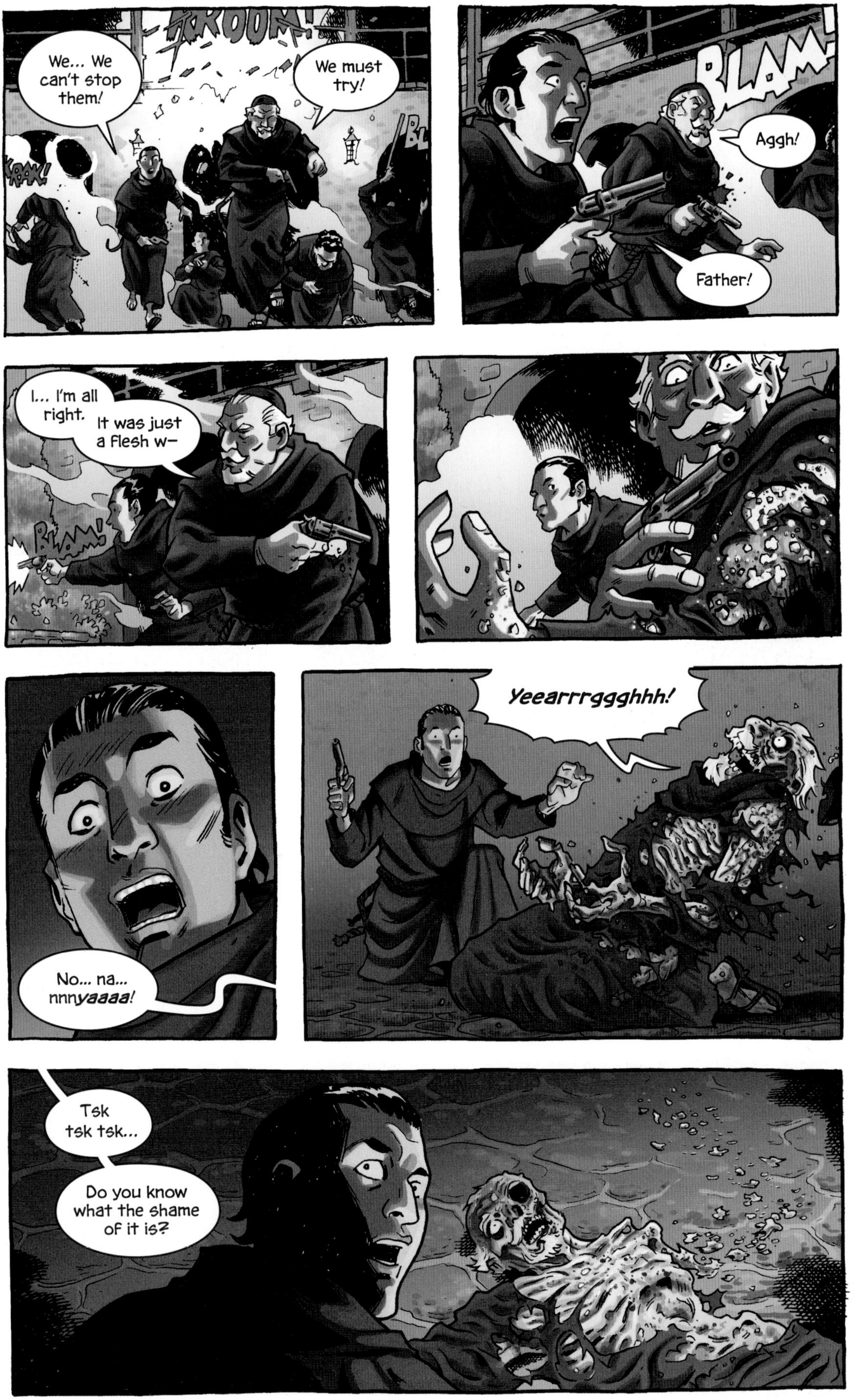
KRAK!
We... We can't stop them!
We must try!
BLAM!
Aggh!
Father!
I... I'm all right.
It was just a flesh w—
BLAM!
No... na... nnn*yaaaa*!
*Yeearrrrggghhh!*
Tsk tsk tsk...
Do you know what the shame of it is?

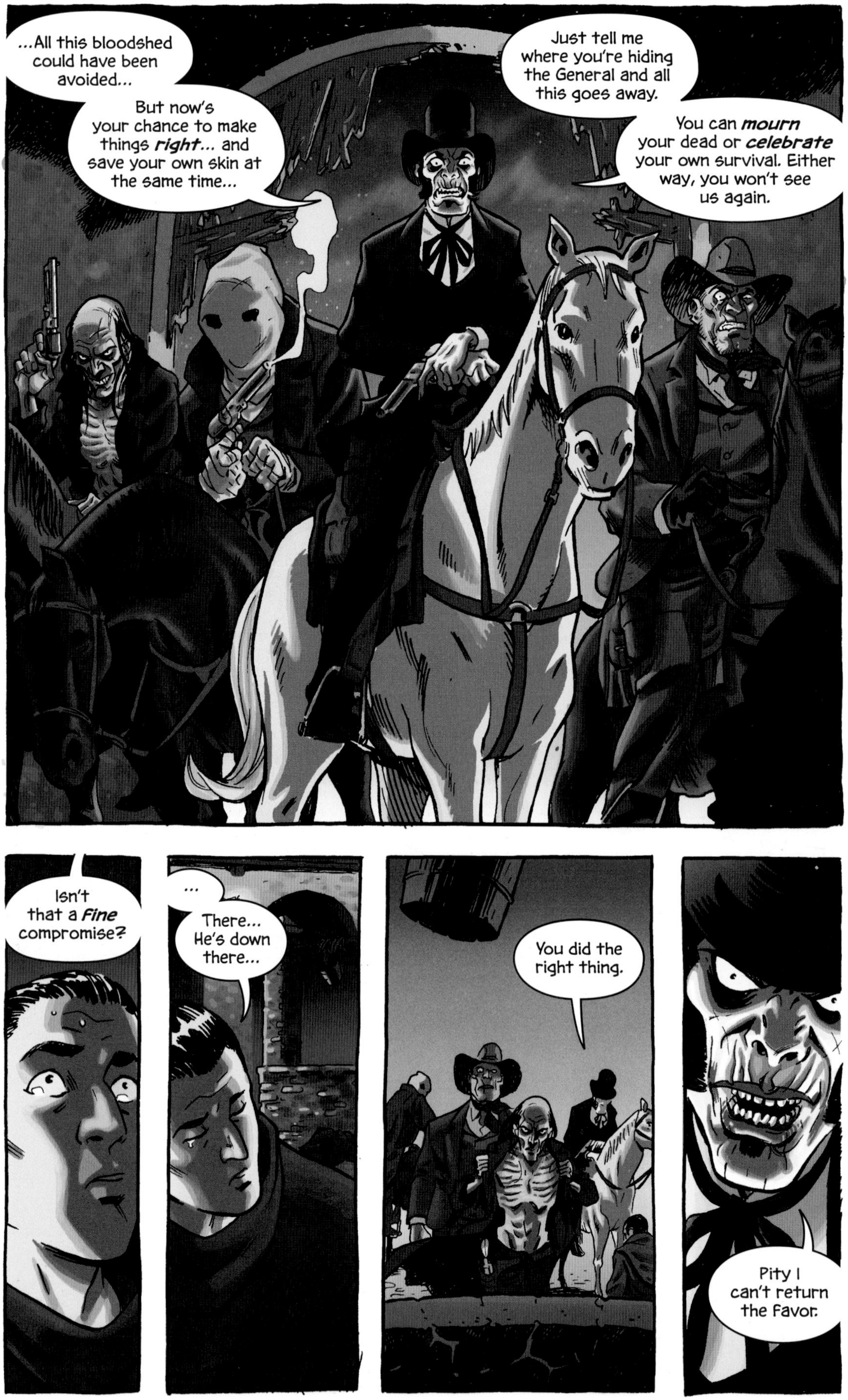

...All this bloodshed could have been avoided...
But now's your chance to make things *right*... and save your own skin at the same time...
Just tell me where you're hiding the General and all this goes away.
You can *mourn* your dead or *celebrate* your own survival. Either way, you won't see us again.
Isn't that a *Fine* compromise?
...
There... He's down there...
You did the right thing.
Pity I can't return the Favor.

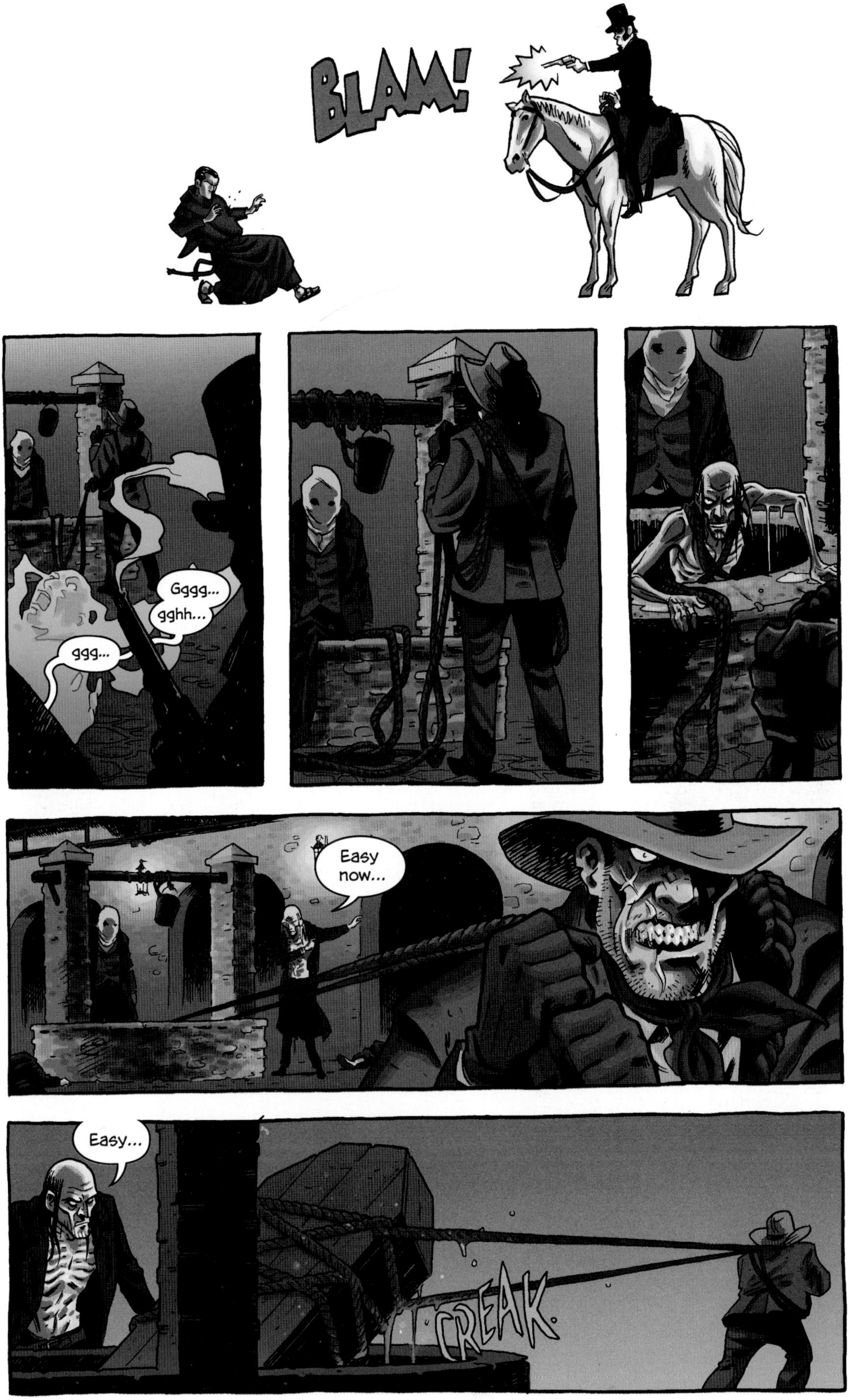
BLAM!
Gggg...
gghh...
ggg...
Easy now...
Easy...
CREAK

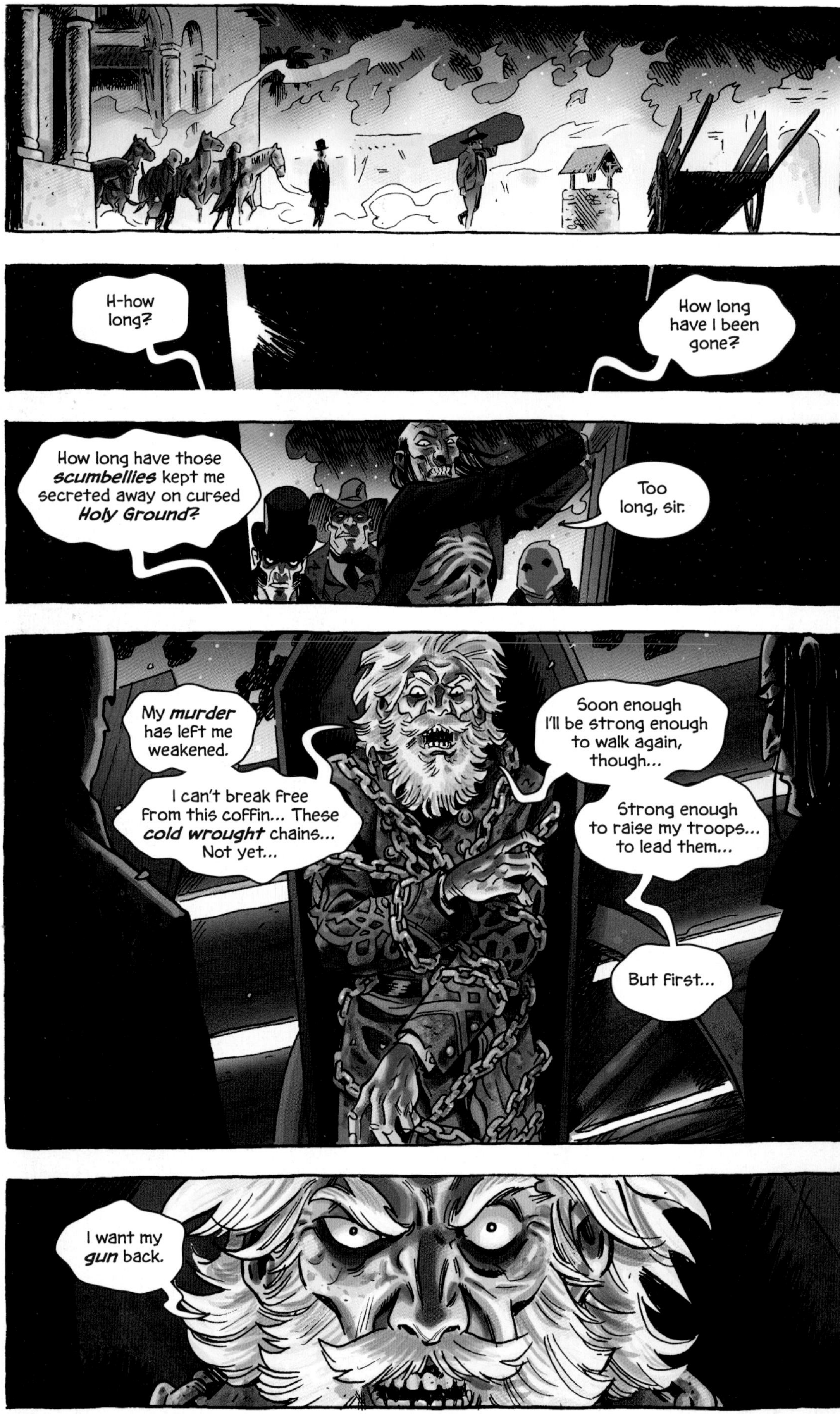

H-how long?
How long have I been gone?
How long have those *scumbellies* kept me secreted away on cursed *Holy Ground?*
Too long, sir.
My *murder* has left me weakened.
I can't break free from this coffin... These *cold wrought* chains... Not yet...
Soon enough I'll be strong enough to walk again, though...
Strong enough to raise my troops... to lead them...
But first...
I want my *gun* back.

# CHAPTER TWO

General Oliander Bedford Hume had been *dead* and *buried* for a right long while.

Yet he *stirred.*

And while his strength had faded in the years since his demise, his *rage* had grown like a wild thing...

Worms, maggots, and grave bugs had burrowed tunnels through his rotting flesh, and those tunnels had filled with a festering *hatred*...

Now, newly risen from a dead man's nightmares, he turned his every thought towards the vengeance his newfound freedom would afford.

The preacher... he was smart...

...wrapping me in these *cold iron* chains the way he did...

Hrr... hrr...

RATTLE CLANK RATTLE

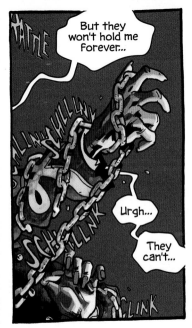

RATTLE

But they won't hold me forever...

Urgh...

They can't...

SCHLLNK SCHLLNK CLINK

I can feel myself growing stronger with each passing moment...

...and I'll be free from this blasted box soon enough...

RATTLE CLANK CLANK RATTLE

In the meanwhile, I'll need troops what will do my bidding.

Silas, would you do me the kindness?

With pleasure.

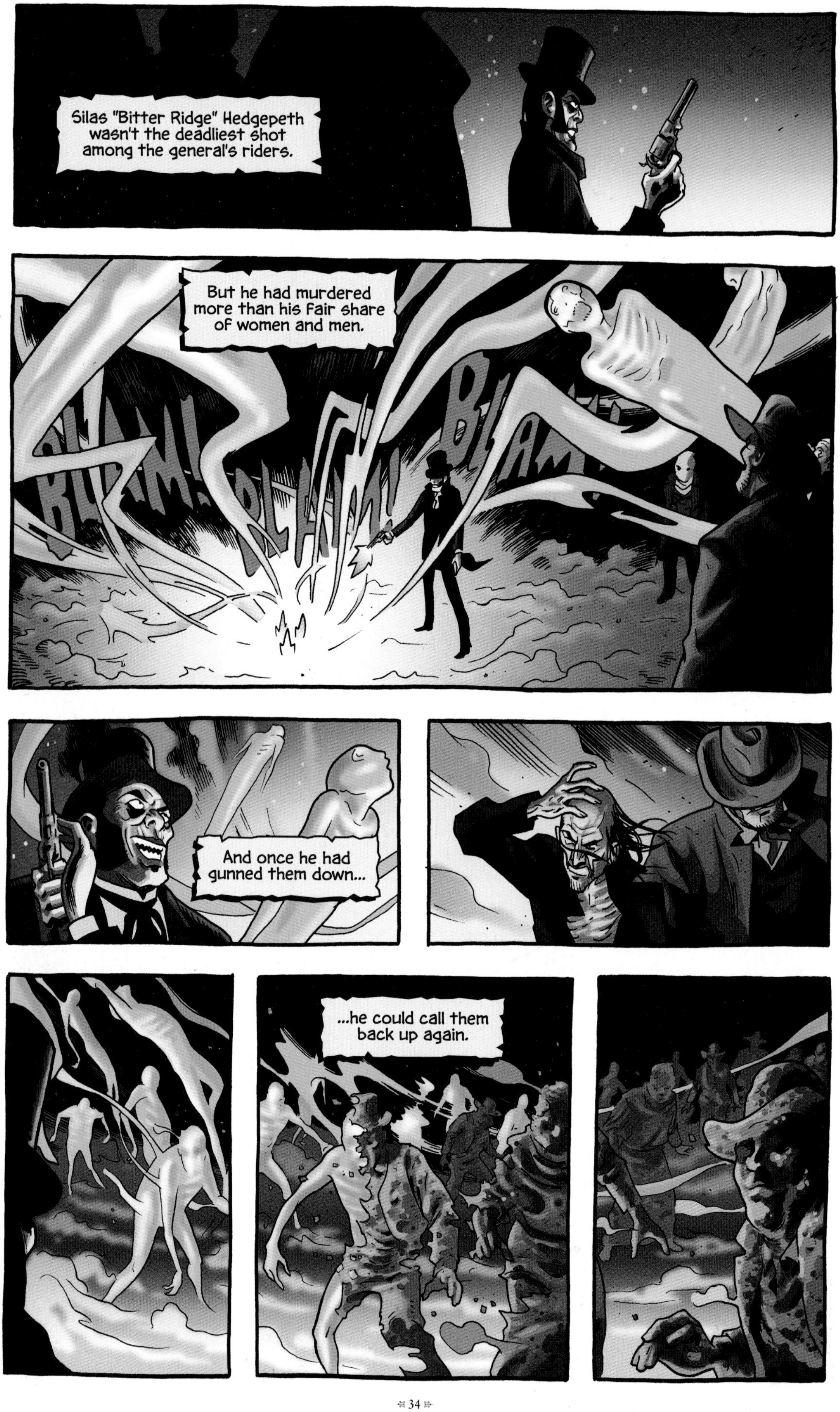

Silas "Bitter Ridge" Hedgepeth wasn't the deadliest shot among the general's riders.
But he had murdered more than his fair share of women and men.
BLAM! BLAM! BLAM!
And once he had gunned them down...
...he could call them back up again.

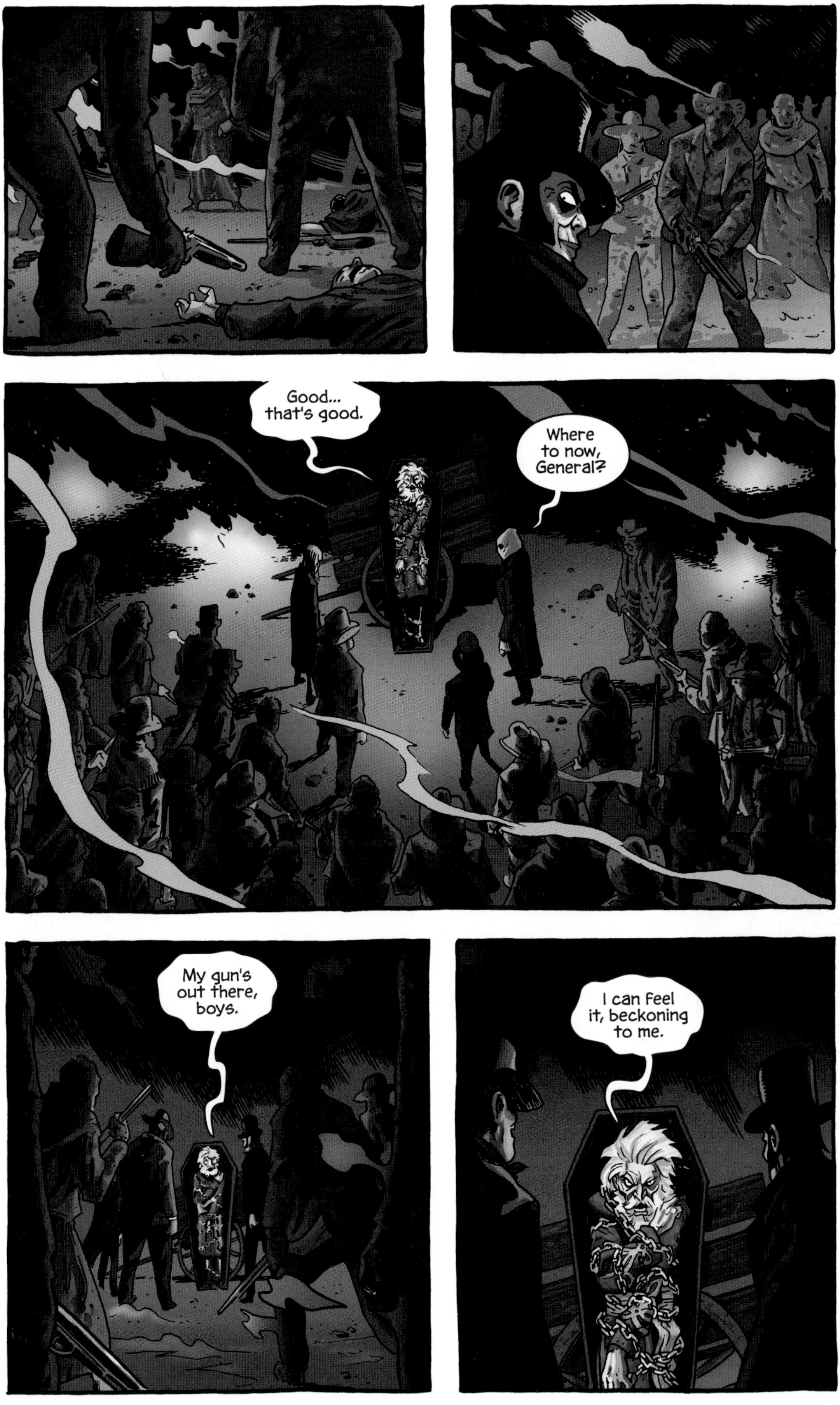
Good... that's good.
Where to now, General?
My gun's out there, boys.
I can feel it, beckoning to me.

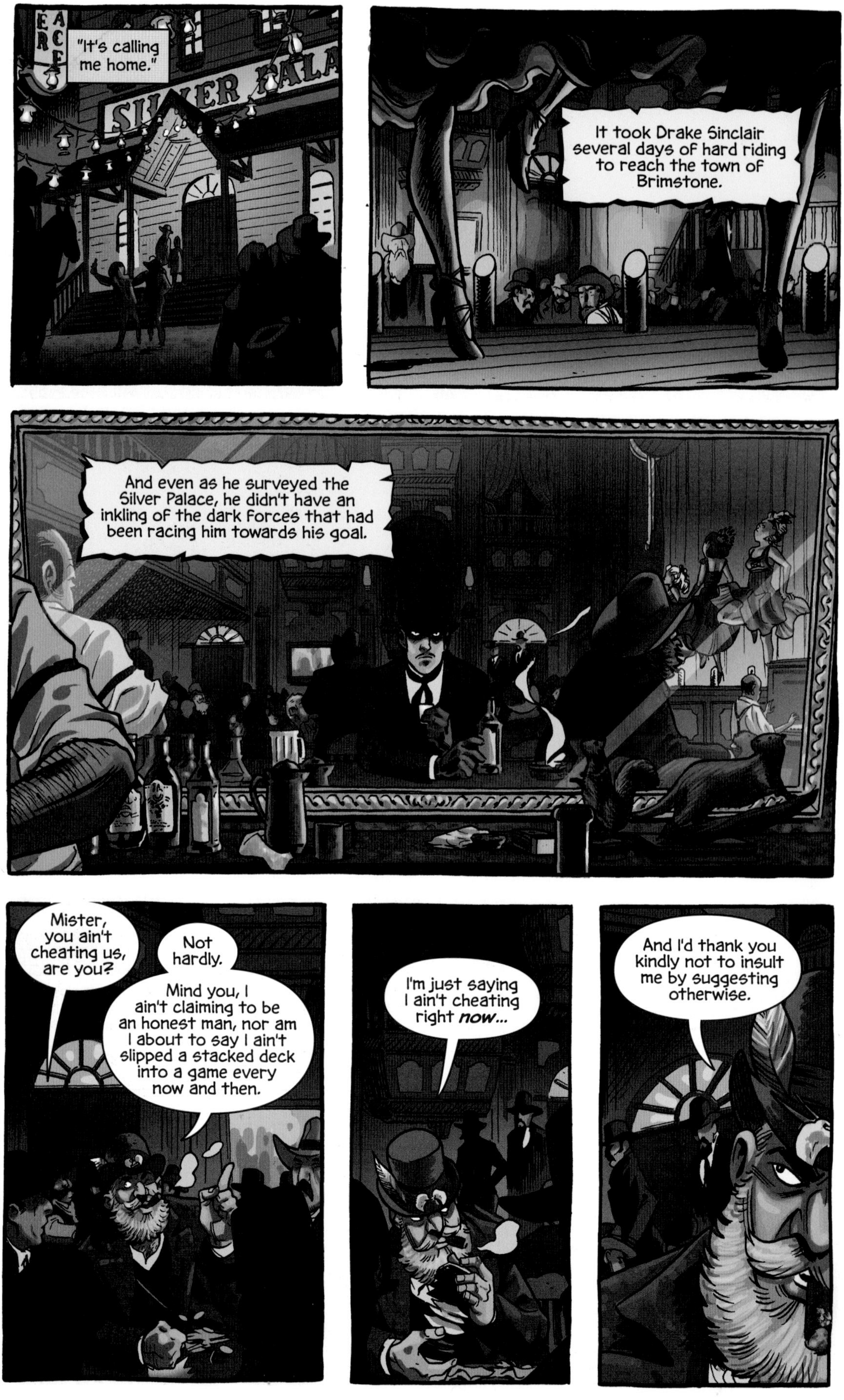
"It's calling me home."
It took Drake Sinclair several days of hard riding to reach the town of Brimstone.
And even as he surveyed the Silver Palace, he didn't have an inkling of the dark forces that had been racing him towards his goal.
Mister, you ain't cheating us, are you?
Not hardly.
Mind you, I ain't claiming to be an honest man, nor am I about to say I ain't slipped a stacked deck into a game every now and then.
I'm just saying I ain't cheating right *now*...
And I'd thank you kindly not to insult me by suggesting otherwise.

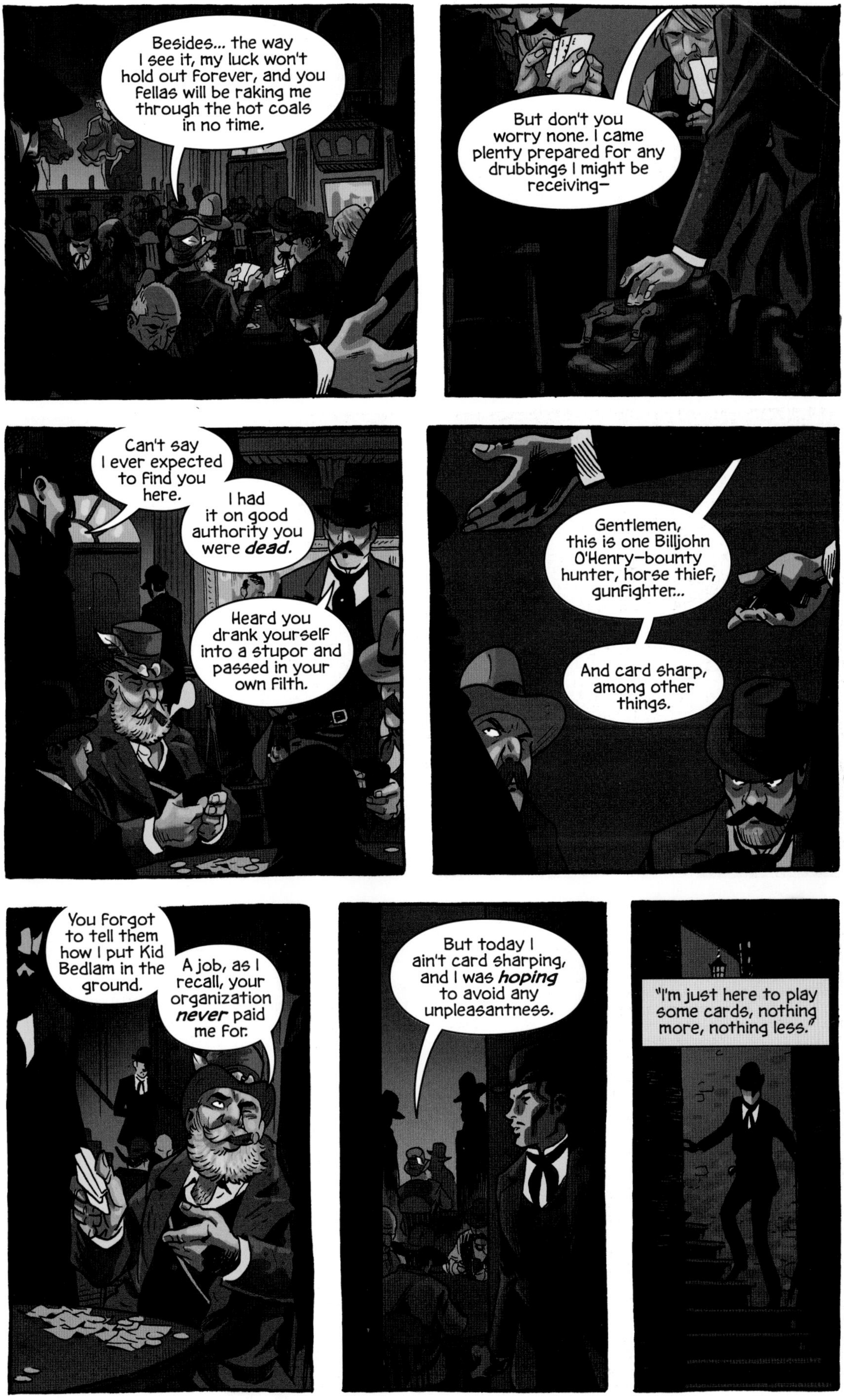
Besides... the way I see it, my luck won't hold out forever, and you fellas will be raking me through the hot coals in no time.
But don't you worry none. I came plenty prepared for any drubbings I might be receiving–
Can't say I ever expected to find you here.
I had it on good authority you were *dead.*
Heard you drank yourself into a stupor and passed in your own filth.
Gentlemen, this is one Billjohn O'Henry–bounty hunter, horse thief, gunfighter...
And card sharp, among other things.
You forgot to tell them how I put Kid Bedlam in the ground.
A job, as I recall, your organization *never* paid me for.
But today I ain't card sharping, and I was *hoping* to avoid any unpleasantness.
"I'm just here to play some cards, nothing more, nothing less."

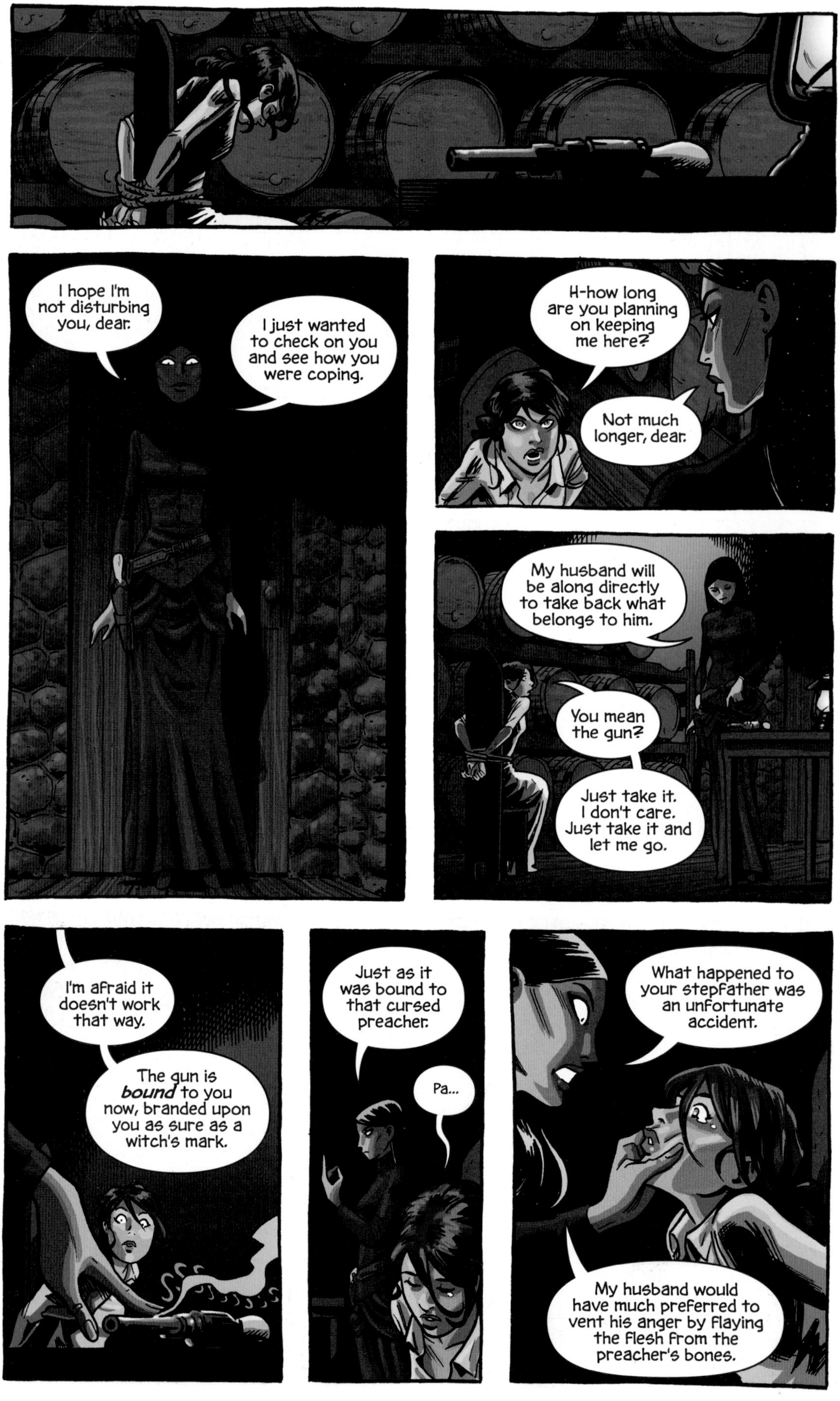
I hope I'm not disturbing you, dear.
I just wanted to check on you and see how you were coping.
H-how long are you planning on keeping me here?
Not much longer, dear.
My husband will be along directly to take back what belongs to him.
You mean the gun?
Just take it. I don't care. Just take it and let me go.
I'm afraid it doesn't work that way.
The gun is *bound* to you now, branded upon you as sure as a witch's mark.
Just as it was bound to that cursed preacher.
Pa...
What happened to your stepfather was an unfortunate accident.
My husband would have much preferred to vent his anger by flaying the flesh from the preacher's bones.

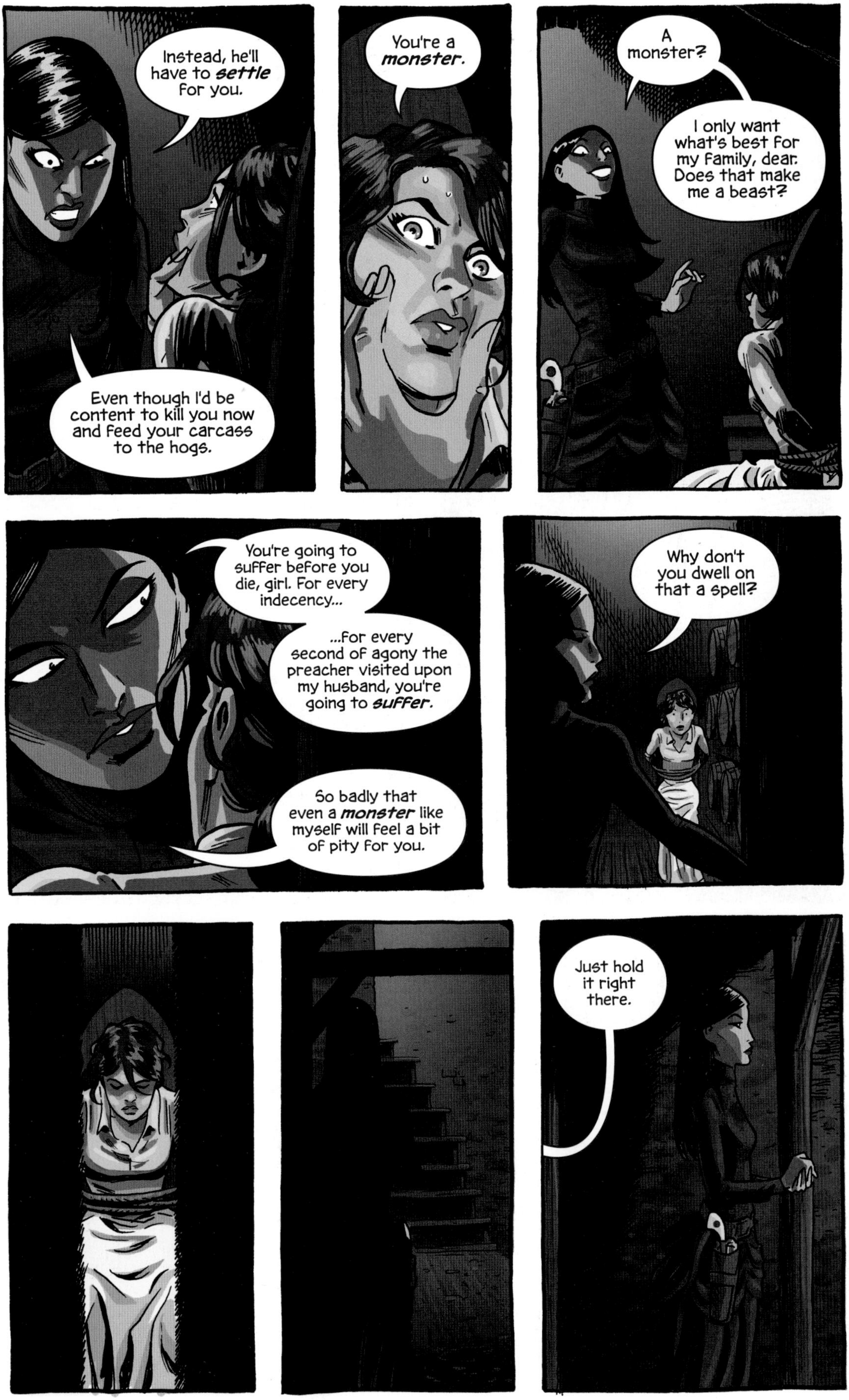
Instead, he'll have to settle for you.
Even though I'd be content to kill you now and feed your carcass to the hogs.
You're a monster.
A monster?
I only want what's best for my family, dear. Does that make me a beast?
You're going to suffer before you die, girl. For every indecency...
...for every second of agony the preacher visited upon my husband, you're going to suffer.
So badly that even a monster like myself will feel a bit of pity for you.
Why don't you dwell on that a spell?
Just hold it right there.

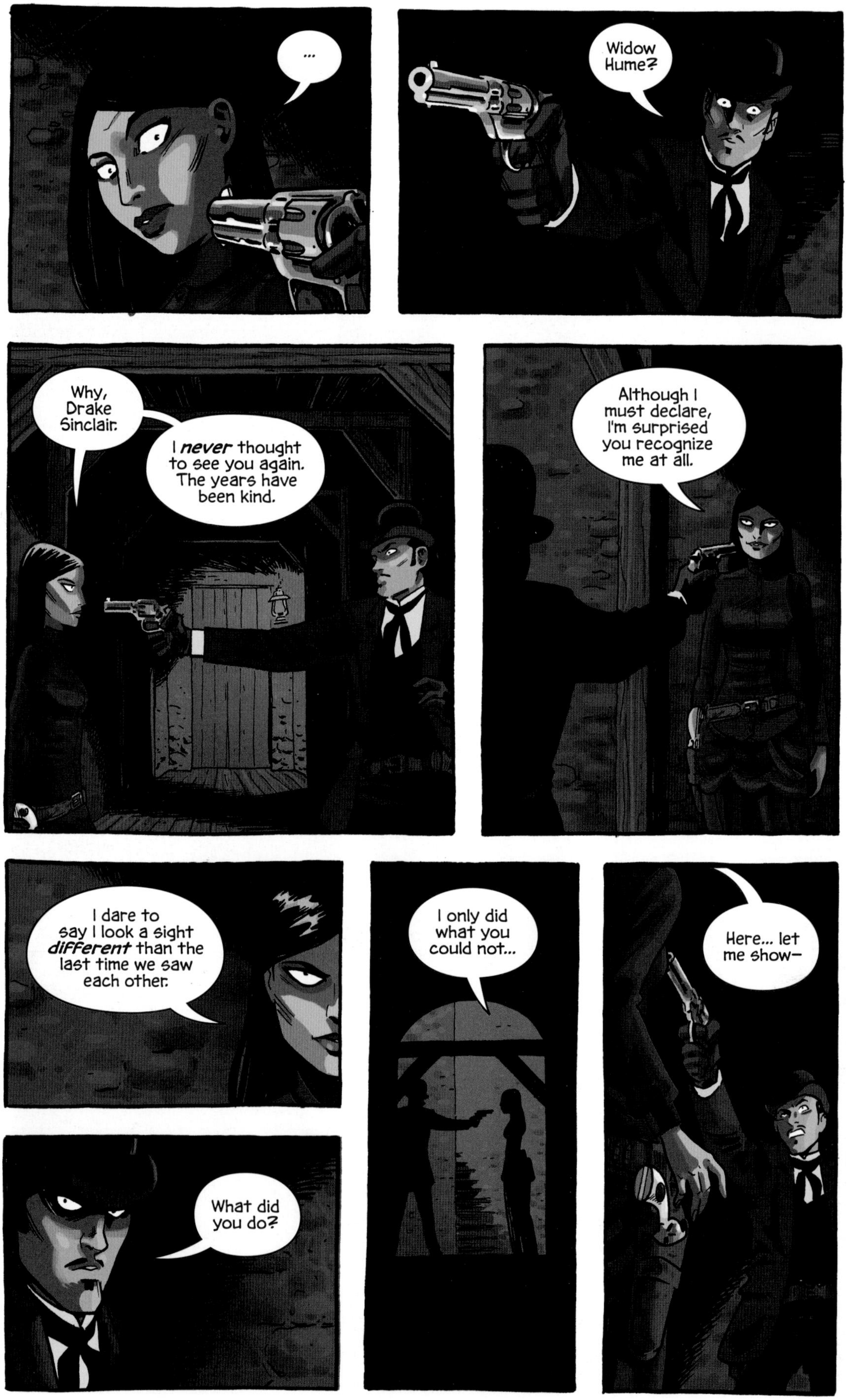
...
Widow Hume?
Why, Drake Sinclair.
I *never* thought to see you again. The years have been kind.
Although I must declare, I'm surprised you recognize me at all.
I dare to say I look a sight *different* than the last time we saw each other.
What did you do?
I only did what you could not...
Here... let me show–

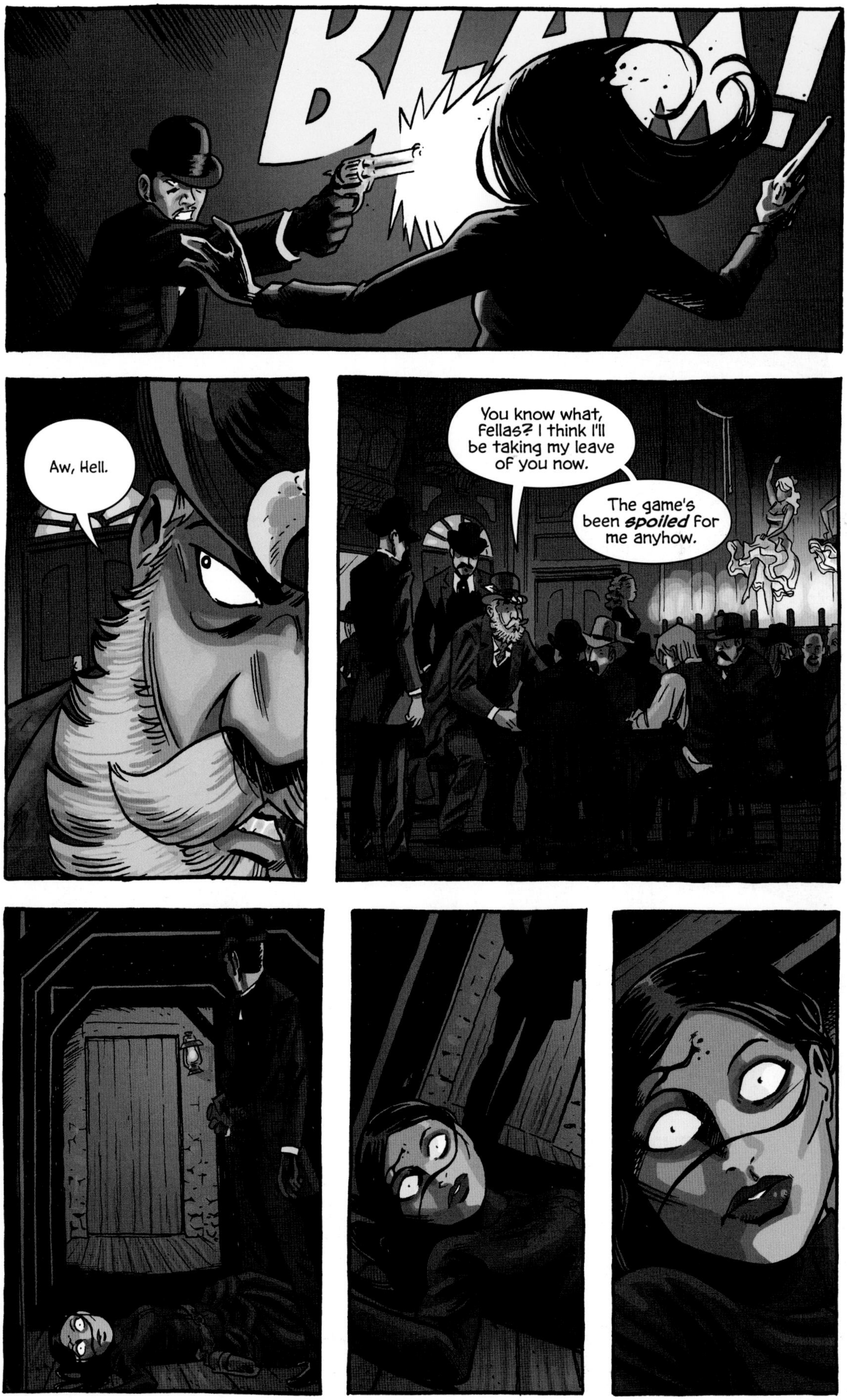
BLAM!
Aw, Hell.
You know what, fellas? I think I'll be taking my leave of you now.
The game's been *spoiled* for me anyhow.

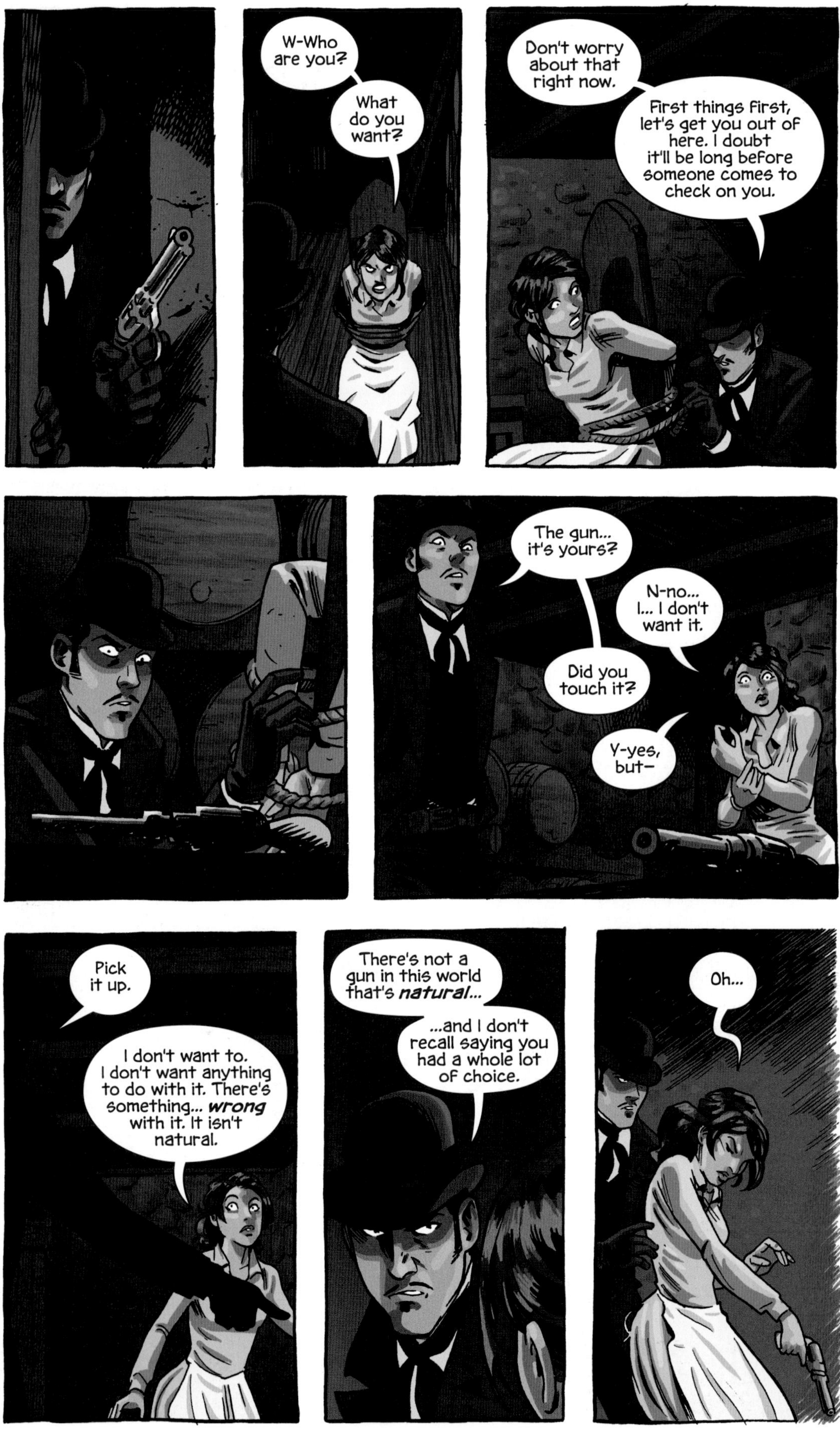
W-Who are you?
What do you want?
Don't worry about that right now.
First things first, let's get you out of here. I doubt it'll be long before someone comes to check on you.
The gun... it's yours?
N-no... I... I don't want it.
Did you touch it?
Y-yes, but–
Pick it up.
I don't want to. I don't want anything to do with it. There's something... *wrong* with it. It isn't natural.
There's not a gun in this world that's *natural*...
...and I don't recall saying you had a whole lot of choice.
Oh...

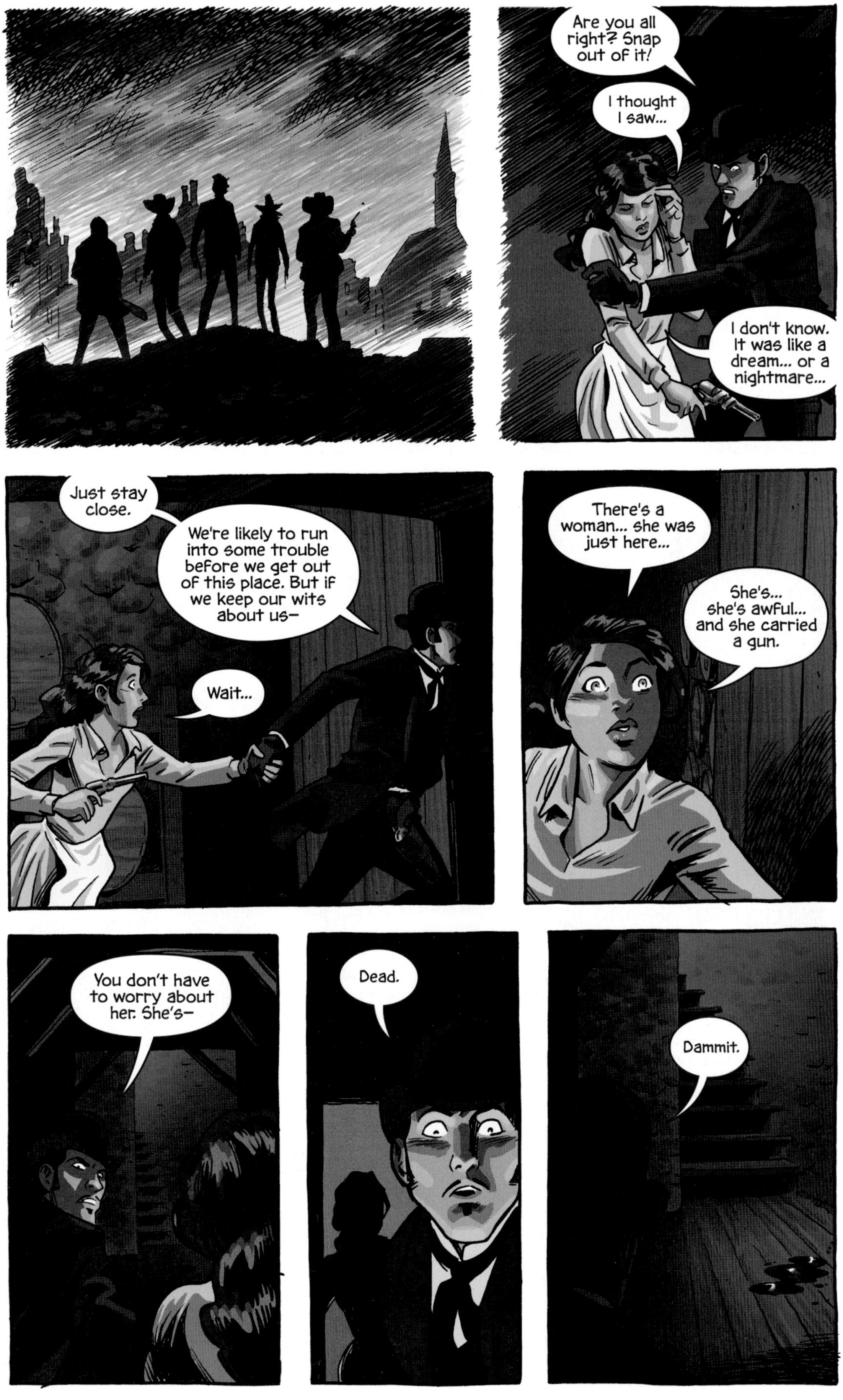

Are you all right? Snap out of it!
I thought I saw...
I don't know. It was like a dream... or a nightmare...
Just stay close.
We're likely to run into some trouble before we get out of this place. But if we keep our wits about us—
Wait...
There's a woman... she was just here...
She's... she's awful... and she carried a gun.
You don't have to worry about her. She's—
Dead.
Dammit.

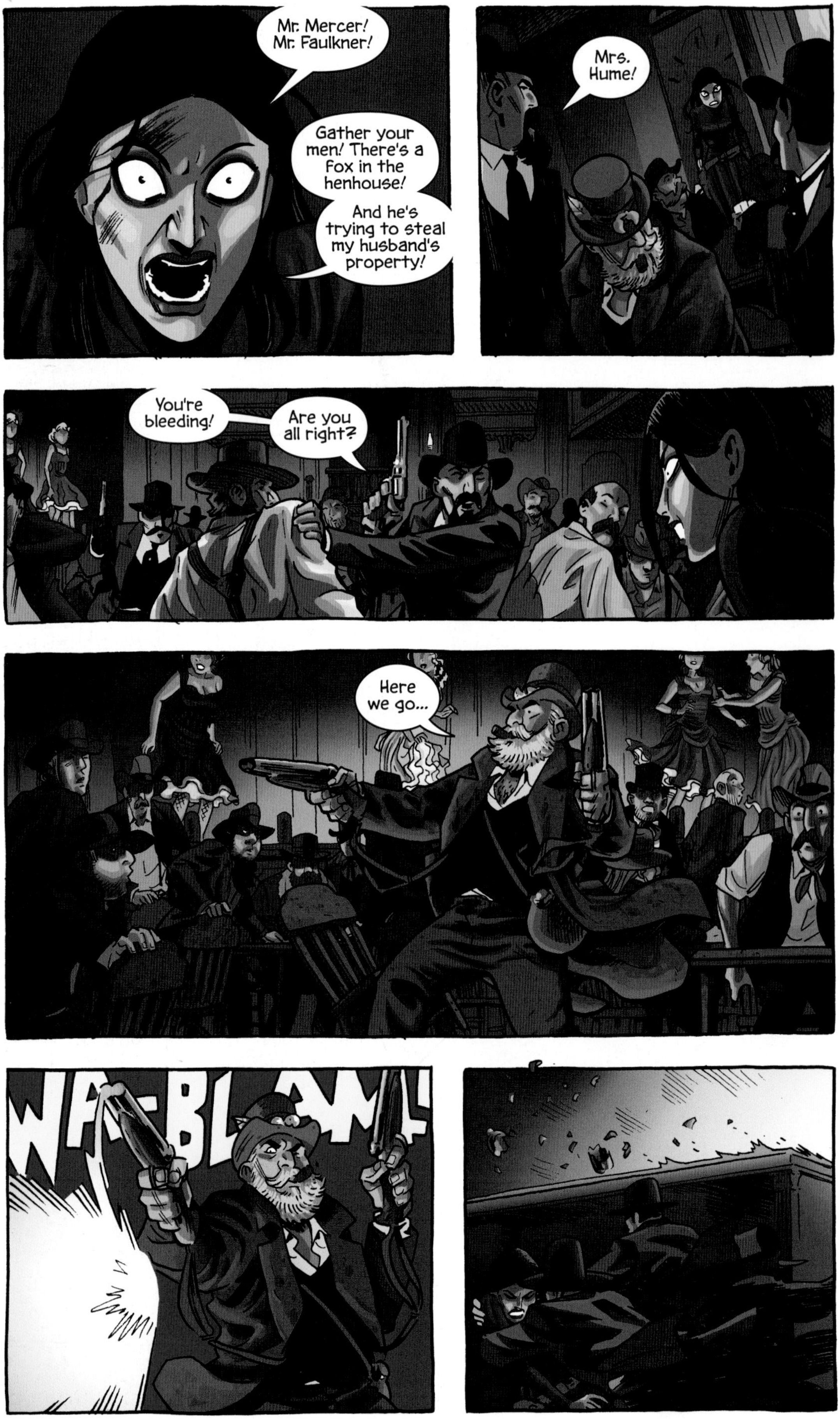
Mr. Mercer! Mr. Faulkner!
Gather your men! There's a fox in the henhouse!
And he's trying to steal my husband's property!
Mrs. Hume!
You're bleeding!
Are you all right?
Here we go...
WA-BLAM!

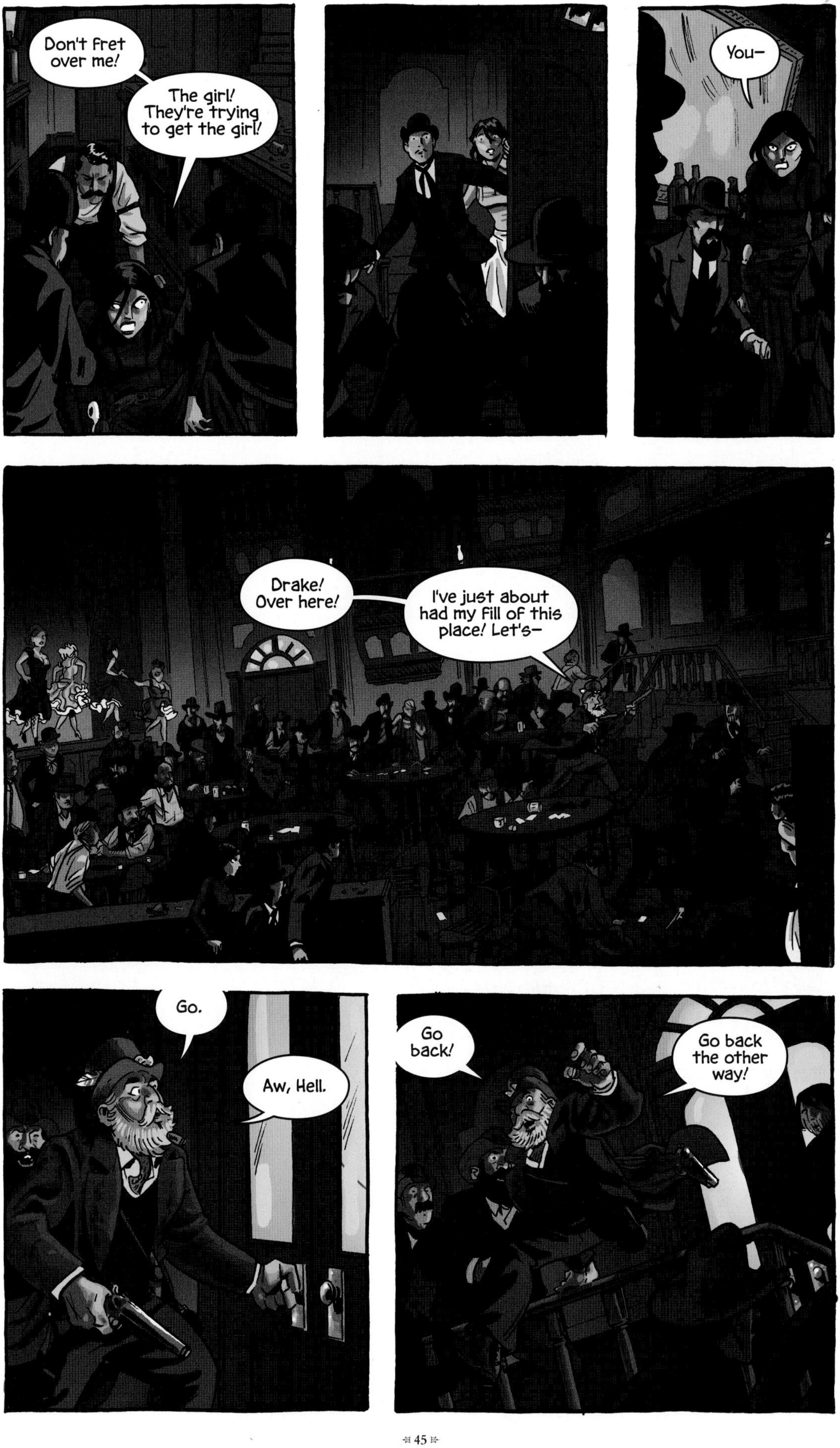
Don't fret over me!
The girl! They're trying to get the girl!
You–
Drake! Over here!
I've just about had my fill of this place! Let's–
Go.
Aw, Hell.
Go back!
Go back the other way!

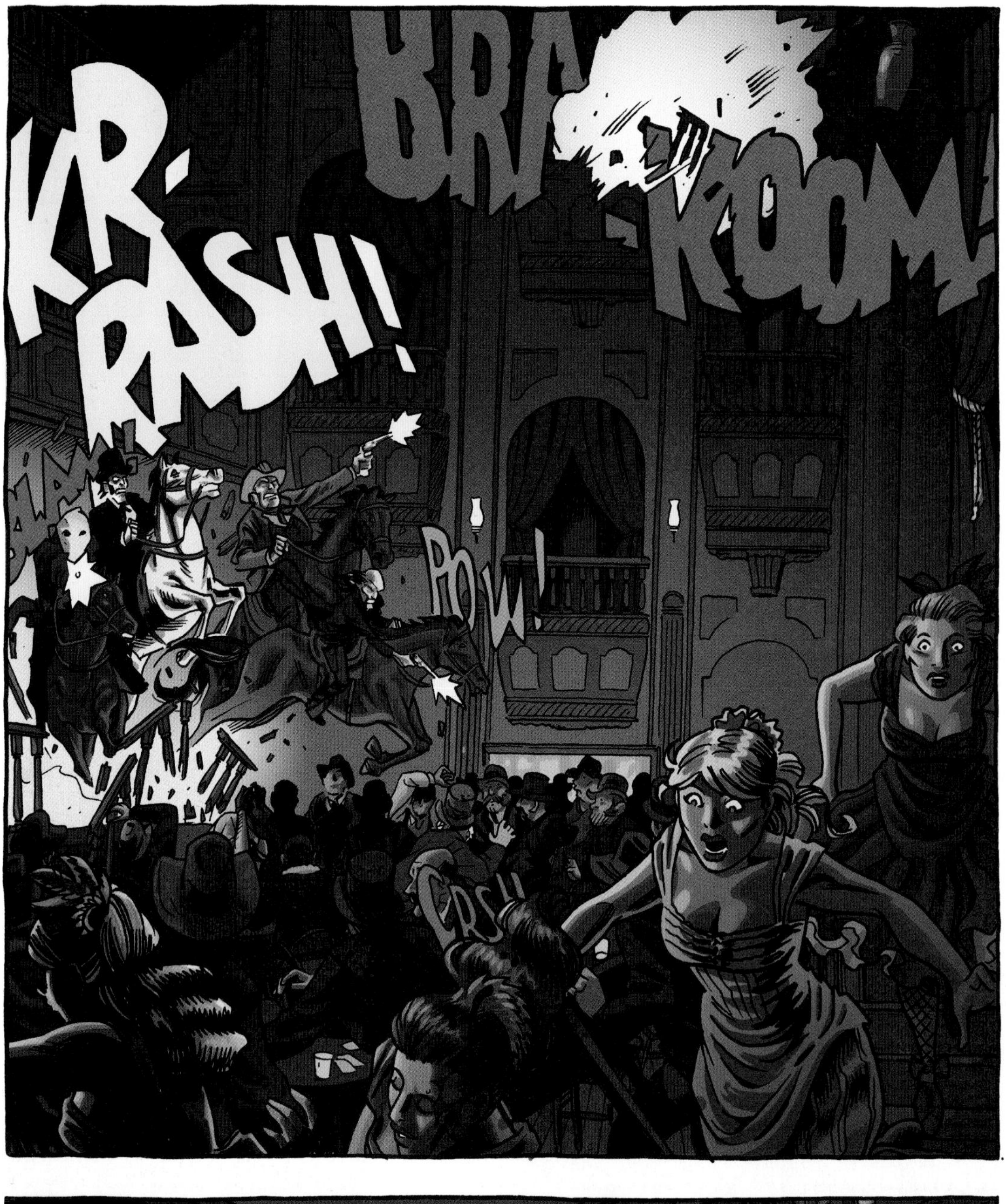
KR-RASH!
BRA-KOOM!
POW!

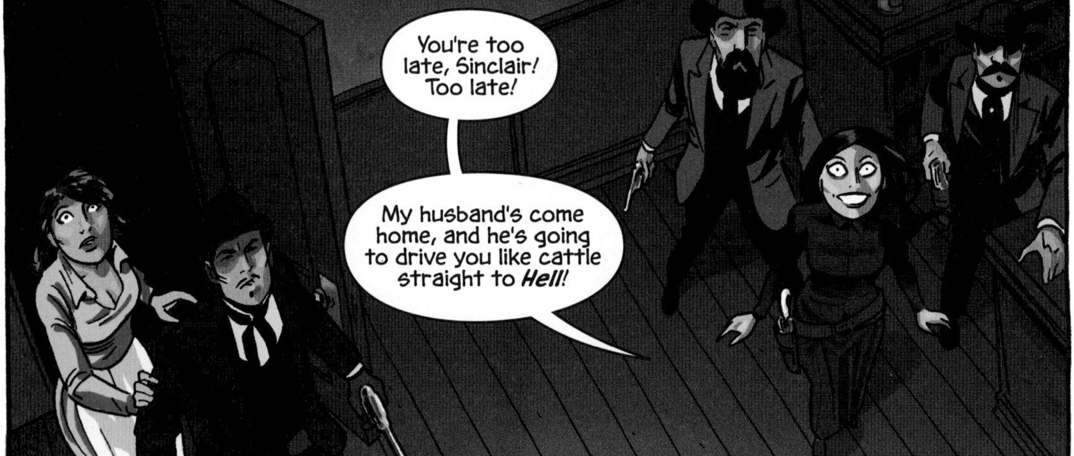
You're too late, Sinclair! Too late!
My husband's come home, and he's going to drive you like cattle straight to *Hell!*

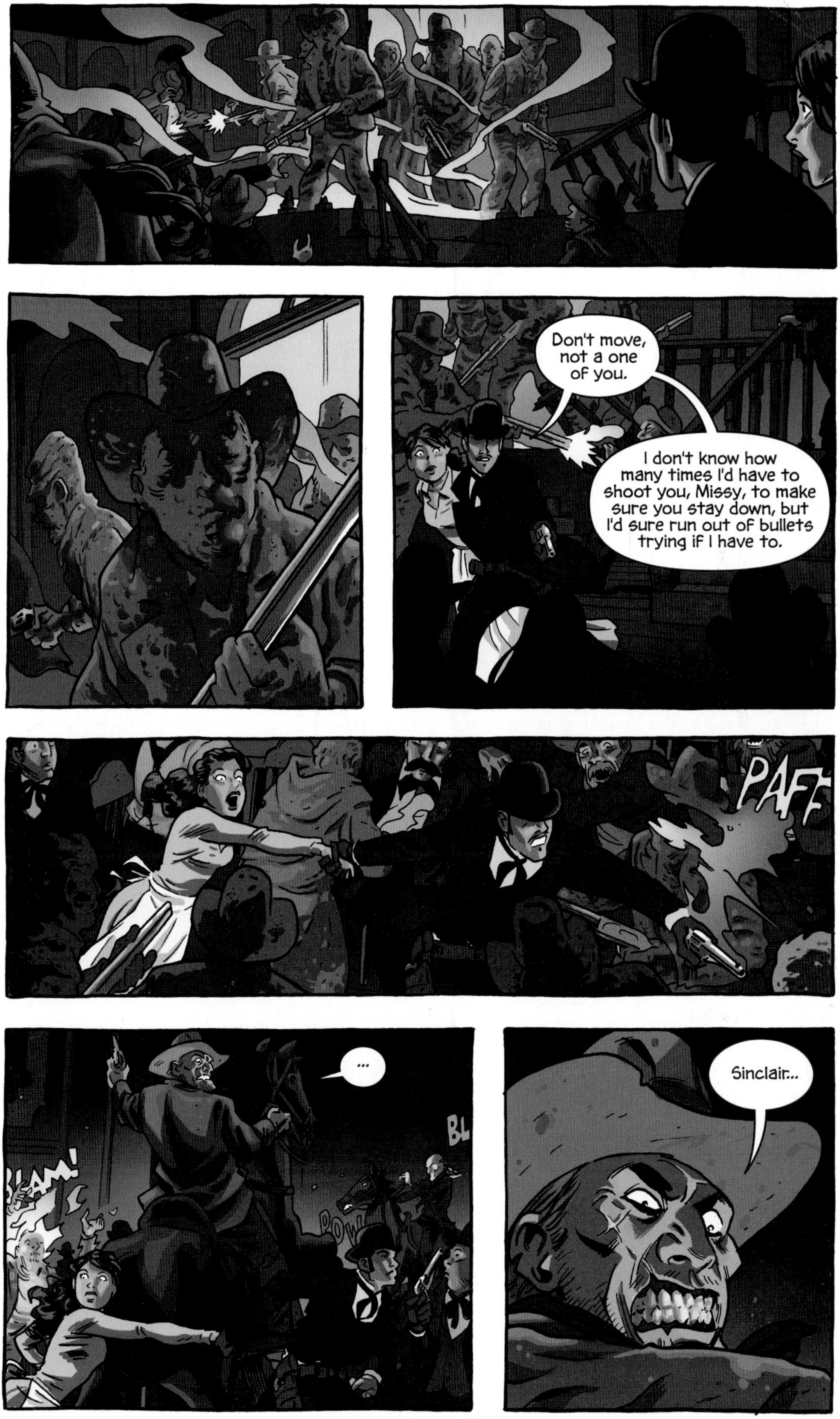
Don't move, not a one of you.
I don't know how many times I'd have to shoot you, Missy, to make sure you stay down, but I'd sure run out of bullets trying if I have to.
PAFF
...
BLAM!
POW
Sinclair...

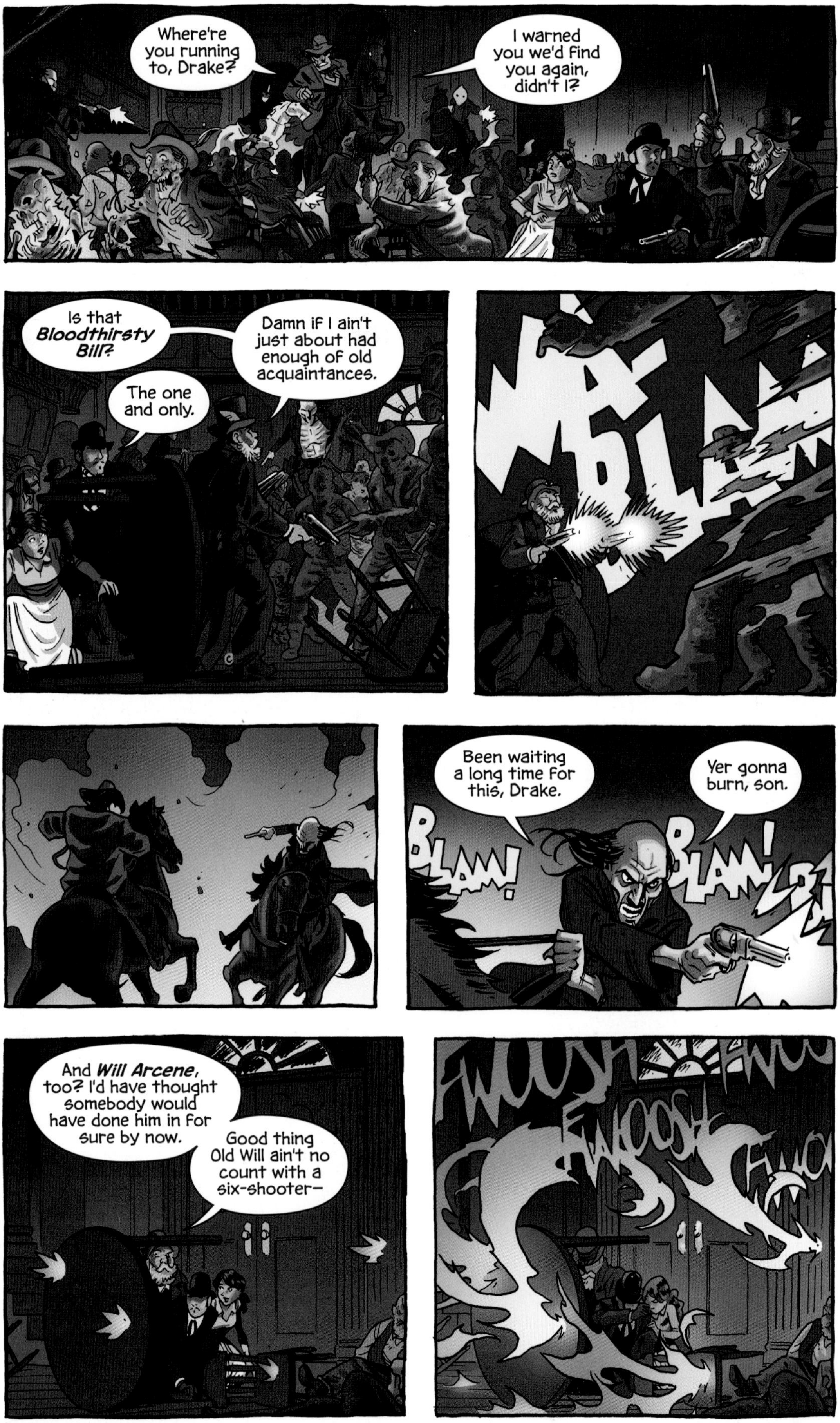

Where're you running to, Drake?
I warned you we'd find you again, didn't I?
Is that Bloodthirsty Bill?
The one and only.
Damn if I ain't just about had enough of old acquaintances.
BLAM
Been waiting a long time for this, Drake.
Yer gonna burn, son.
BLAM!
BLAM!
And Will Arcene, too? I'd have thought somebody would have done him in for sure by now.
Good thing Old Will ain't no count with a six-shooter—
FWOOSH
FWOOSH

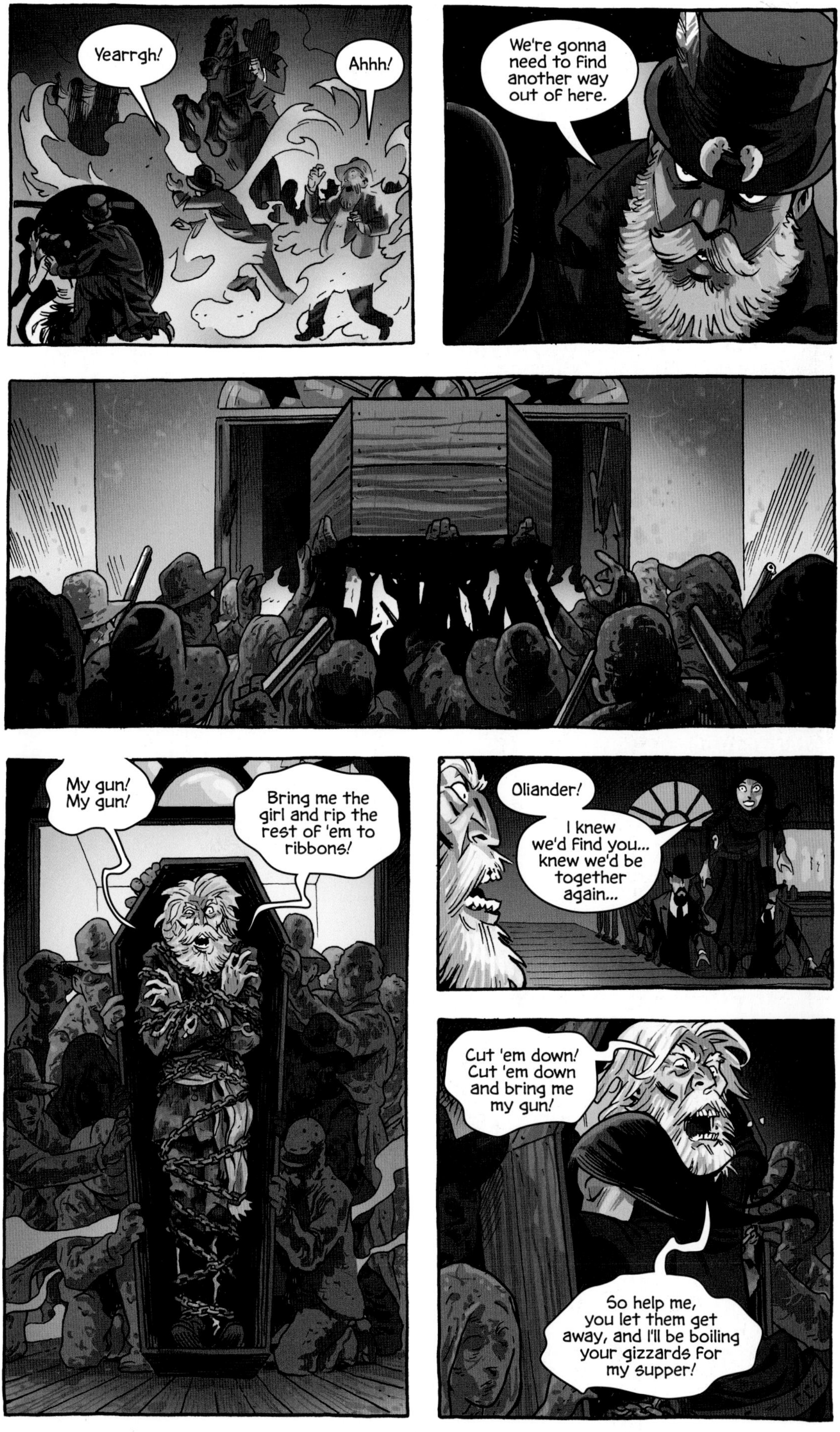
Yearrgh!
Ahhh!
We're gonna need to find another way out of here.
My gun! My gun!
Bring me the girl and rip the rest of 'em to ribbons!
Oliander!
I knew we'd find you... knew we'd be together again...
Cut 'em down! Cut 'em down and bring me my gun!
So help me, you let them get away, and I'll be boiling your gizzards for my supper!

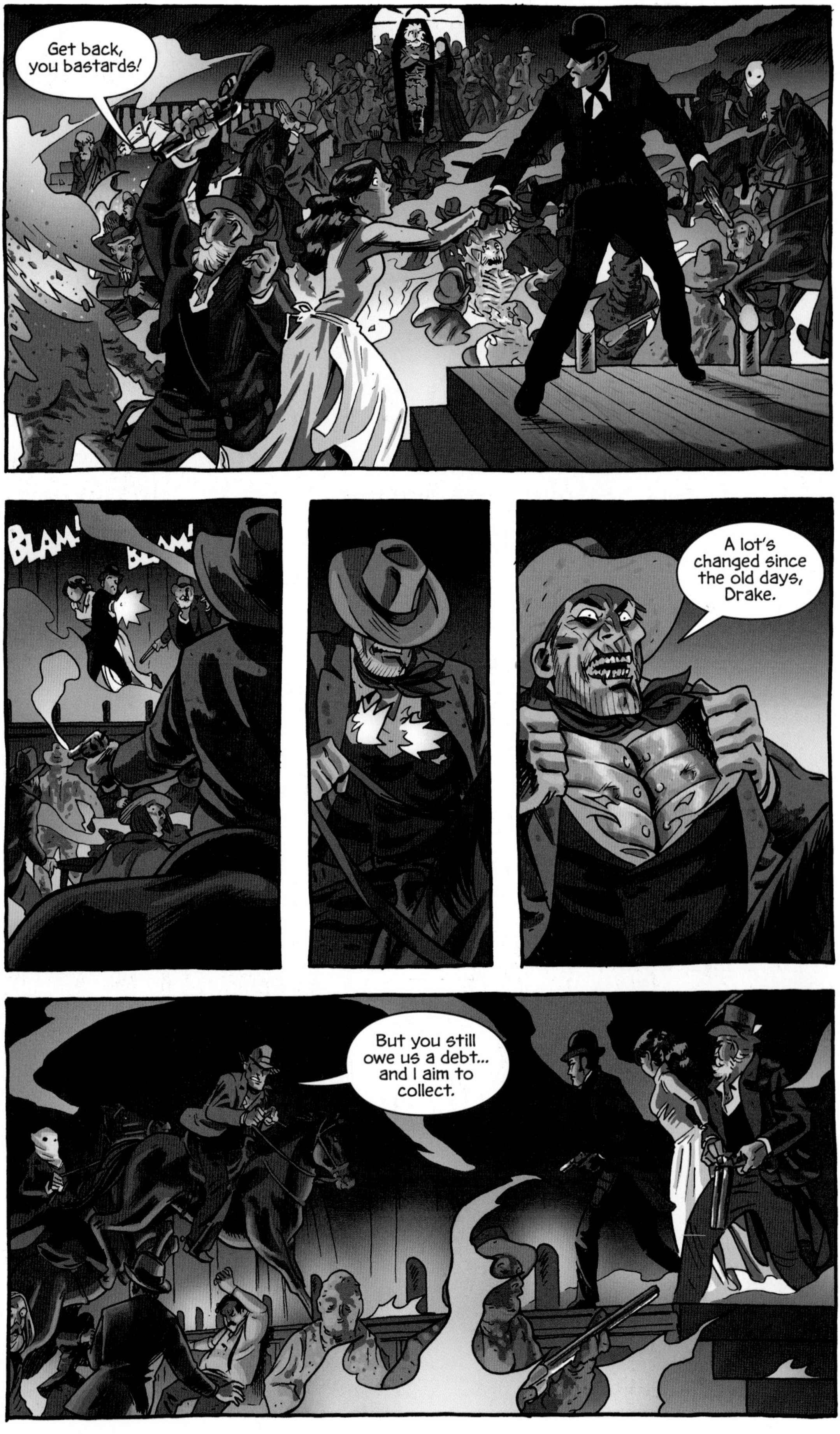
Get back, you bastards!
BLAM!
A lot's changed since the old days, Drake.
But you still owe us a debt... and I aim to collect.

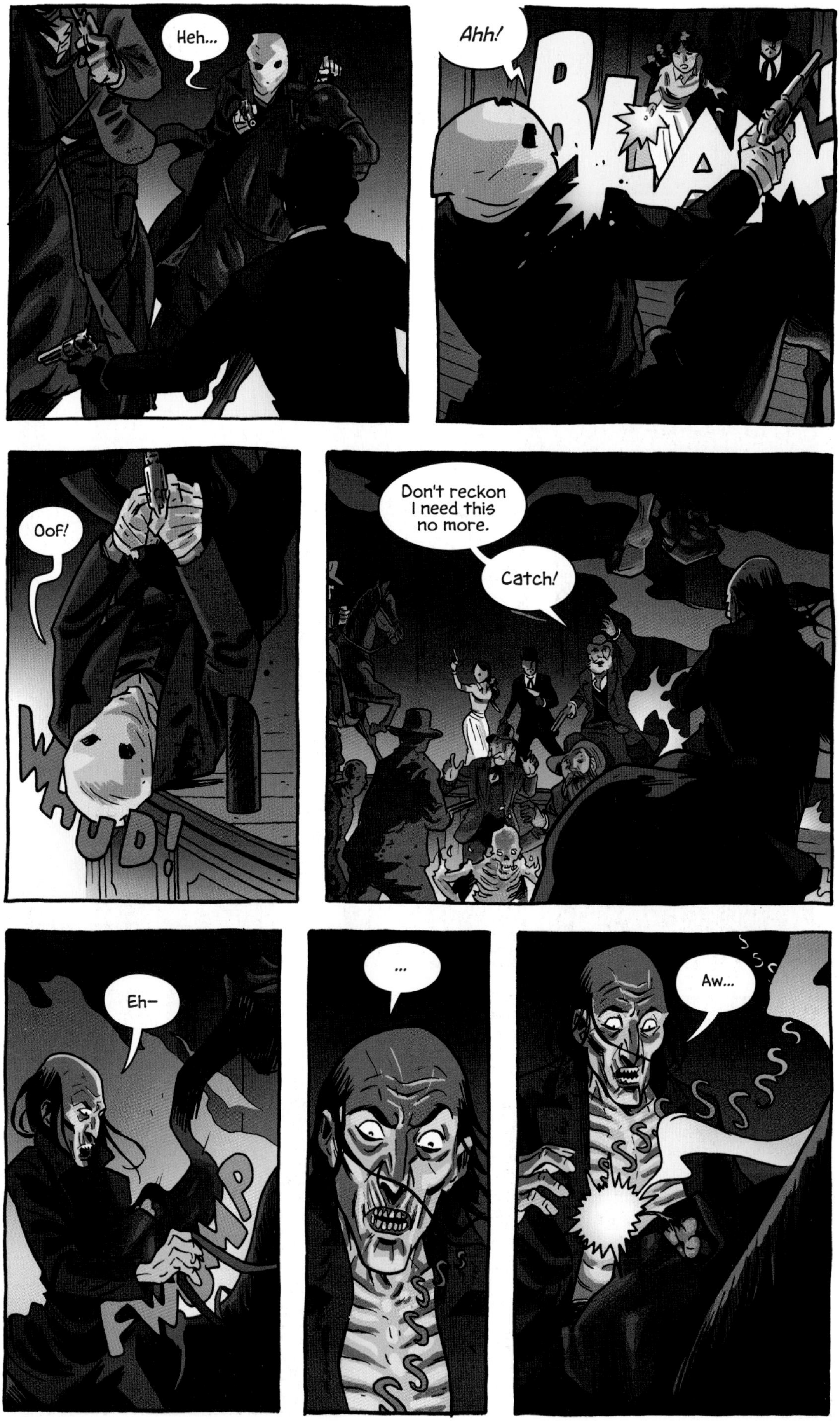
Heh...
Ahh!
BLAM!
Oof!
WHUD!
Don't reckon I need this no more.
Catch!
Eh–
FWOMP
...
Aw...

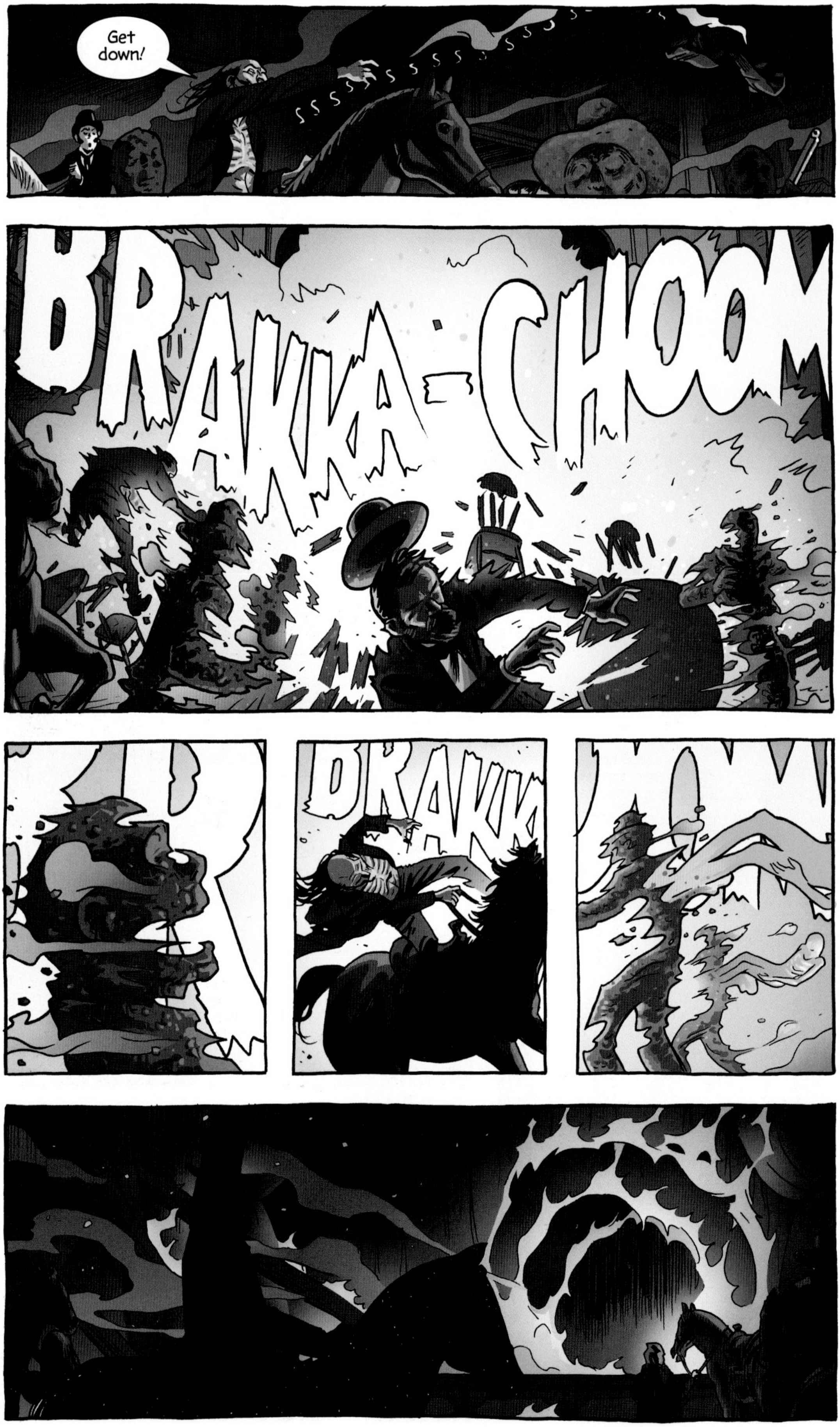
Get down!
BRAKKA-CHOOM
BRAKK

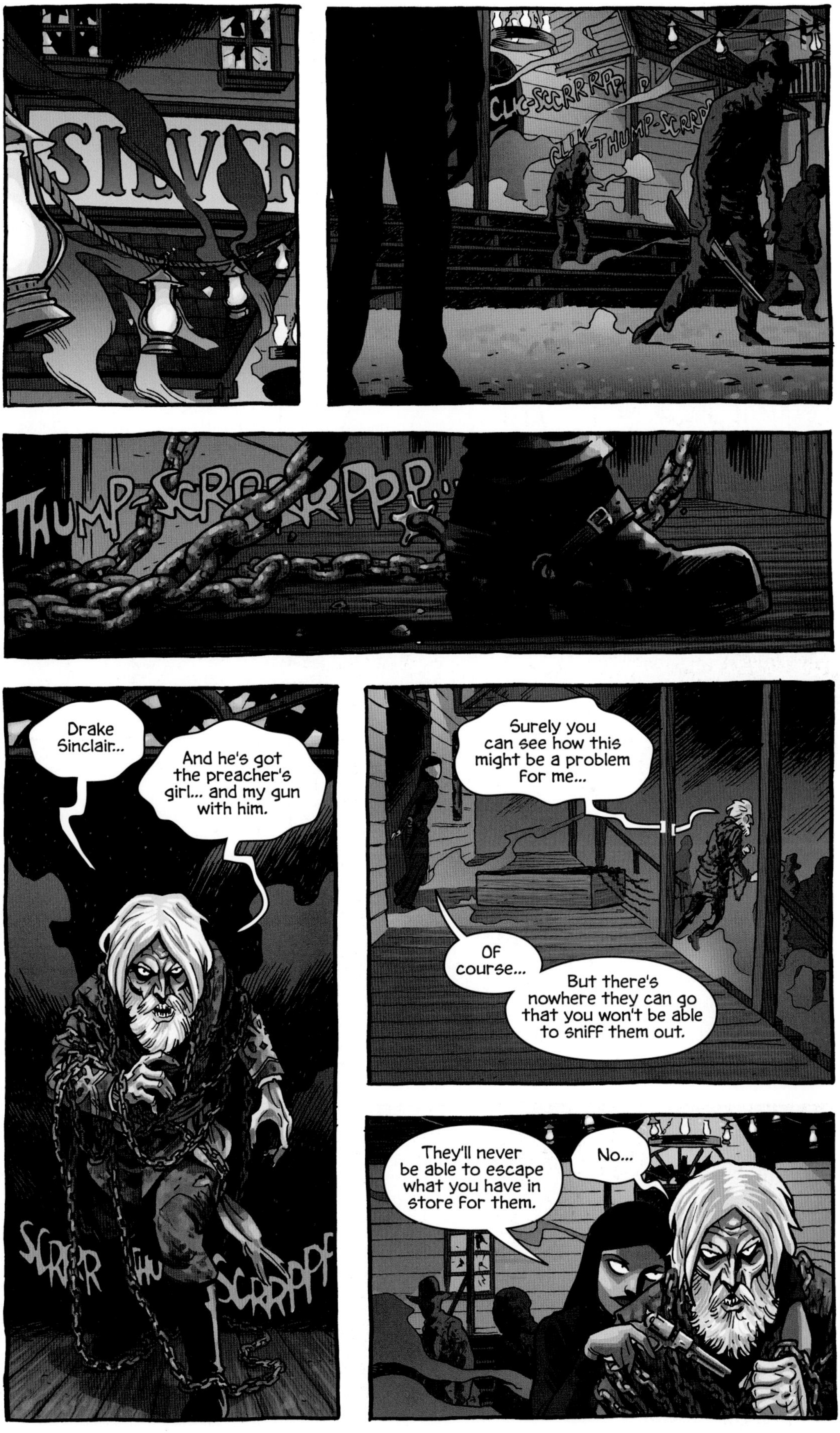
CLIC-SCRRRRPPP
CLIK-THUMP-SCRRPP
THUMP-SCRRRRRPPP...
Drake Sinclair...
And he's got the preacher's girl... and my gun with him.
SCRRR
THU
SCRRPPF
Surely you can see how this might be a problem for me...
Of course...
But there's nowhere they can go that you won't be able to sniff them out.
They'll never be able to escape what you have in store for them.
No...

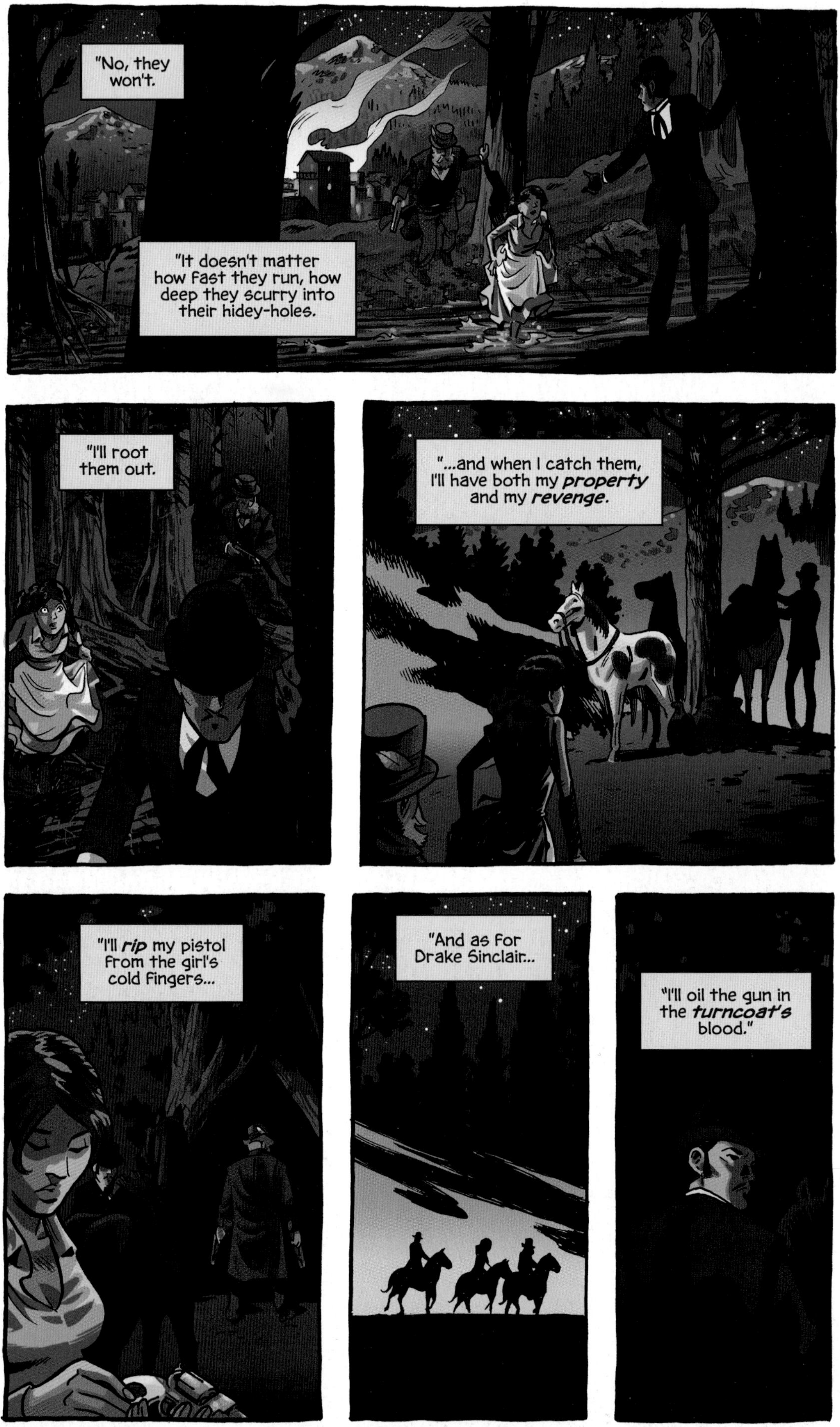
"No, they won't.
"It doesn't matter how fast they run, how deep they scurry into their hidey-holes.
"I'll root them out.
"...and when I catch them, I'll have both my *property* and my *revenge*.
"I'll *rip* my pistol from the girl's cold fingers...
"And as for Drake Sinclair...
"I'll oil the gun in the *turncoat's* blood."

# CHAPTER THREE

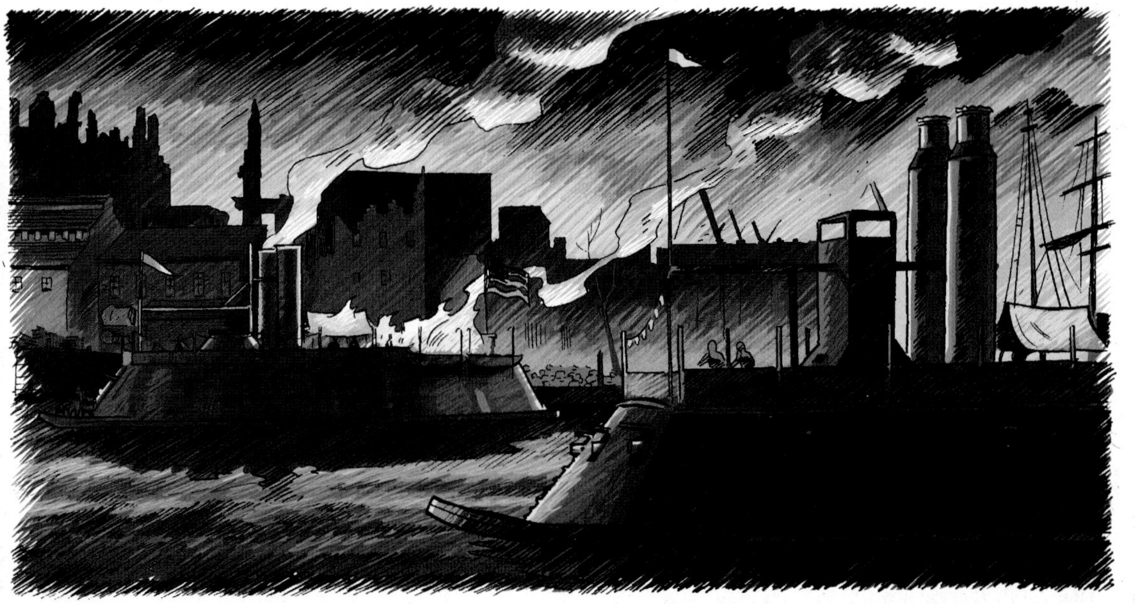

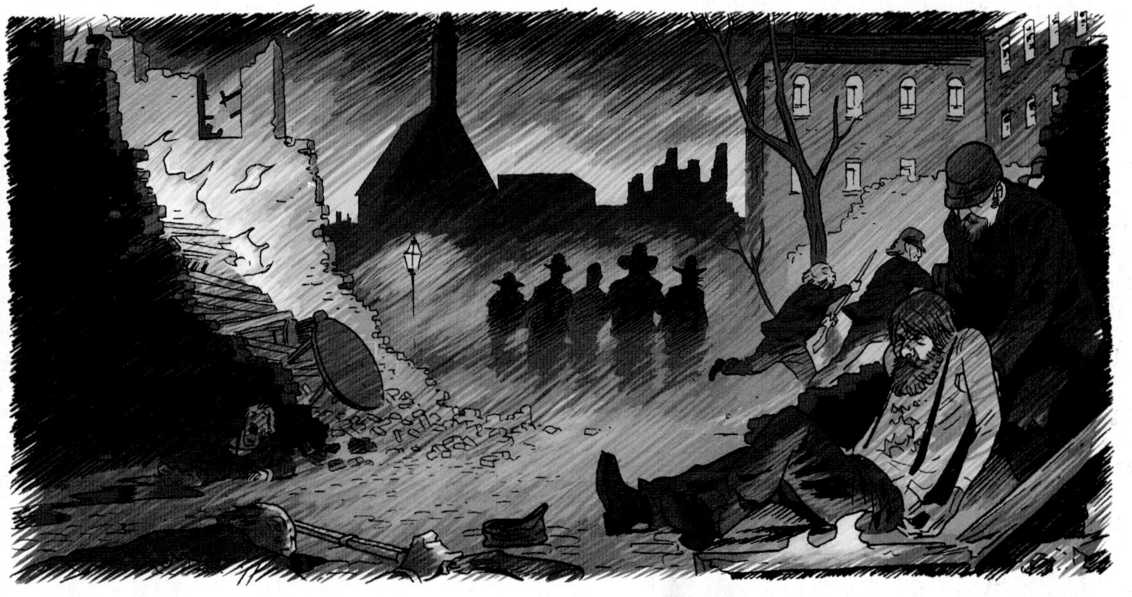

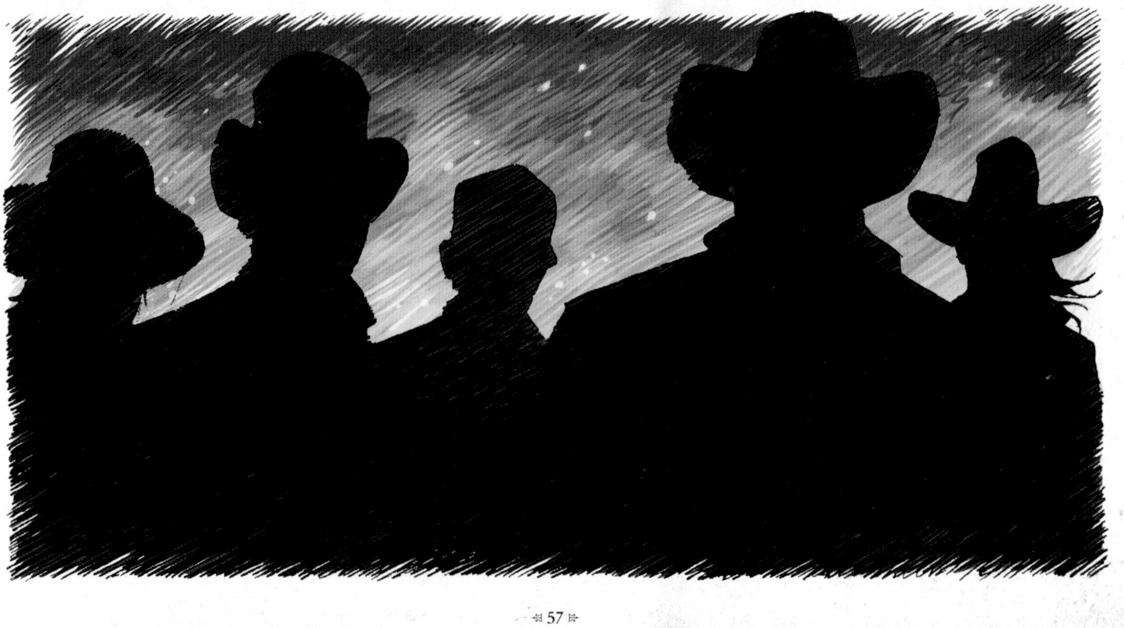

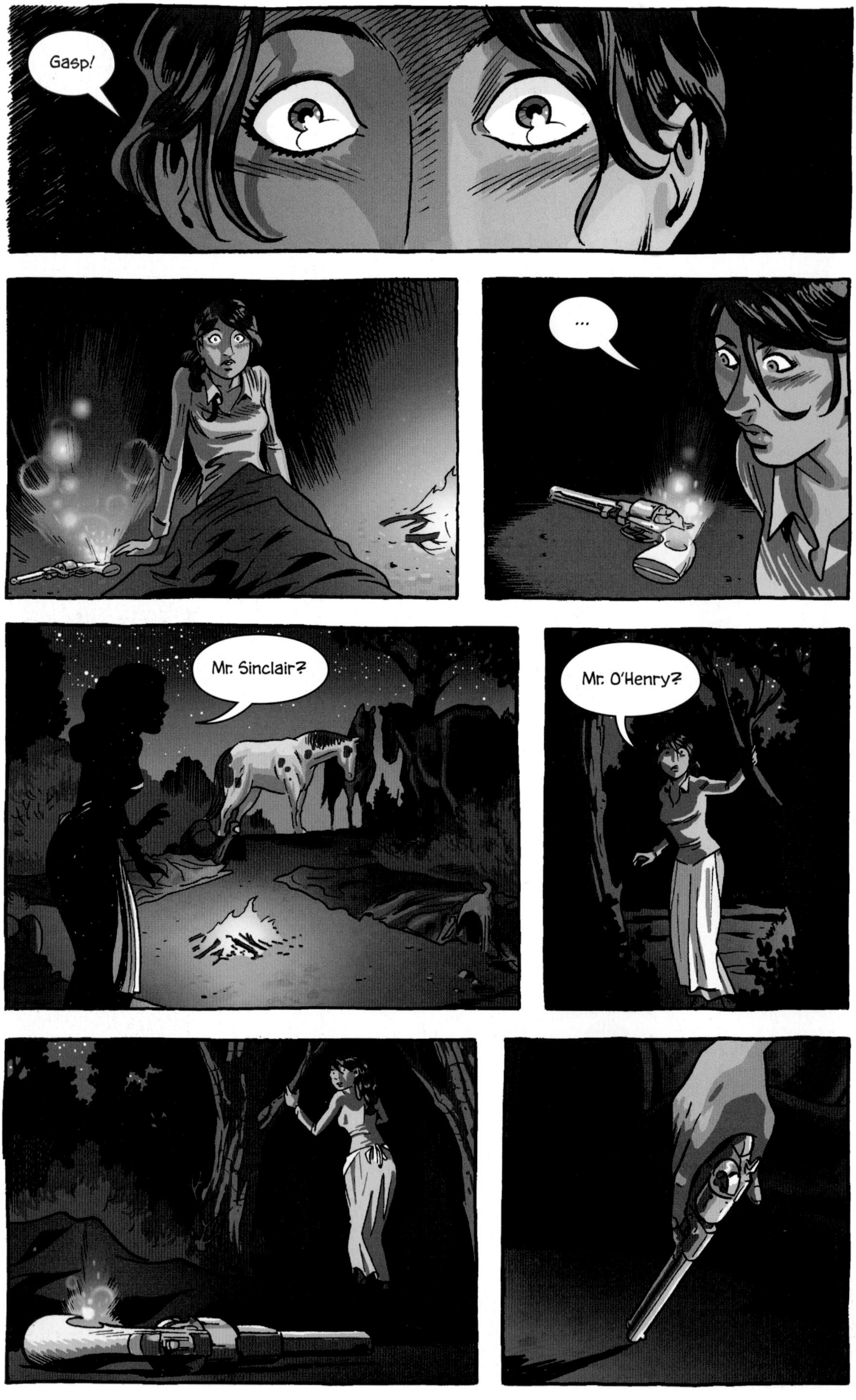
Gasp!
...
Mr. Sinclair?
Mr. O'Henry?

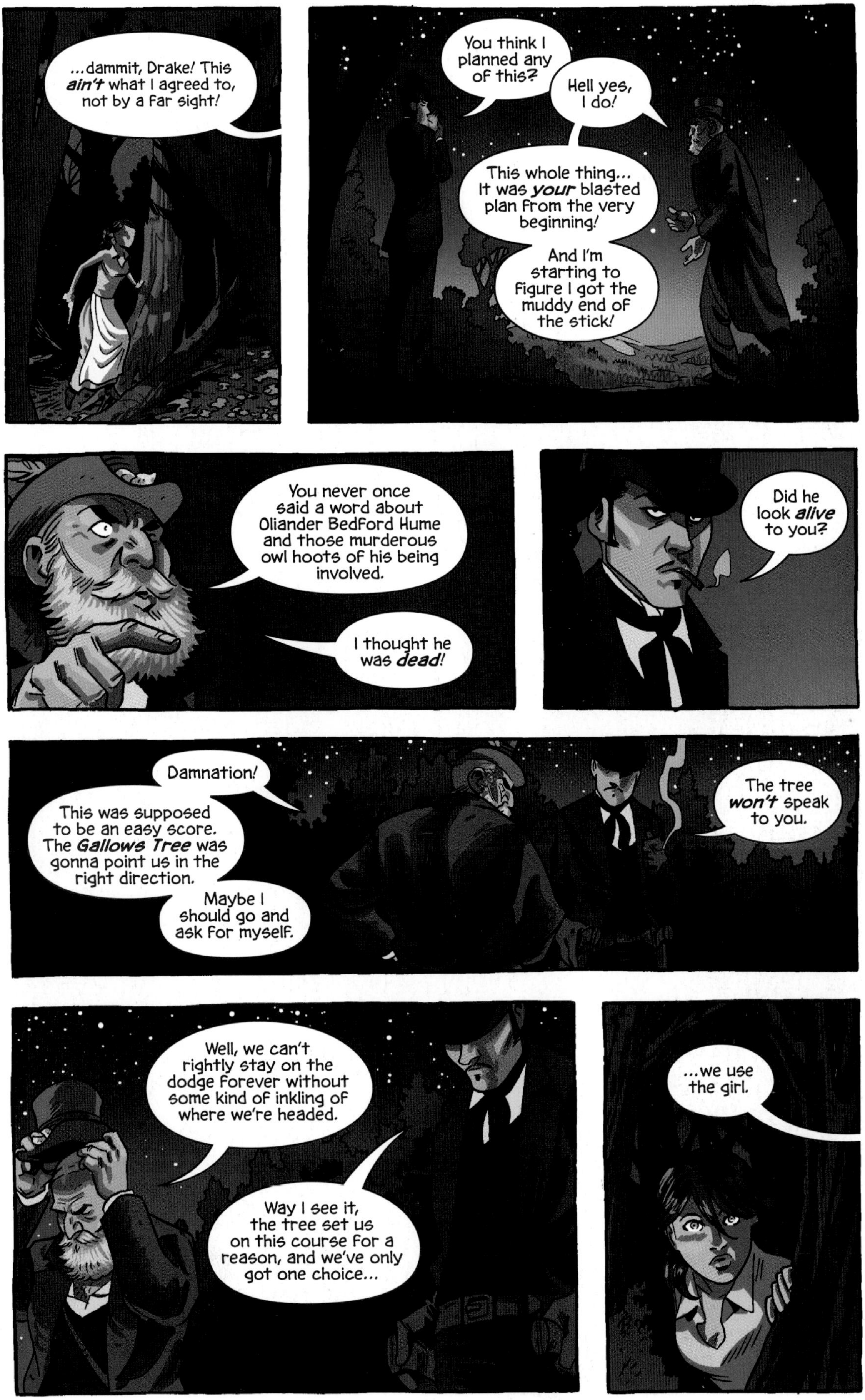

...dammit, Drake! This ain't what I agreed to, not by a far sight!
You think I planned any of this?
Hell yes, I do!
This whole thing... It was your blasted plan from the very beginning!
And I'm starting to figure I got the muddy end of the stick!
You never once said a word about Oliander Bedford Hume and those murderous owl hoots of his being involved.
I thought he was dead!
Did he look alive to you?
Damnation!
This was supposed to be an easy score. The Gallows Tree was gonna point us in the right direction.
Maybe I should go and ask for myself.
The tree won't speak to you.
Well, we can't rightly stay on the dodge forever without some kind of inkling of where we're headed.
Way I see it, the tree set us on this course for a reason, and we've only got one choice...
...we use the girl.

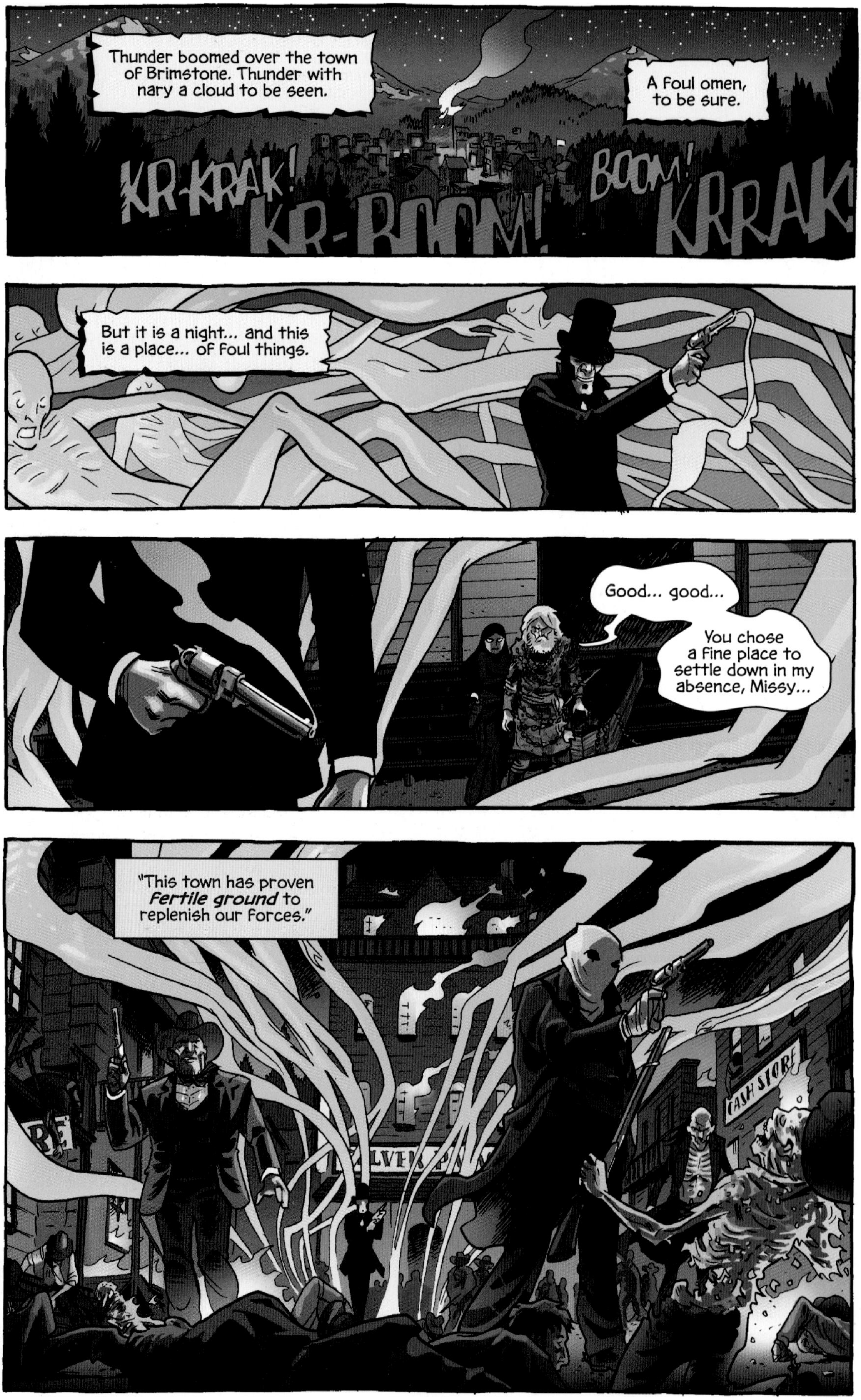

Thunder boomed over the town of Brimstone. Thunder with nary a cloud to be seen.
A foul omen, to be sure.
KR-KRAK!
KR-BOOM!
BOOM!
KRRAK!
But it is a night... and this is a place... of foul things.
Good... good...
You chose a fine place to settle down in my absence, Missy...
"This town has proven *fertile ground* to replenish our forces."
CASH STORE

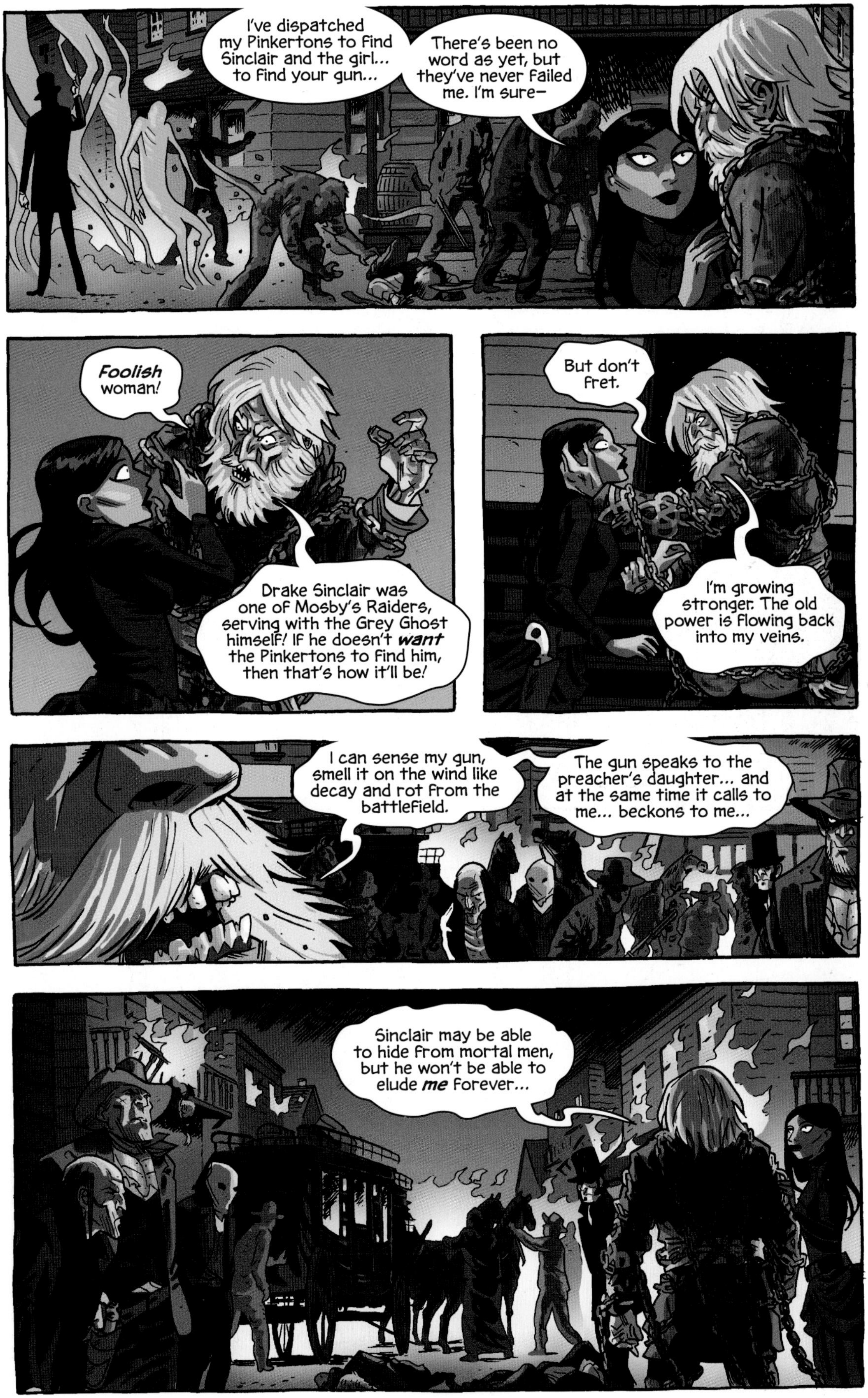

I've dispatched my Pinkertons to find Sinclair and the girl... to find your gun...
There's been no word as yet, but they've never failed me. I'm sure—
*Foolish* woman!
Drake Sinclair was one of Mosby's Raiders, serving with the Grey Ghost himself! If he doesn't *want* the Pinkertons to find him, then that's how it'll be!
But don't fret.
I'm growing stronger. The old power is flowing back into my veins.
I can sense my gun, smell it on the wind like decay and rot from the battlefield.
The gun speaks to the preacher's daughter... and at the same time it calls to me... beckons to me...
Sinclair may be able to hide from mortal men, but he won't be able to elude *me* forever...

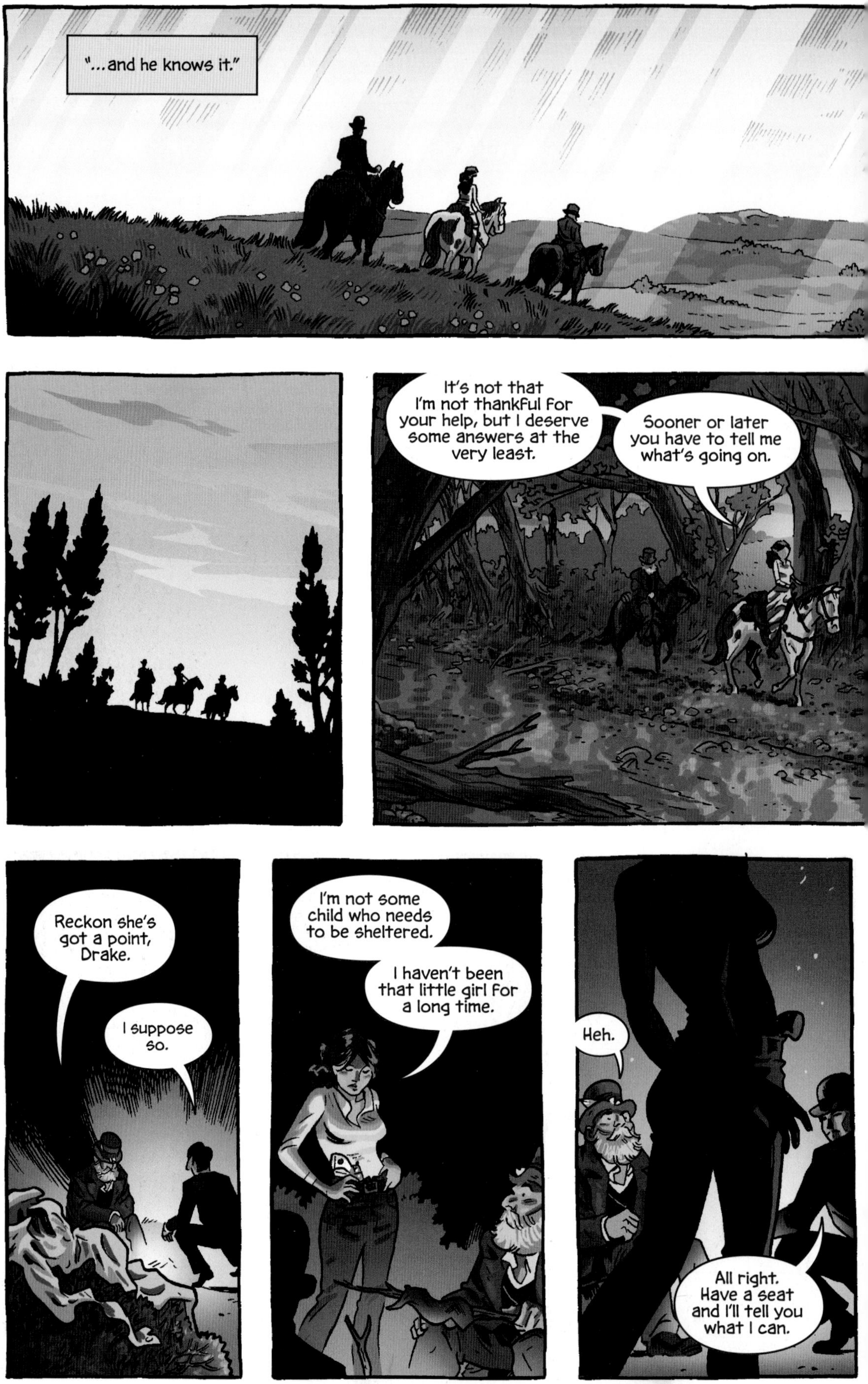
"...and he knows it."
It's not that I'm not thankful for your help, but I deserve some answers at the very least.
Sooner or later you have to tell me what's going on.
Reckon she's got a point, Drake.
I suppose so.
I'm not some child who needs to be sheltered.
I haven't been that little girl for a long time.
Heh.
All right. Have a seat and I'll tell you what I can.

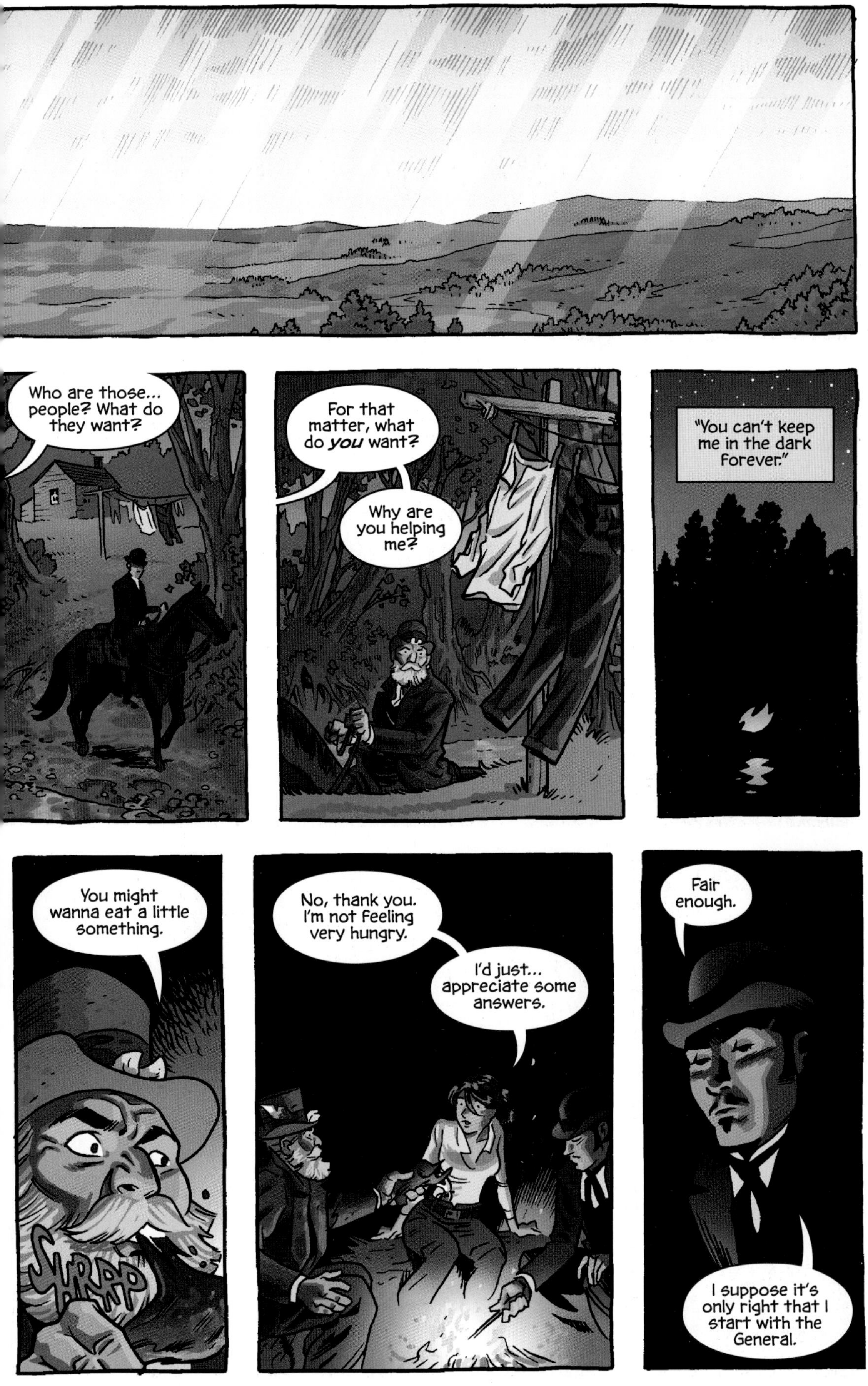

Who are those... people? What do they want?
For that matter, what do *you* want?
Why are you helping me?
"You can't keep me in the dark forever."
You might wanna eat a little something.
SHRRP
No, thank you. I'm not feeling very hungry.
I'd just... appreciate some answers.
Fair enough.
I suppose it's only right that I start with the General.

"Oliandar Bedford Hume was one of the most feared... and the most *reviled* generals of the Confederacy.

"He was a brilliant strategist, leading his troops to victory after victory. It was said that if you followed Hume, you followed him to glory.

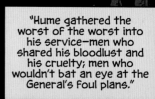

"But he was also a bloodthirsty madman...

"...the kind of man who inspired all manner of dark rumors and god-awful stories.

"Only, no matter how awful the stories were, the *truth* was far more frightening.

"Hume gathered the worst of the worst into his service—men who shared his bloodlust and his cruelty; men who wouldn't bat an eye at the General's foul plans."

What about the guns?

I don't know if anyone other than the General himself knows where the guns came from.

Some say he conjured them up using sorcery. Others say he found them in some forgotten ruin.

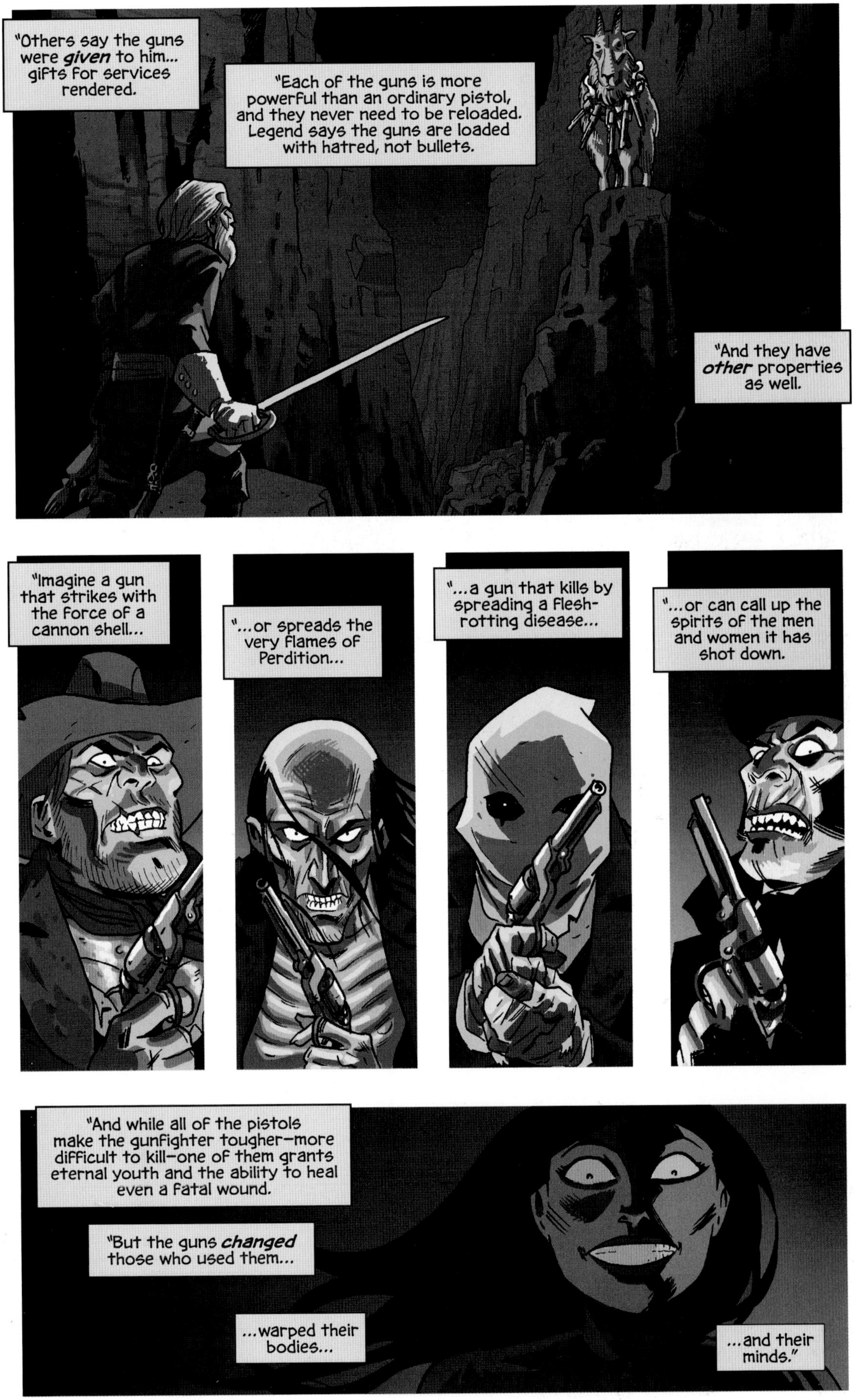
"Others say the guns were *given* to him... gifts for services rendered.
"Each of the guns is more powerful than an ordinary pistol, and they never need to be reloaded. Legend says the guns are loaded with hatred, not bullets.
"And they have *other* properties as well.
"Imagine a gun that strikes with the force of a cannon shell...
"...or spreads the very flames of Perdition...
"...a gun that kills by spreading a flesh-rotting disease...
"...or can call up the spirits of the men and women it has shot down.
"And while all of the pistols make the gunfighter tougher—more difficult to kill—one of them grants eternal youth and the ability to heal even a fatal wound.
"But the guns *changed* those who used them...
...warped their bodies...
...and their minds."

W-what about *this* gun?

Is it going to... to *change* me?

I don't know.

That gun speaks to you... shows you things that have happened... and circumstances that have yet to pass.

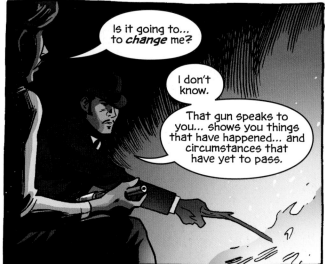

It's said General Hume was such a brilliant warmonger because he knew the way a battle was going to play out long before it took place.

"He saw the *future*."

The Future...

Only, all the fortune-telling in the world didn't keep him from getting killed, did it?

That's on account that no man, no matter how insightful, can know the cause of his demise.

How... how did he die?

A man with that much anger and bloodlust... with all that dark knowledge... can't ever really die.

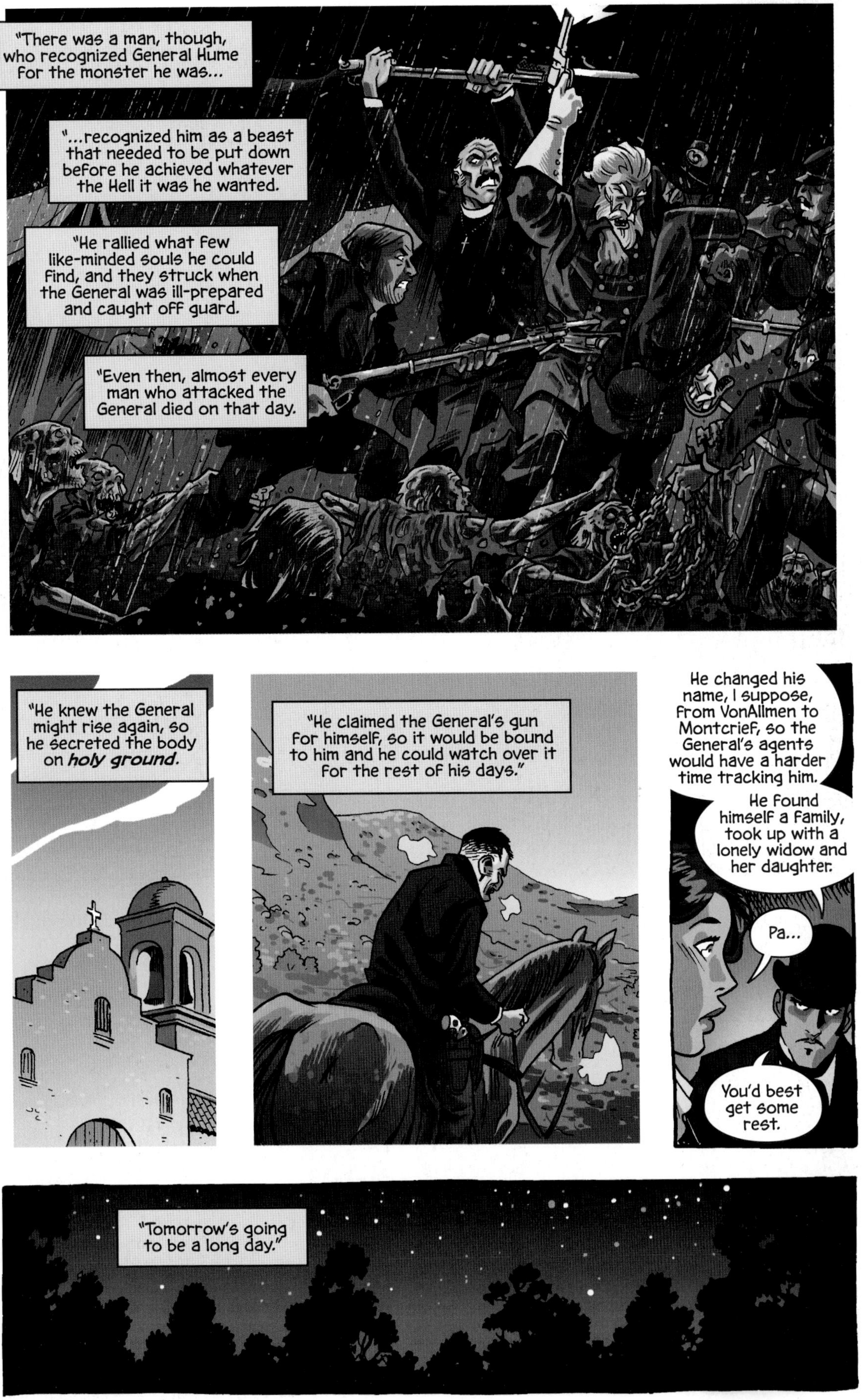
"There was a man, though, who recognized General Hume for the monster he was...
"...recognized him as a beast that needed to be put down before he achieved whatever the Hell it was he wanted.
"He rallied what few like-minded souls he could find, and they struck when the General was ill-prepared and caught off guard.
"Even then, almost every man who attacked the General died on that day.
"He knew the General might rise again, so he secreted the body on *holy ground*.
"He claimed the General's gun for himself, so it would be bound to him and he could watch over it for the rest of his days."
He changed his name, I suppose, from VonAllmen to Montcrief, so the General's agents would have a harder time tracking him.
He found himself a family, took up with a lonely widow and her daughter.
Pa...
You'd best get some rest.
"Tomorrow's going to be a long day."

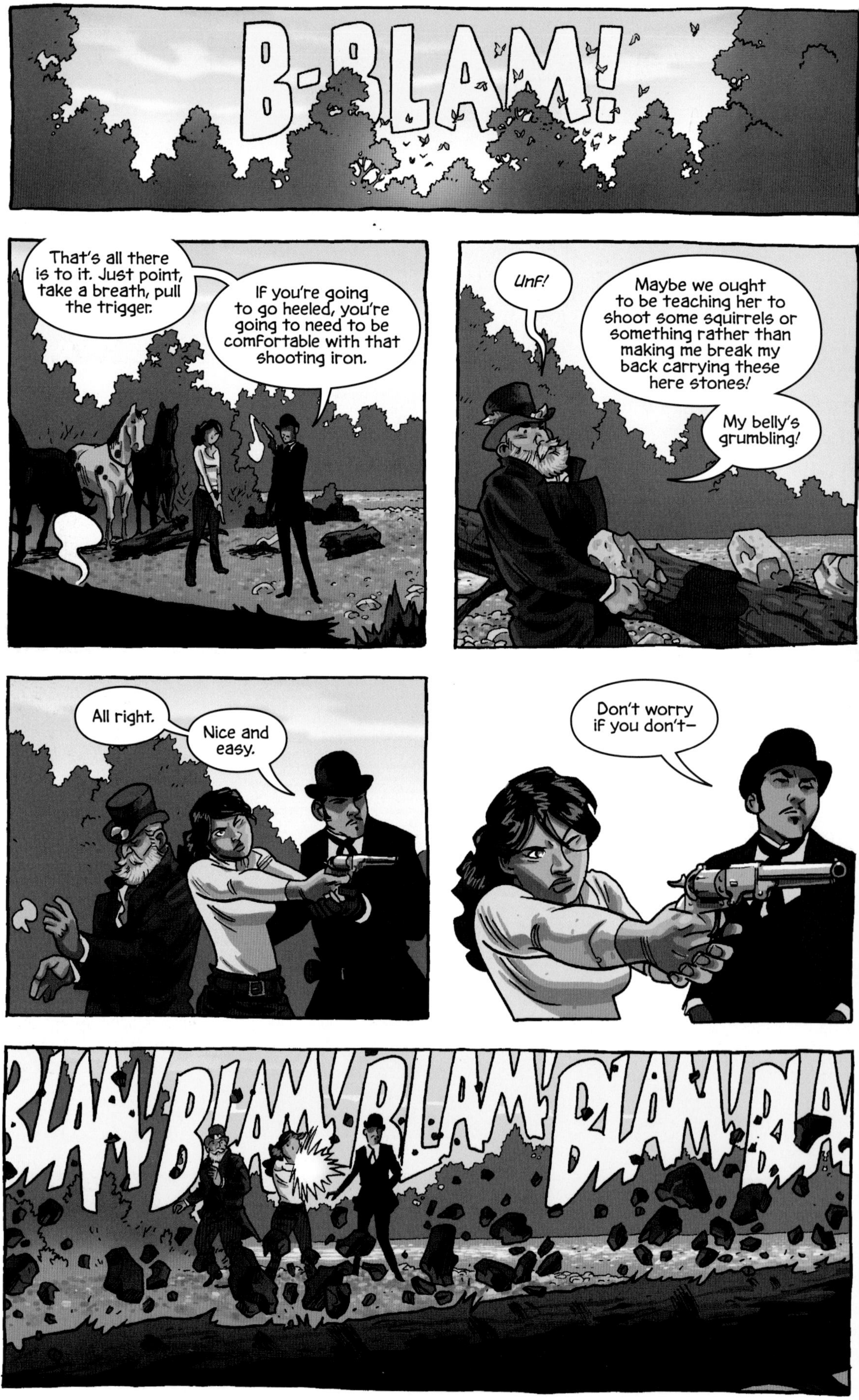
B-BLAM!
That's all there is to it. Just point, take a breath, pull the trigger.
If you're going to go heeled, you're going to need to be comfortable with that shooting iron.
Unf!
Maybe we ought to be teaching her to shoot some squirrels or something rather than making me break my back carrying these here stones!
My belly's grumbling!
All right.
Nice and easy.
Don't worry if you don't—
BLAM BLAM BLAM BLAM BLAM

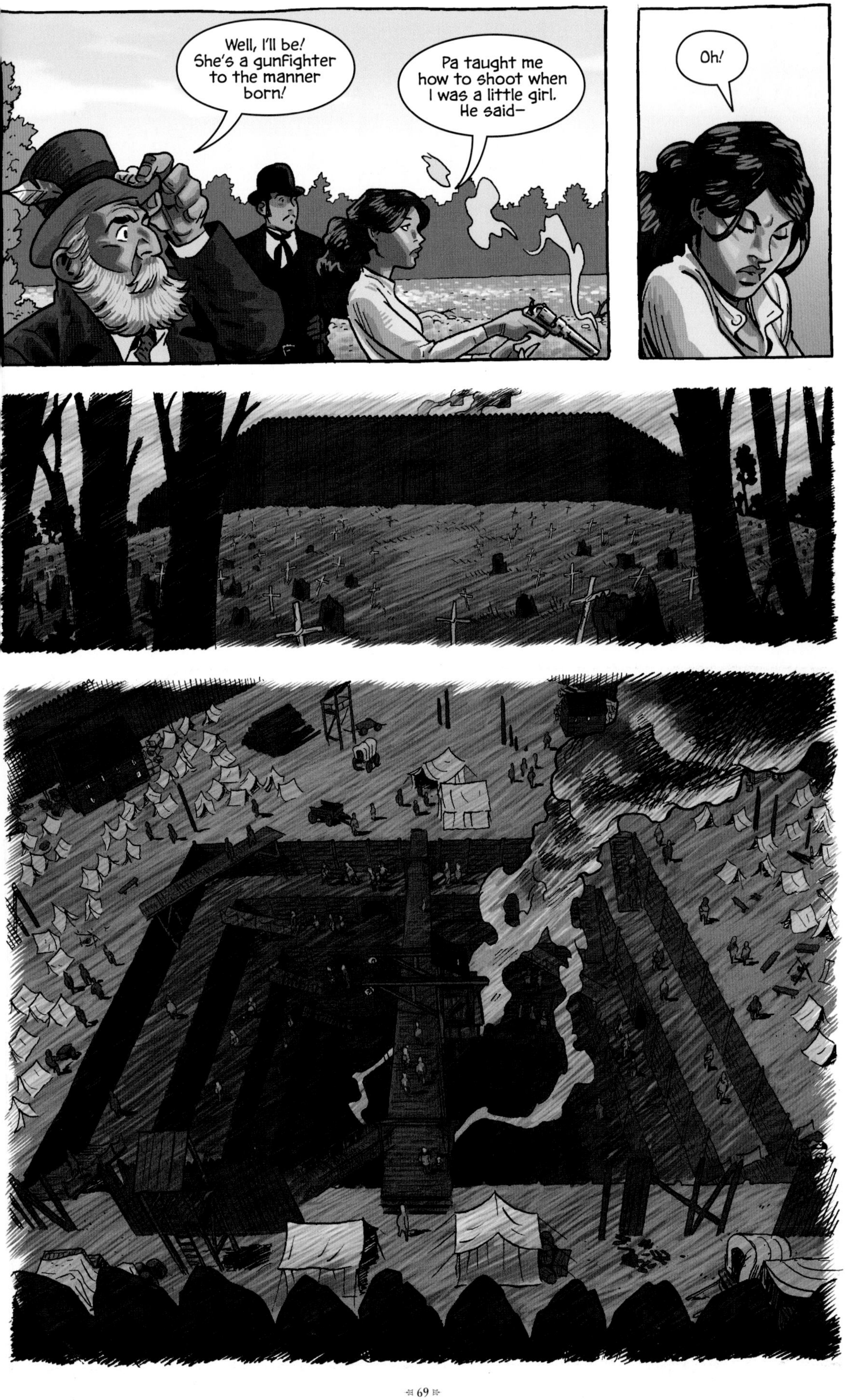

Well, I'll be! She's a gunfighter to the manner born!
Pa taught me how to shoot when I was a little girl. He said—
Oh!

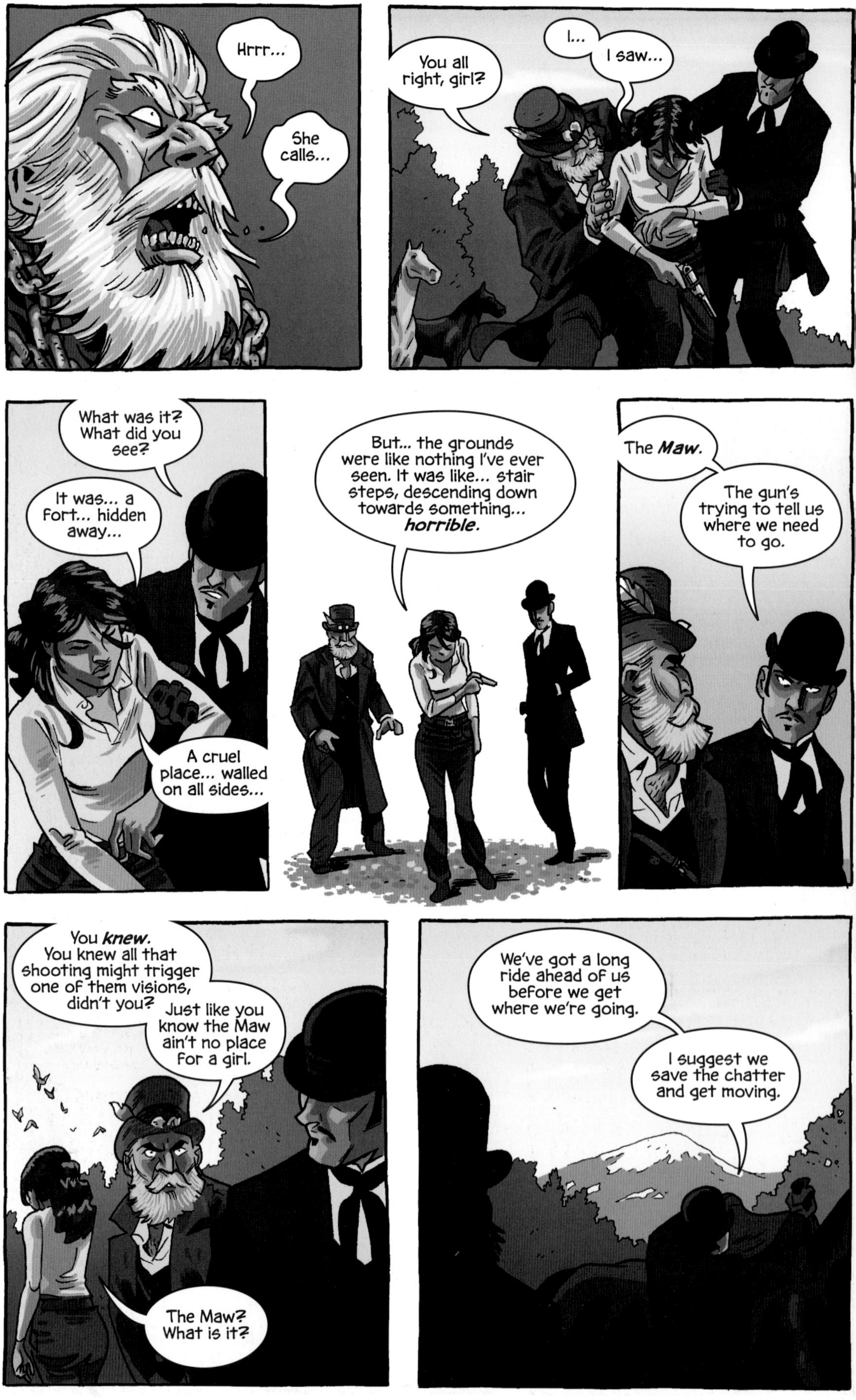

Hrrr...
She calls...
I...
You all right, girl?
I saw...
What was it? What did you see?
It was... a fort... hidden away...
A cruel place... walled on all sides...
But... the grounds were like nothing I've ever seen. It was like... stair steps, descending down towards something... ***horrible***.
The ***Maw***.
The gun's trying to tell us where we need to go.
You ***knew***. You knew all that shooting might trigger one of them visions, didn't you?
Just like you know the Maw ain't no place for a girl.
The Maw? What is it?
We've got a long ride ahead of us before we get where we're going.
I suggest we save the chatter and get moving.

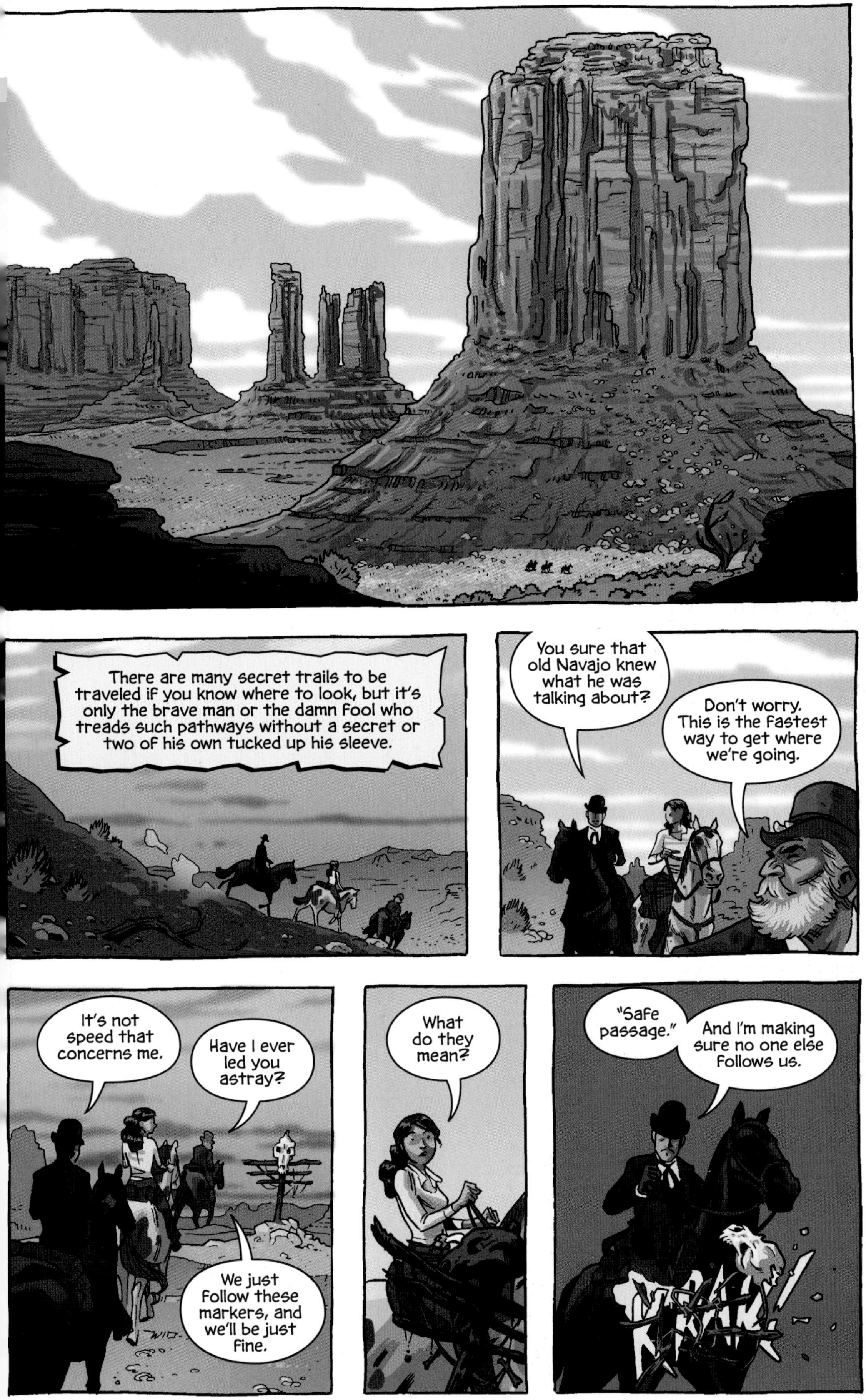
There are many secret trails to be traveled if you know where to look, but it's only the brave man or the damn fool who treads such pathways without a secret or two of his own tucked up his sleeve.
You sure that old Navajo knew what he was talking about?
Don't worry. This is the fastest way to get where we're going.
It's not speed that concerns me.
Have I ever led you astray?
We just follow these markers, and we'll be just fine.
What do they mean?
"Safe passage."
And I'm making sure no one else follows us.
KRAK!

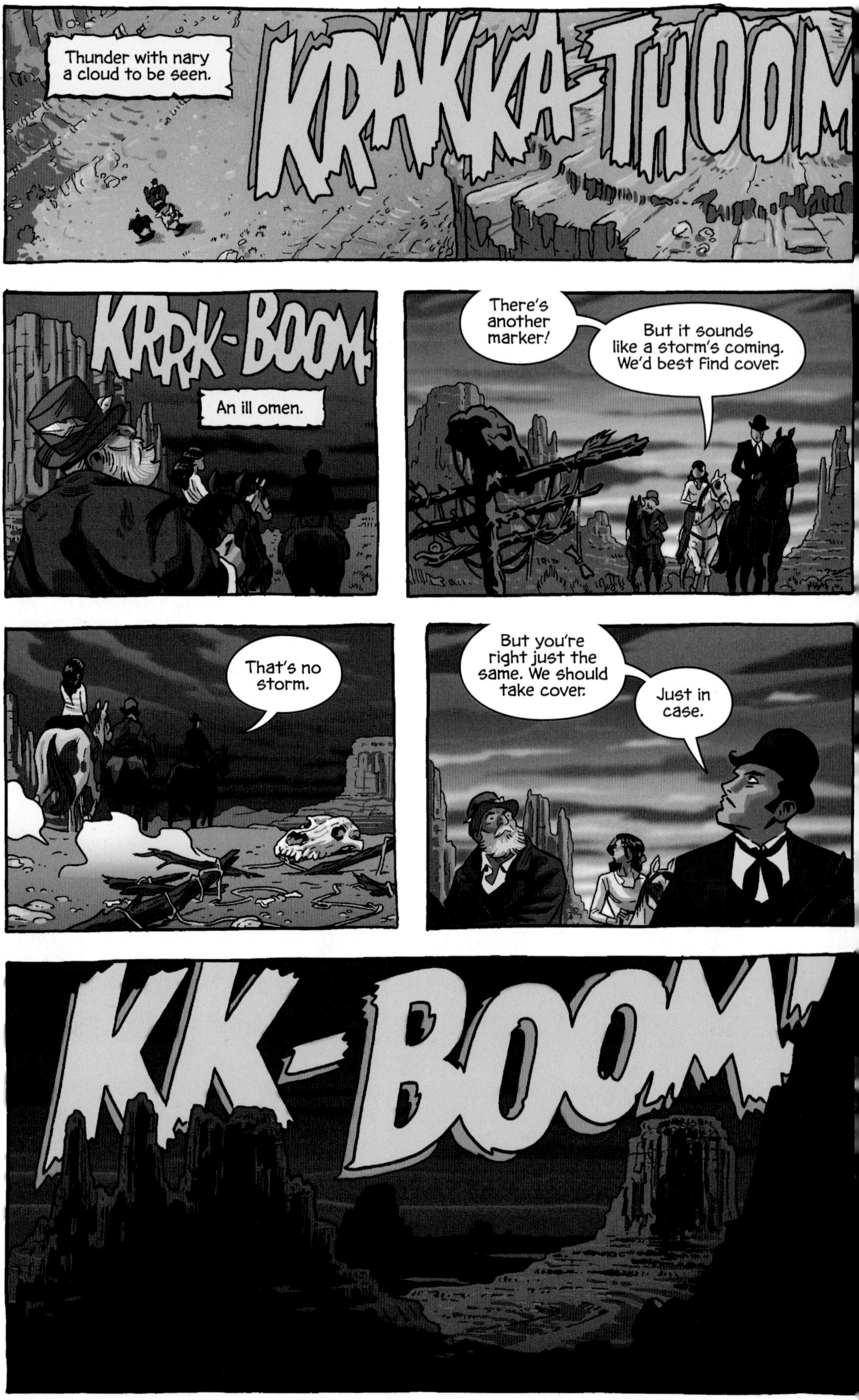
Thunder with nary a cloud to be seen.
KRAKKA-THOOM
KRRK-BOOM
An ill omen.
There's another marker!
But it sounds like a storm's coming. We'd best find cover.
That's no storm.
But you're right just the same. We should take cover.
Just in case.
KK-BOOM

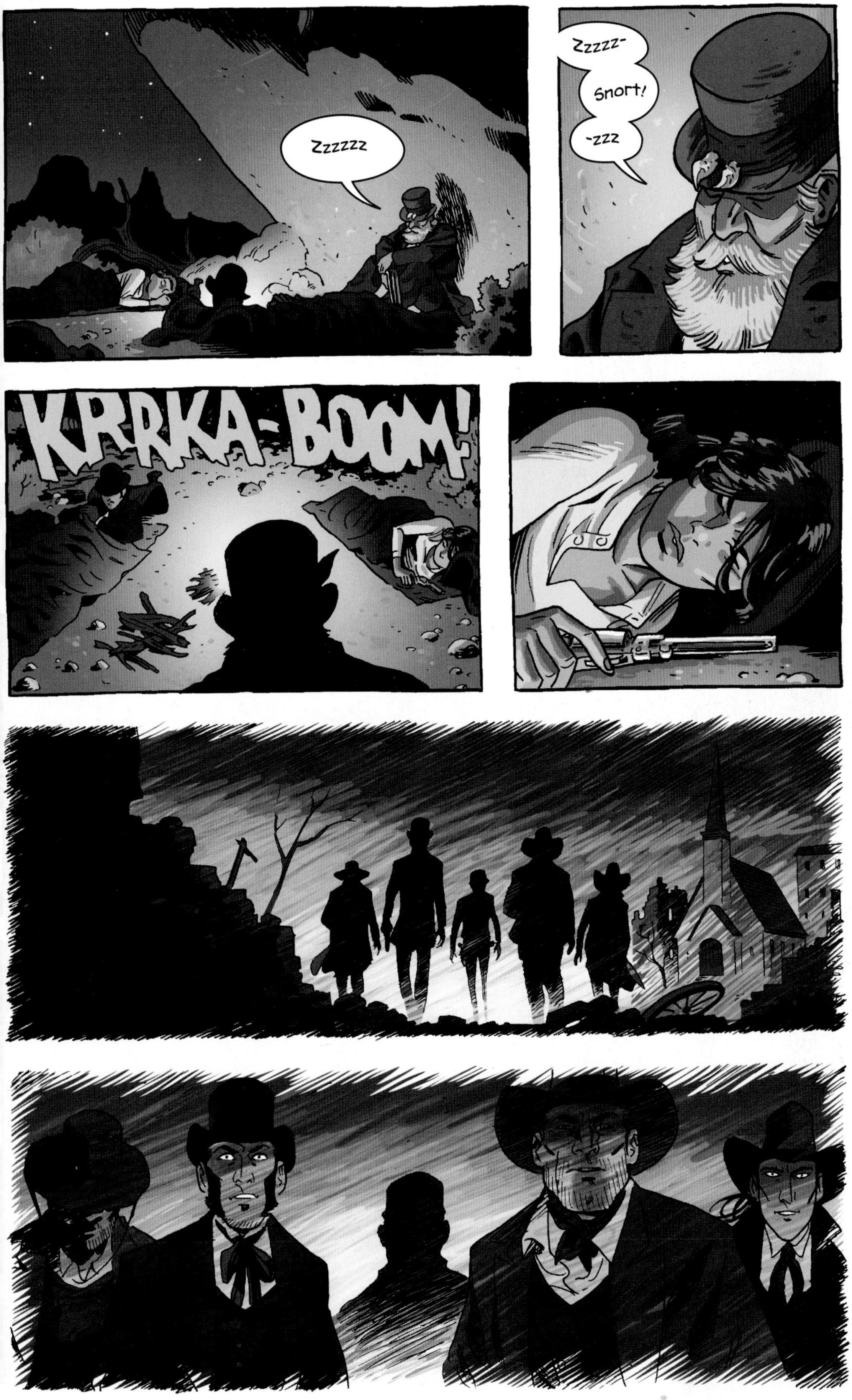
Zzzzzz
Zzzzz-
Snort!
-zzz
KRRKA-BOOM!

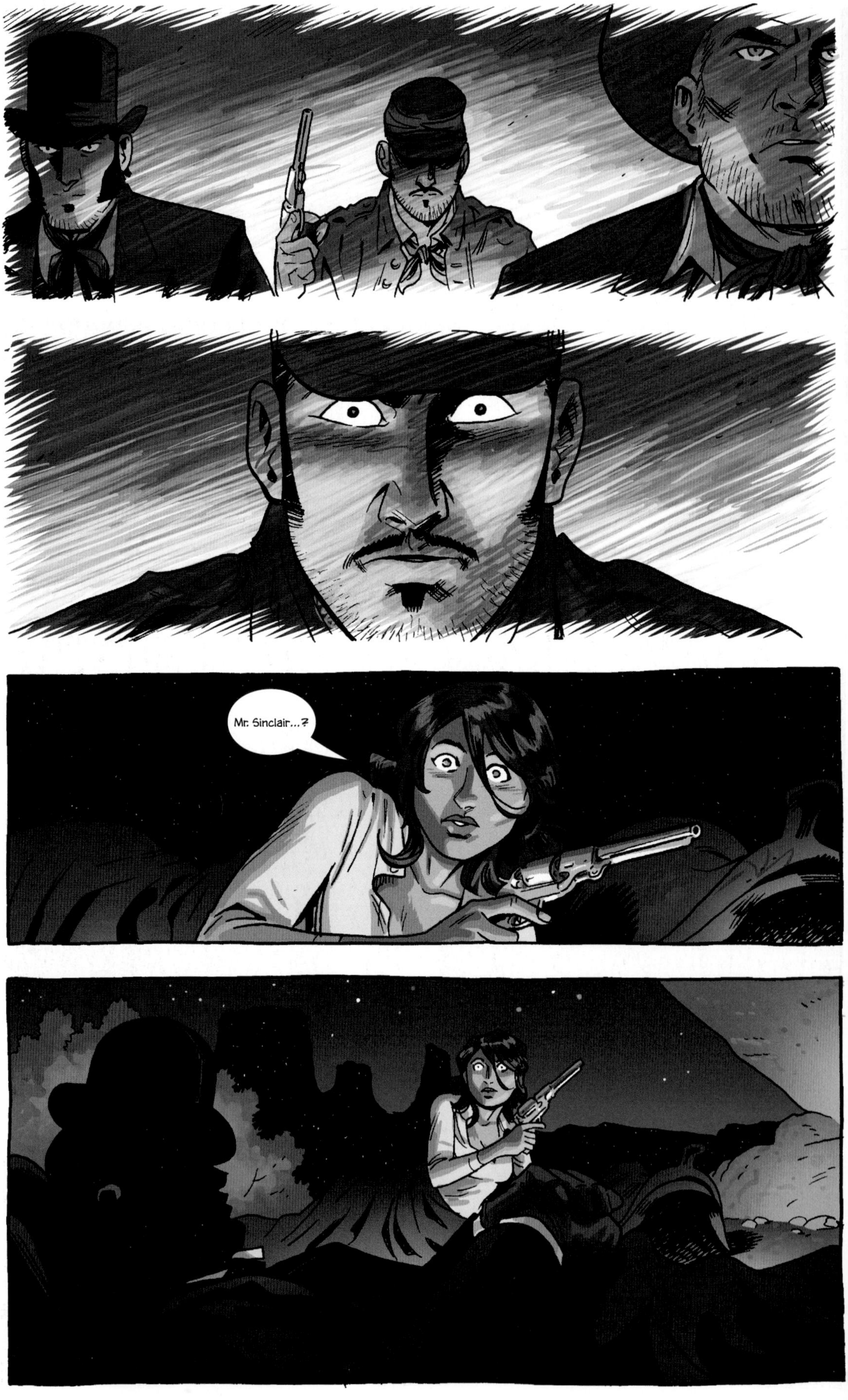
Mr. Sinclair...?

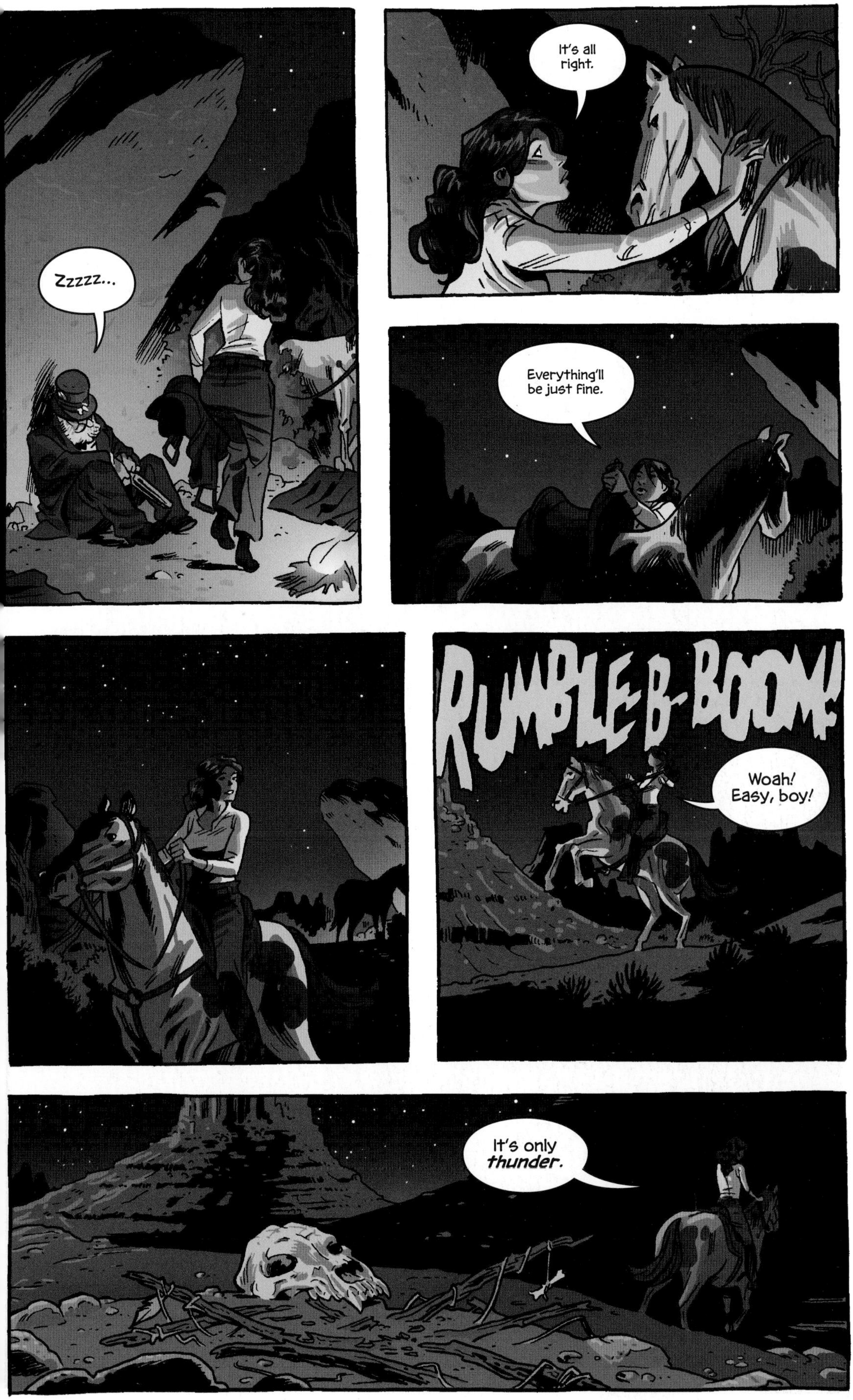
Zzzzz...
It's all right.
Everything'll be just fine.
RUMBLE B-BOOM!
Woah! Easy, boy!
It's only *thunder*.

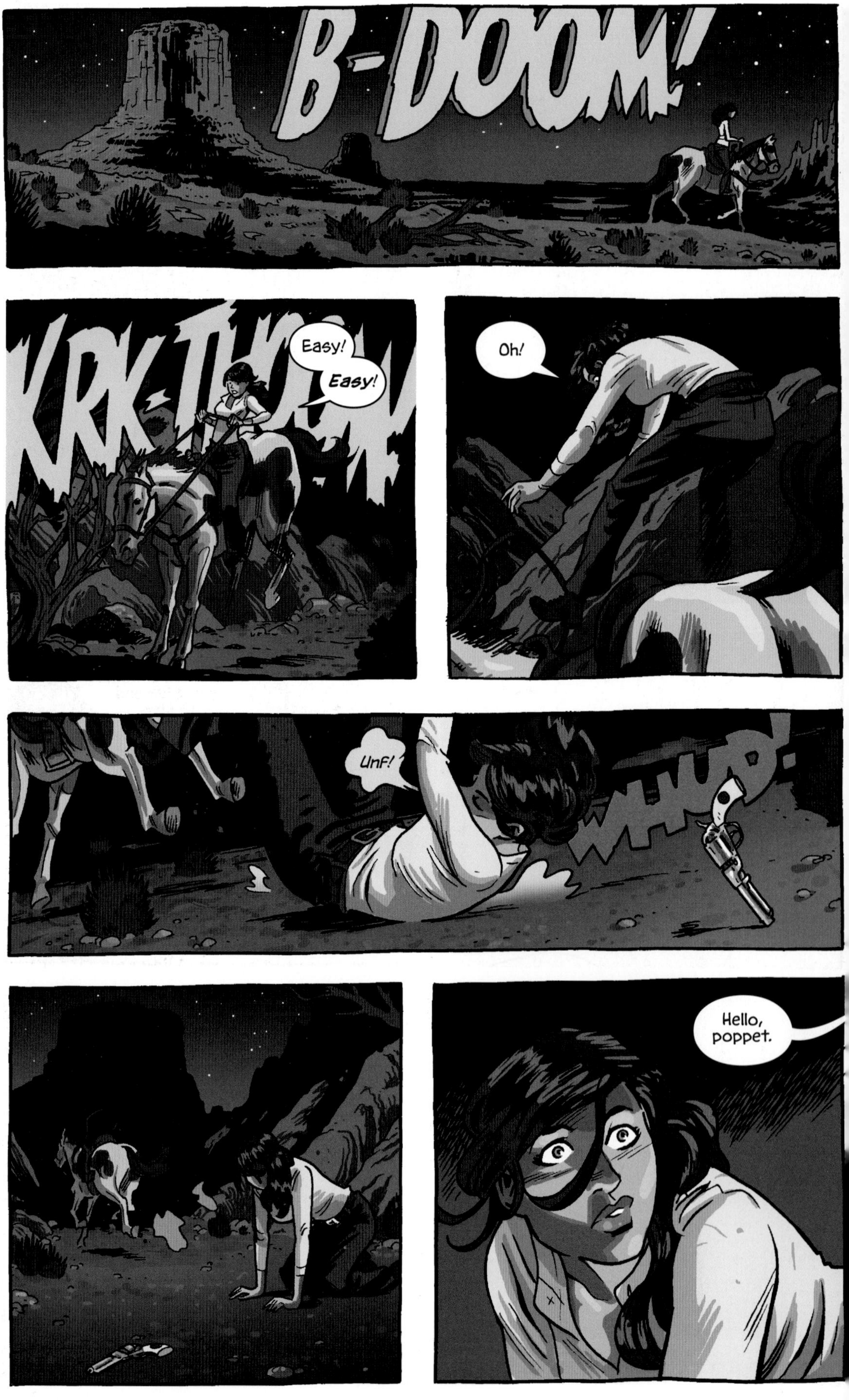
B-DOOM!
KRK-TUNK
Easy!
Easy!
Oh!
Unf!
WHUD!
Hello, poppet.

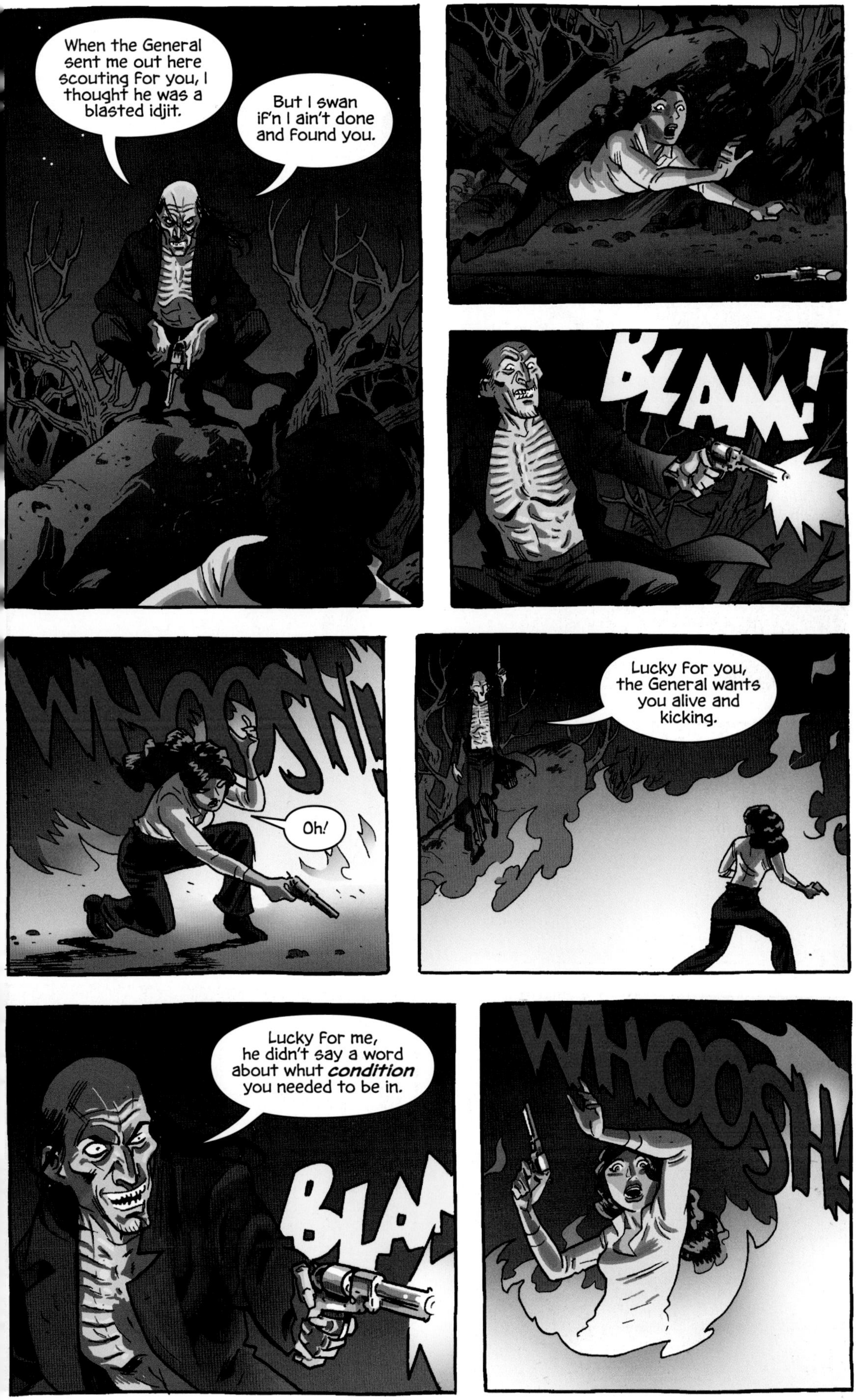
When the General sent me out here scouting for you, I thought he was a blasted idjit.
But I swan if'n I ain't done and found you.
BLAM!
WHOOSH!
Oh!
Lucky for you, the General wants you alive and kicking.
Lucky for me, he didn't say a word about whut *condition* you needed to be in.
BLA
WHOOSH

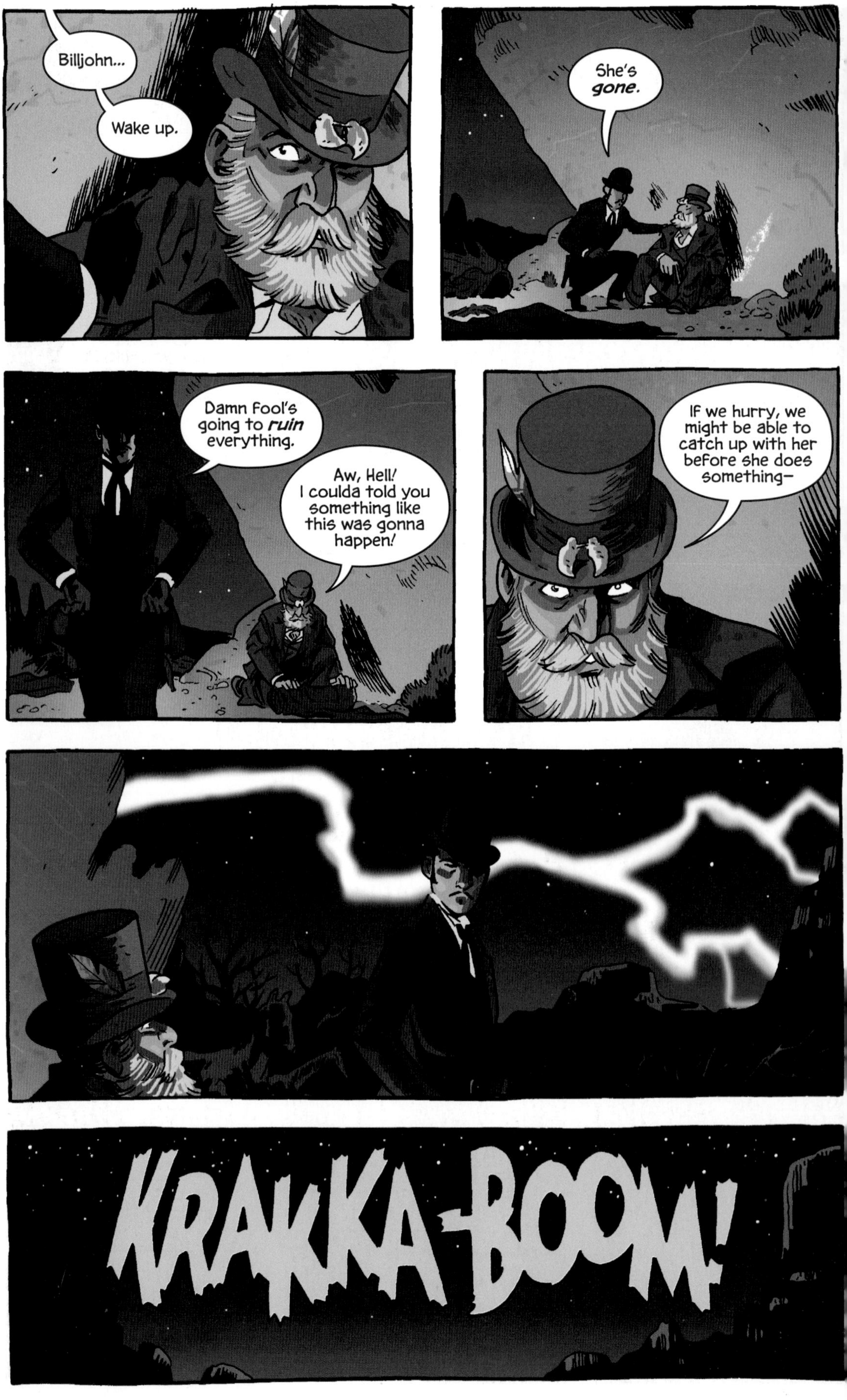
Billjohn...
Wake up.
She's *gone*.
Damn Fool's going to *ruin* everything.
Aw, Hell! I coulda told you something like this was gonna happen!
If we hurry, we might be able to catch up with her before she does something—
KRAKKA-BOOM!

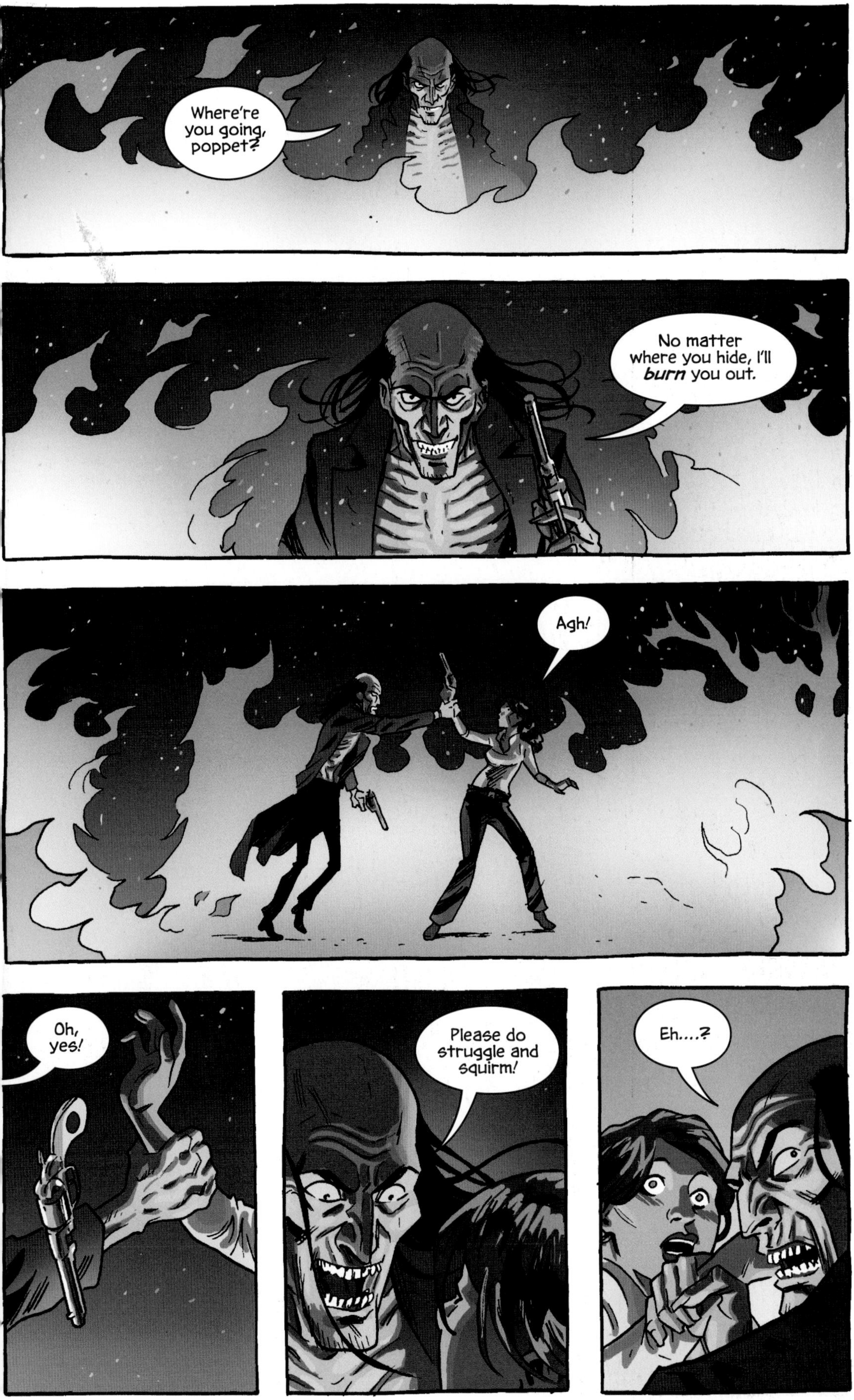
Where're you going, poppet?
No matter where you hide, I'll *burn* you out.
Agh!
Oh, yes!
Please do struggle and squirm!
Eh....?

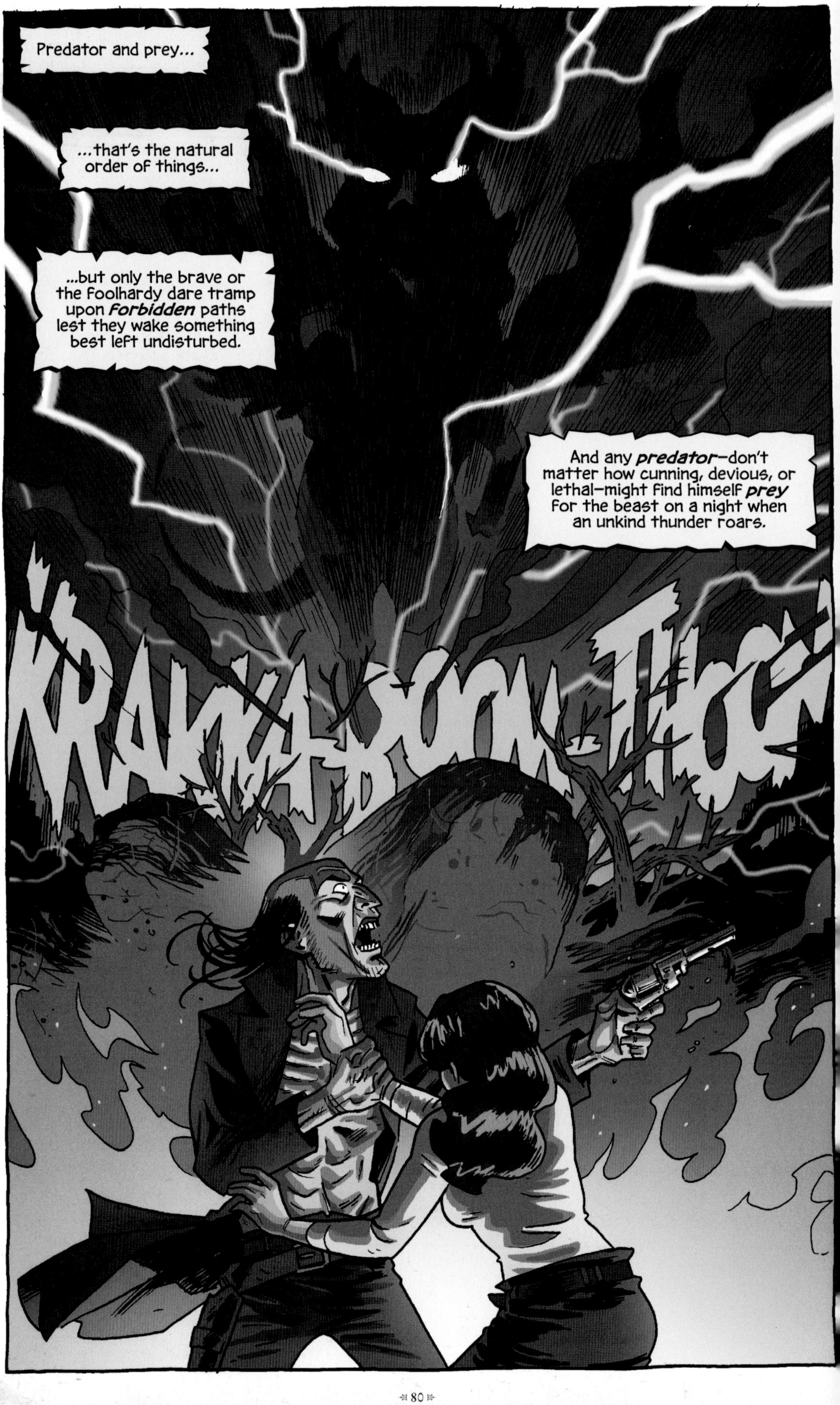

Predator and prey...
...that's the natural order of things...
...but only the brave or the foolhardy dare tramp upon *forbidden* paths lest they wake something best left undisturbed.
And any *predator*—don't matter how cunning, devious, or lethal—might find himself *prey* for the beast on a night when an unkind thunder roars.

# CHAPTER FOUR

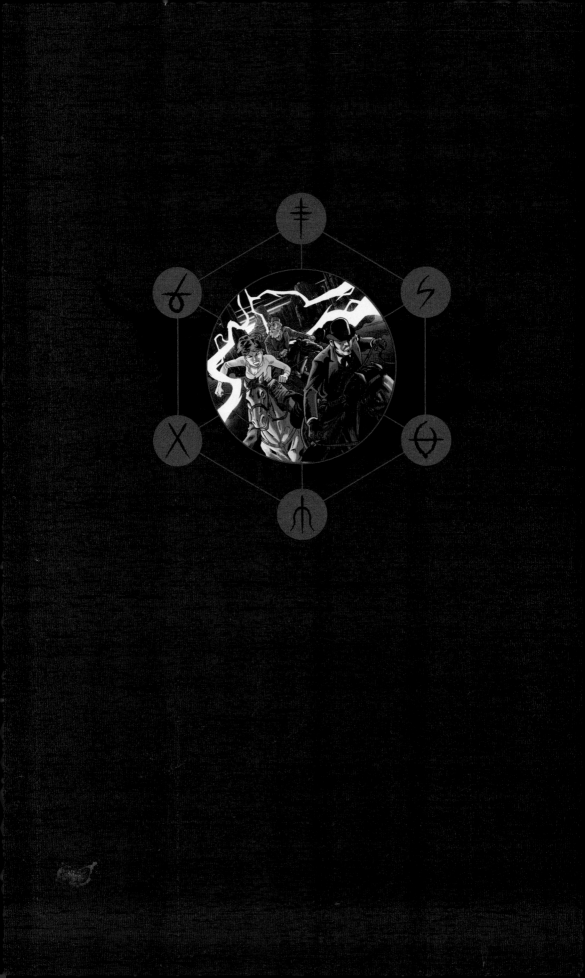

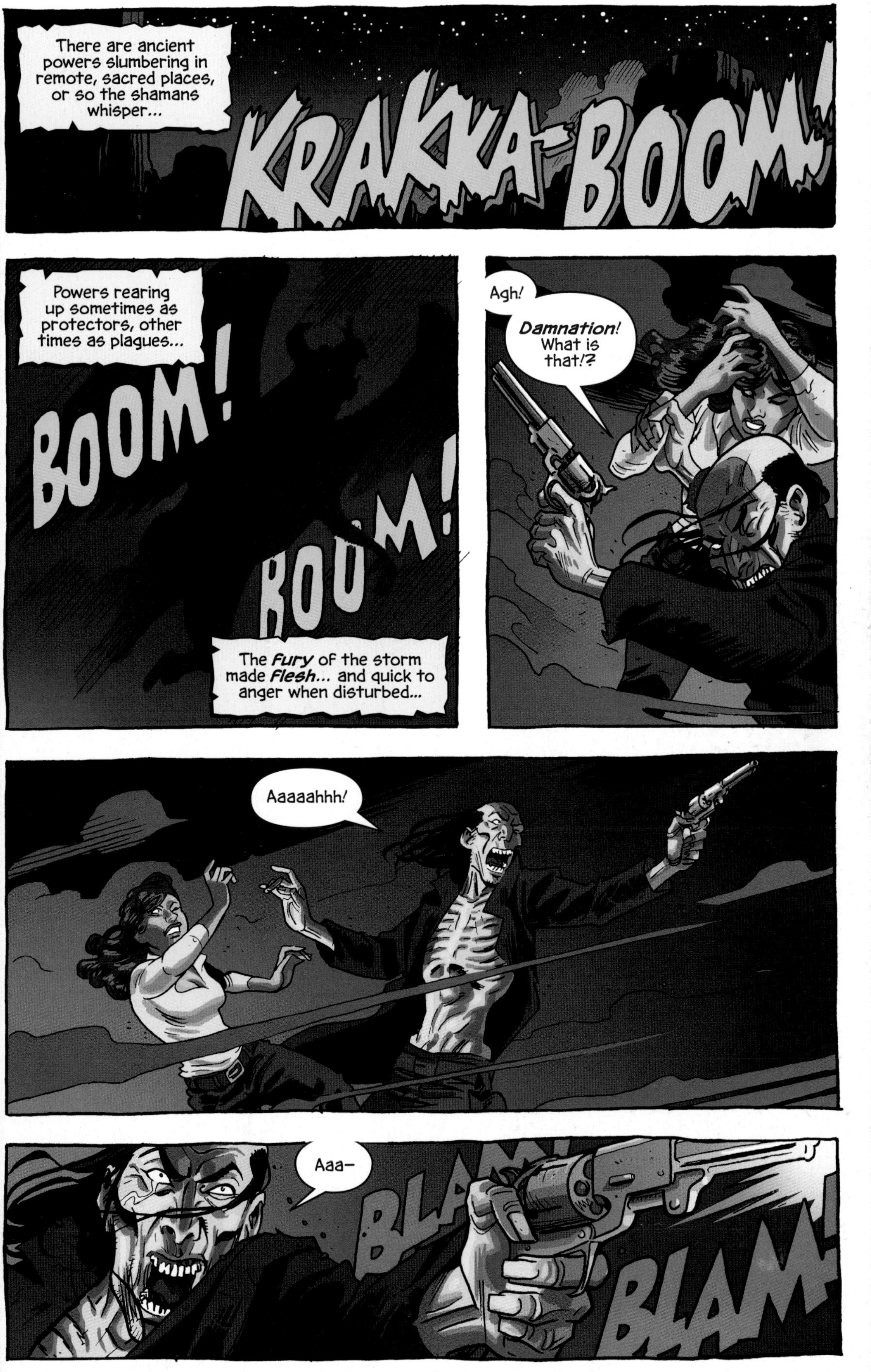
There are ancient powers slumbering in remote, sacred places, or so the shamans whisper...
KRAKKA-BOOM!
Powers rearing up sometimes as protectors, other times as plagues...
BOOM!
BOOM!
The *Fury* of the storm made *Flesh*... and quick to anger when disturbed...
Agh!
*Damnation*! What is that!?
Aaaaahhh!
Aaa—
BLAM!
BLAM

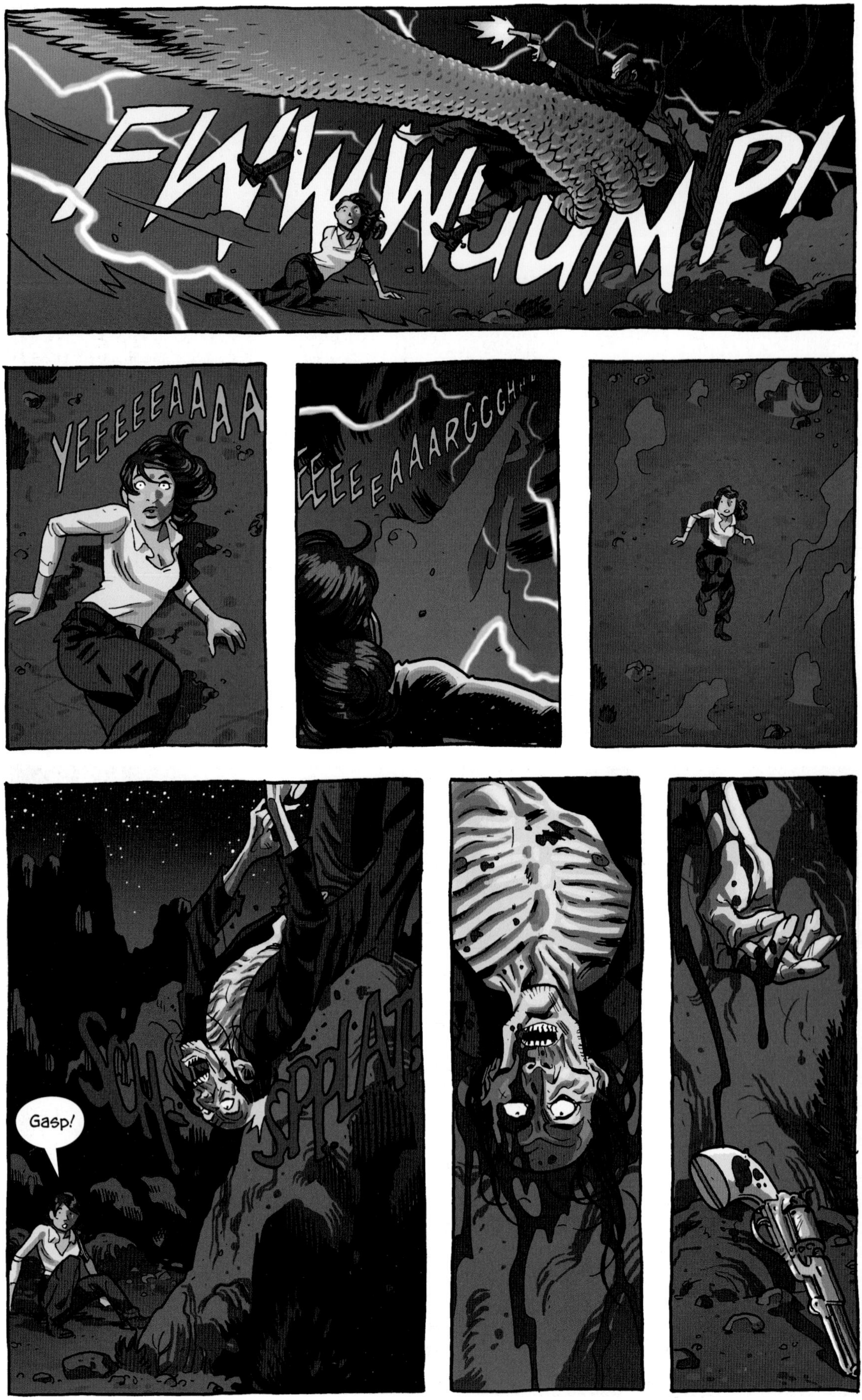
FWWWUUMP!
YEEEEEAAAA
EEEEEAAARGGGH
SCHLUK
SPLAT
Gasp!

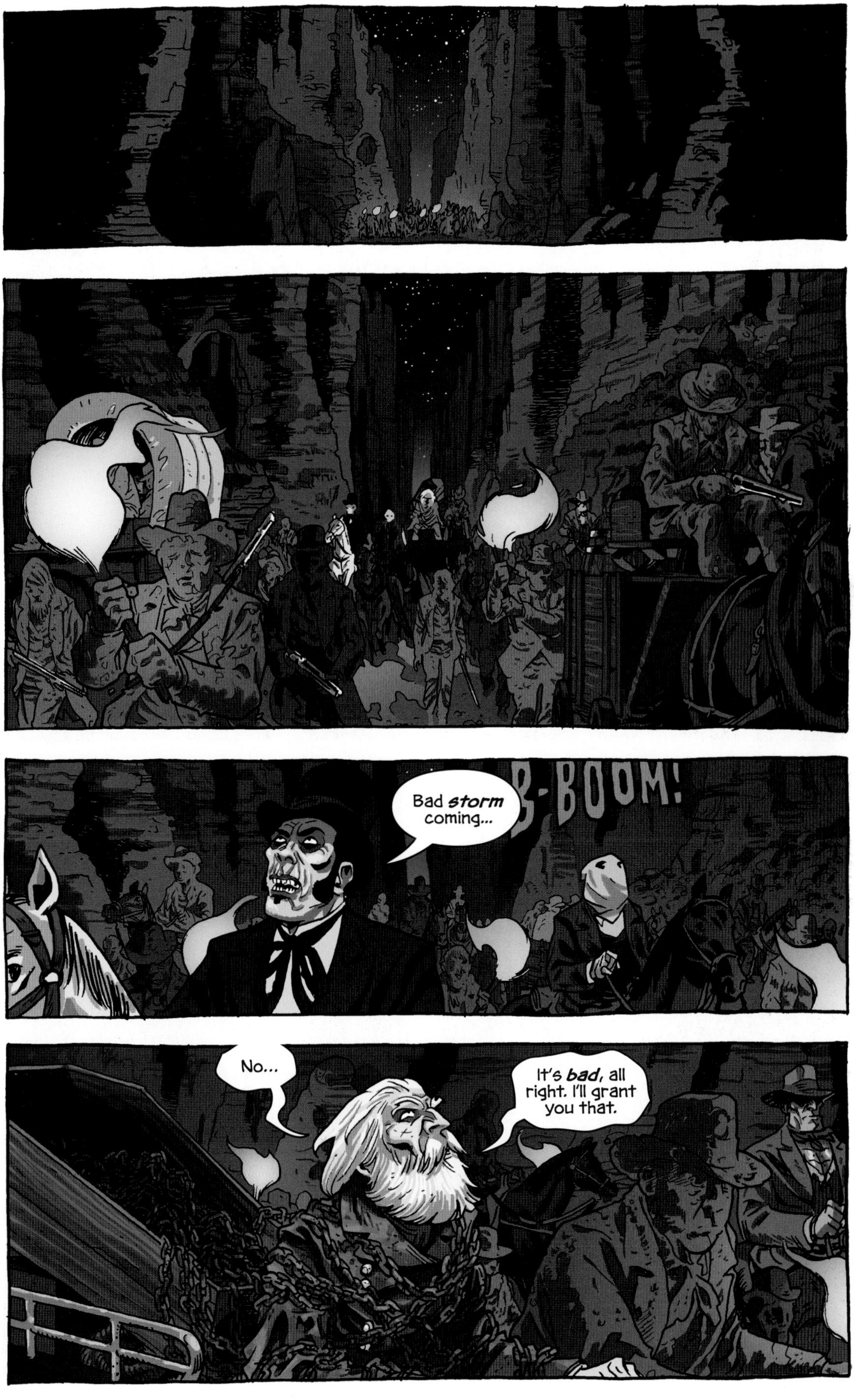
Bad *storm* coming...
B-BOOM!
No...
It's *bad,* all right. I'll grant you that.

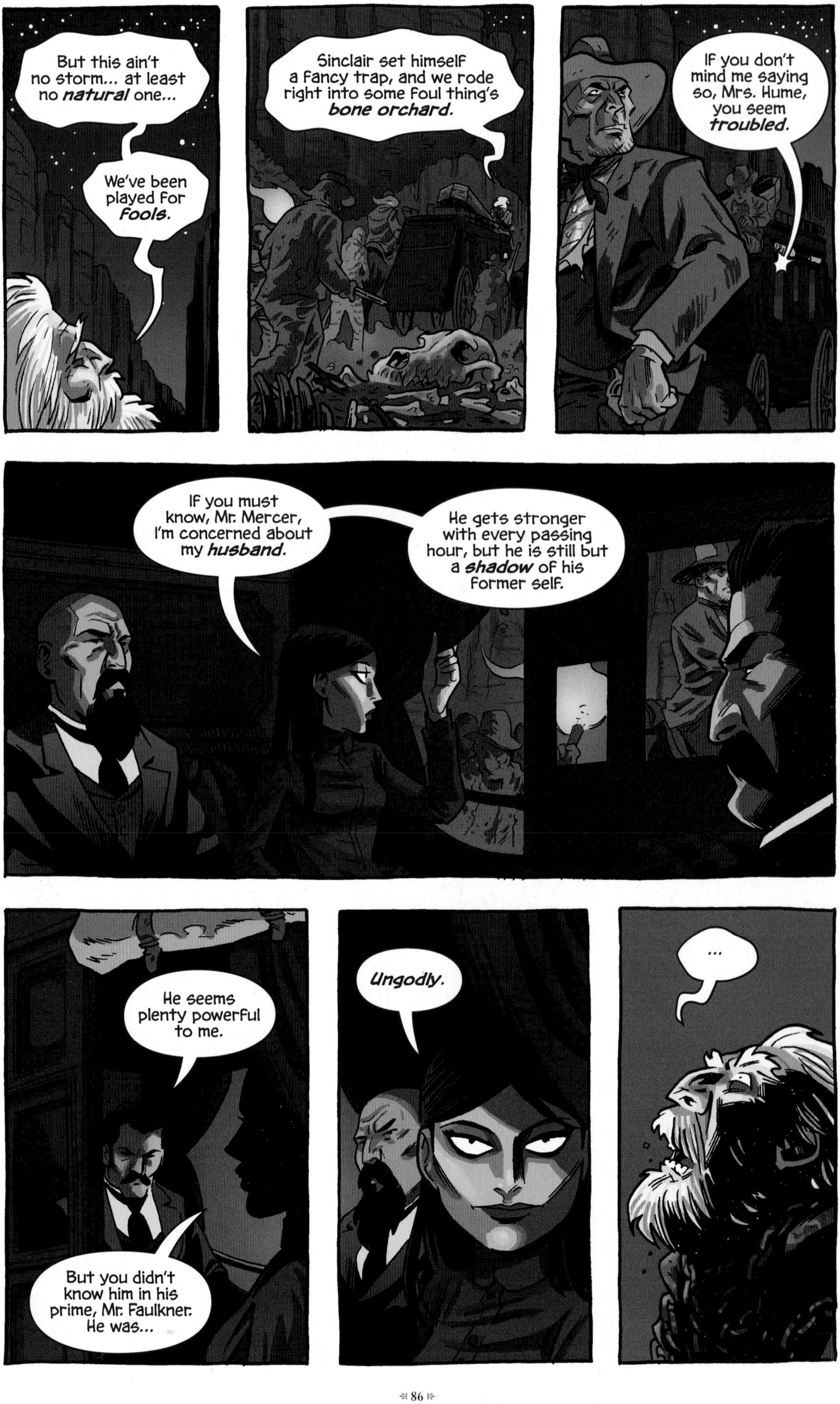
But this ain't no storm... at least no *natural* one...
We've been played for *fools.*
Sinclair set himself a fancy trap, and we rode right into some foul thing's *bone orchard.*
If you don't mind me saying so, Mrs. Hume, you seem *troubled.*
If you must know, Mr. Mercer, I'm concerned about my *husband.*
He gets stronger with every passing hour, but he is still but a *shadow* of his former self.
He seems plenty powerful to me.
But you didn't know him in his prime, Mr. Faulkner. He was...
*Ungodly.*
...

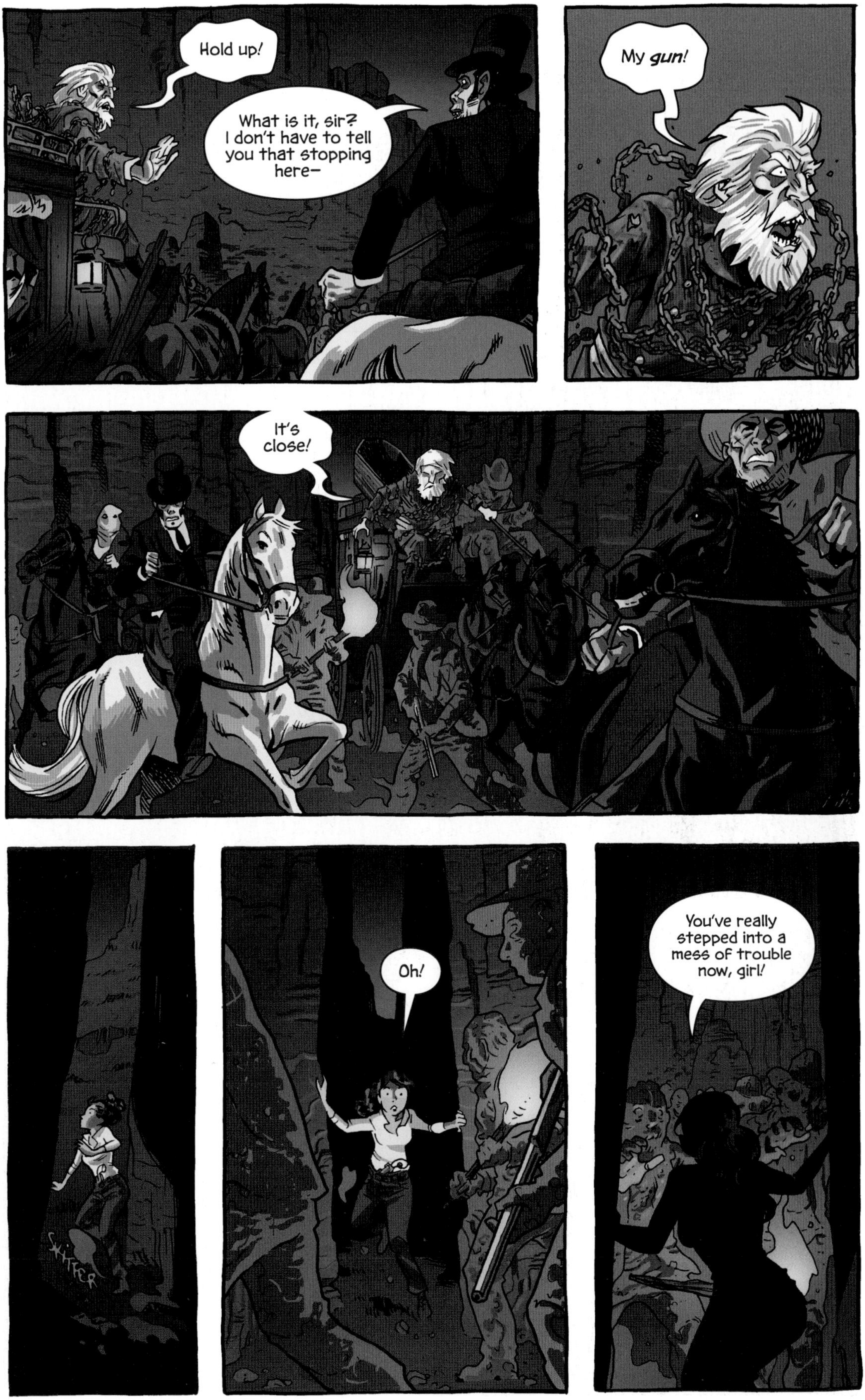
Hold up!
What is it, sir? I don't have to tell you that stopping here–
My gun!
It's close!
SKITTER
Oh!
You've really stepped into a mess of trouble now, girl!

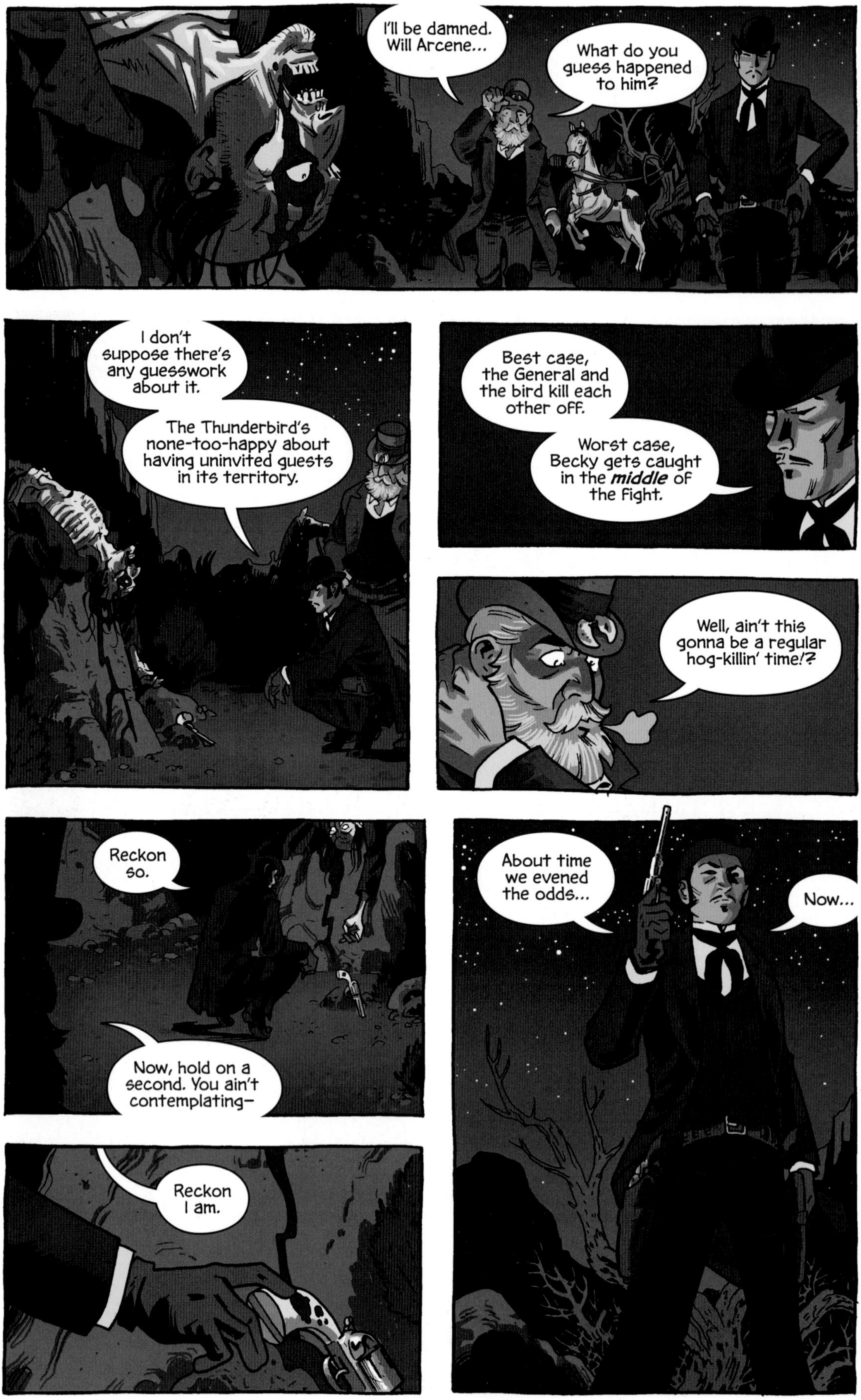
I'll be damned. Will Arcene...
What do you guess happened to him?
I don't suppose there's any guesswork about it.
The Thunderbird's none-too-happy about having uninvited guests in its territory.
Best case, the General and the bird kill each other off.
Worst case, Becky gets caught in the *middle* of the fight.
Well, ain't this gonna be a regular hog-killin' time!?
Reckon so.
Now, hold on a second. You ain't contemplating–
Reckon I am.
About time we evened the odds...
Now...

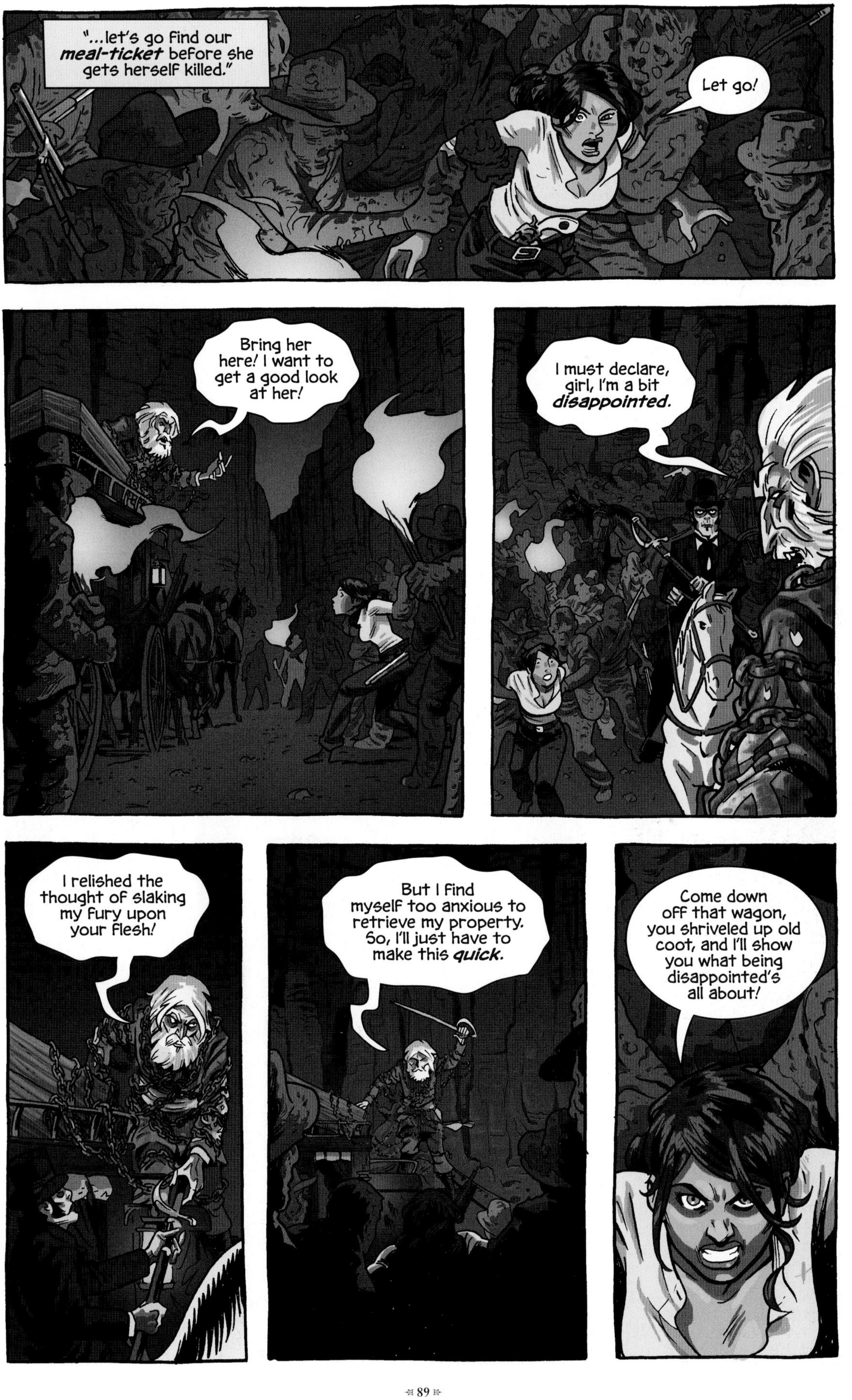
"...let's go find our meal-ticket before she gets herself killed."
Let go!
Bring her here! I want to get a good look at her!
I must declare, girl, I'm a bit disappointed.
I relished the thought of slaking my fury upon your flesh!
But I find myself too anxious to retrieve my property. So, I'll just have to make this quick.
Come down off that wagon, you shriveled up old coot, and I'll show you what being disappointed's all about!

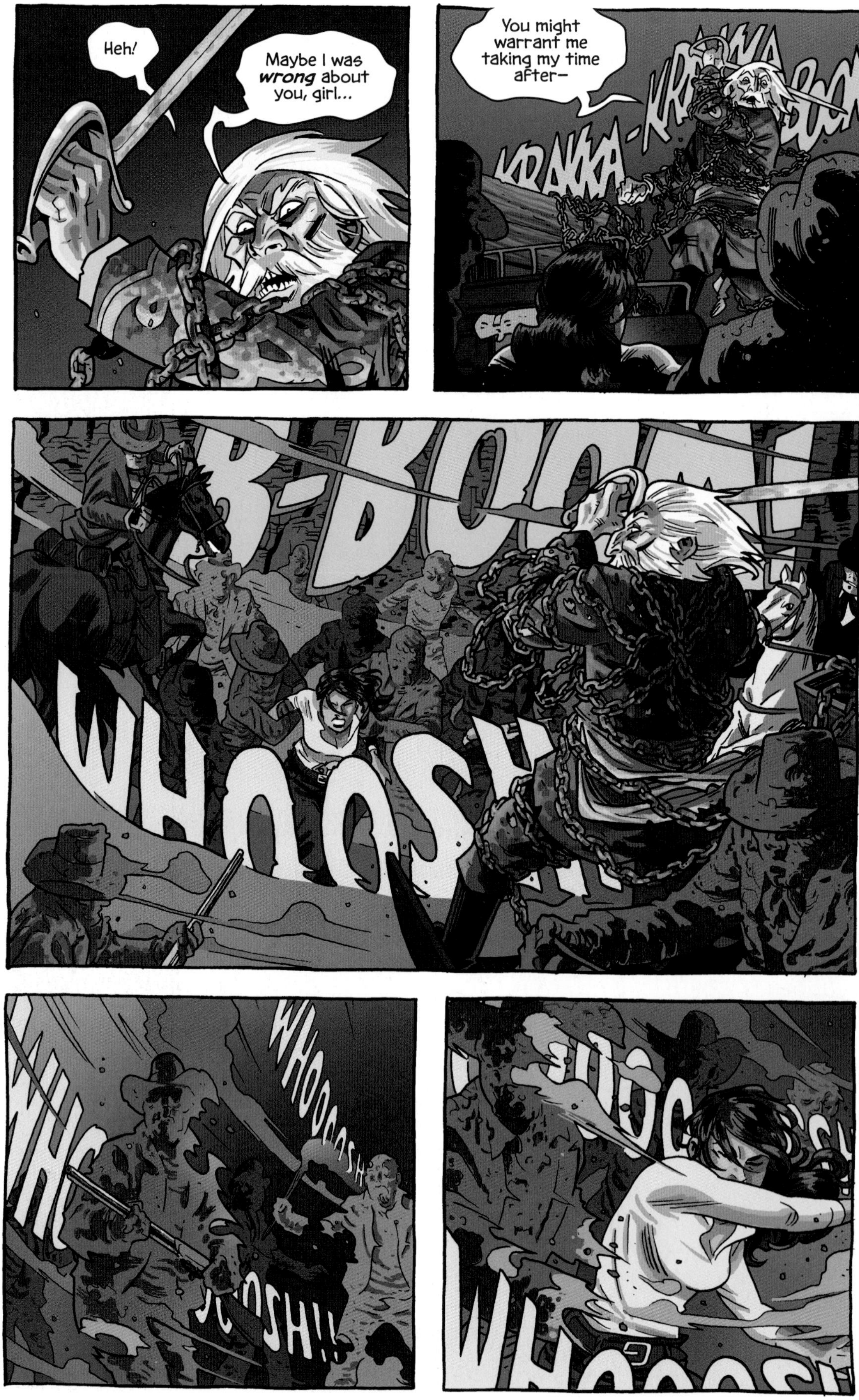
Heh!
Maybe I was **wrong** about you, girl...
You might warrant me taking my time after–
KRAKKA-KRAKKA-BOOM
B-BOOM
WHOOSH
WHOOOOSH
WHO
WHOOSH!!
WHOOOSH
WHOOOSH

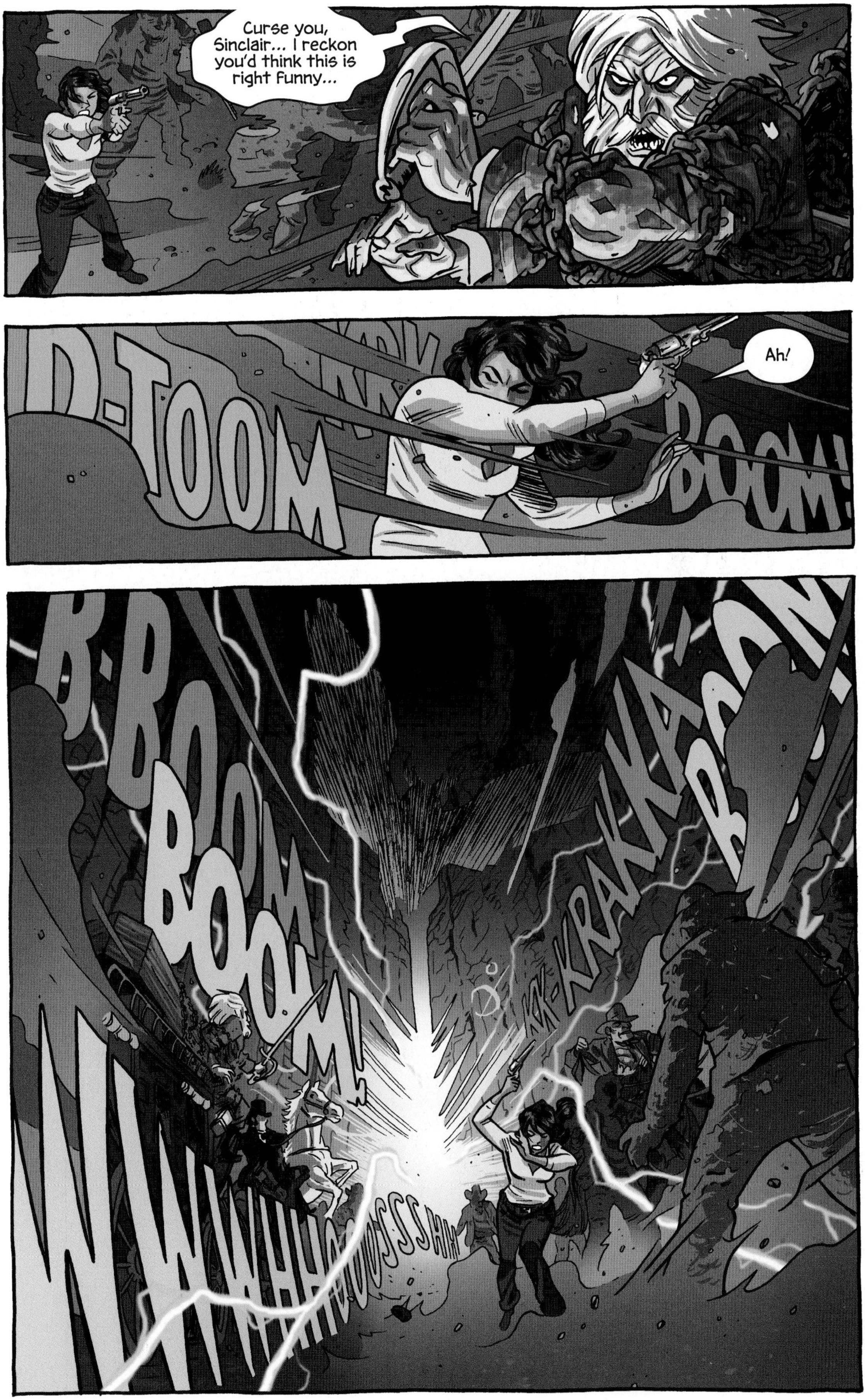
Curse you, Sinclair... I reckon you'd think this is right funny...
D-TOOM
BOOM!
Ah!
B-BOOM
BOOOM!
KK-KRAKA
WHAWHHOOSSSSHH!

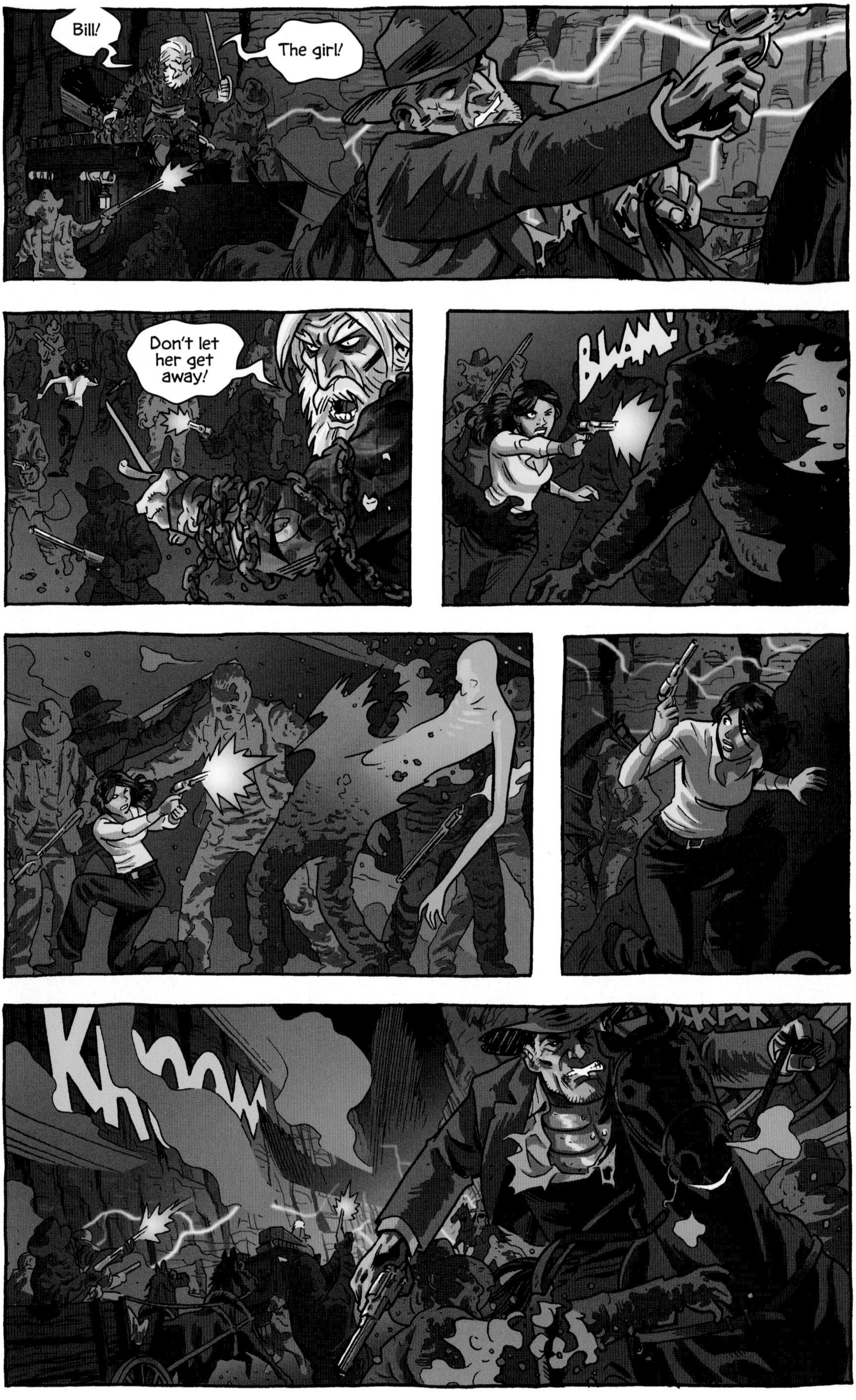
Bill!
The girl!
Don't let her get away!
BLAM!

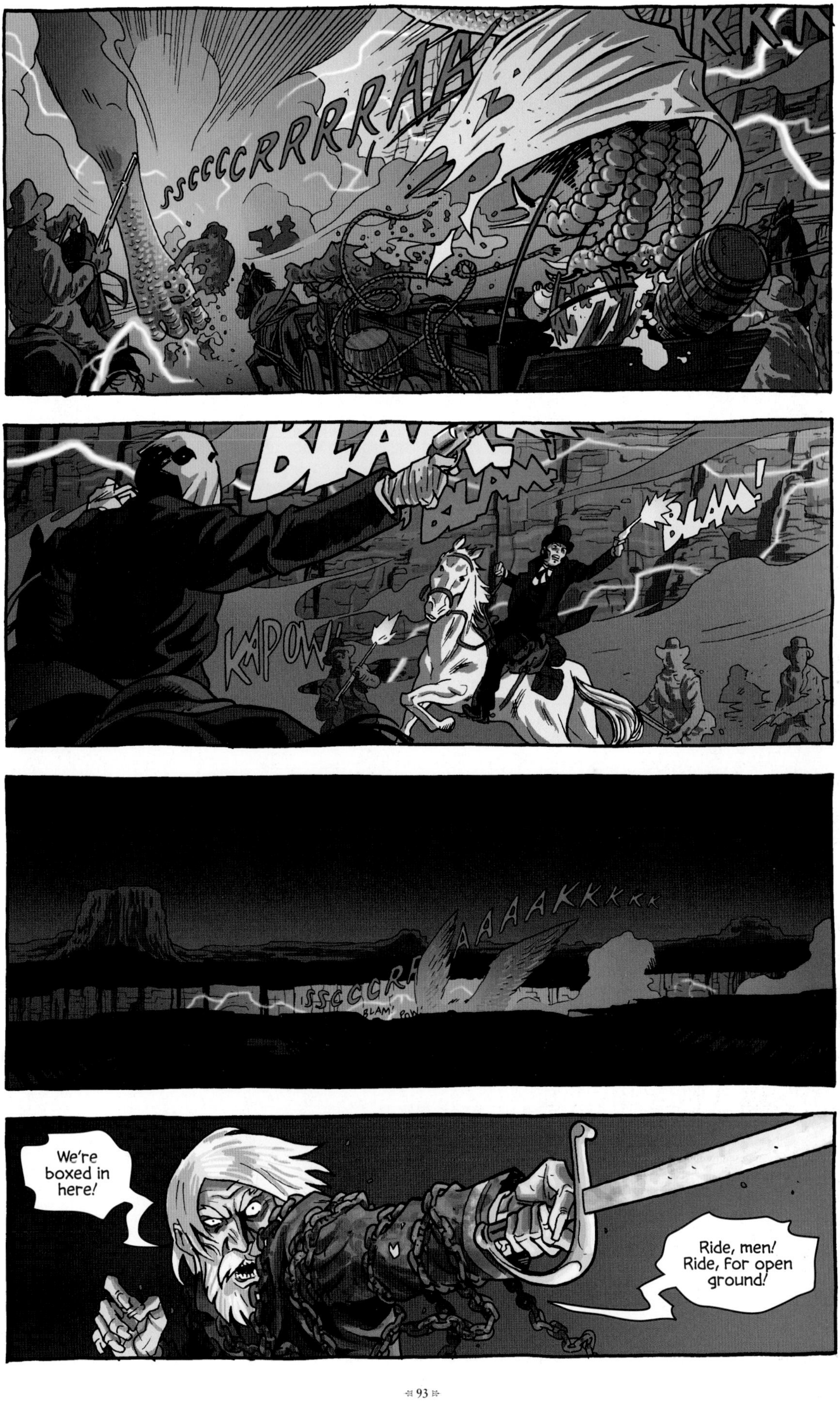
SSCCCCRRRRRRAAK!
BLAM!
BLAM!
KAPOW!
AAAAAKKKKK
SSCCCRA
BLAM!
POW
We're boxed in here!
Ride, men! Ride, for open ground!

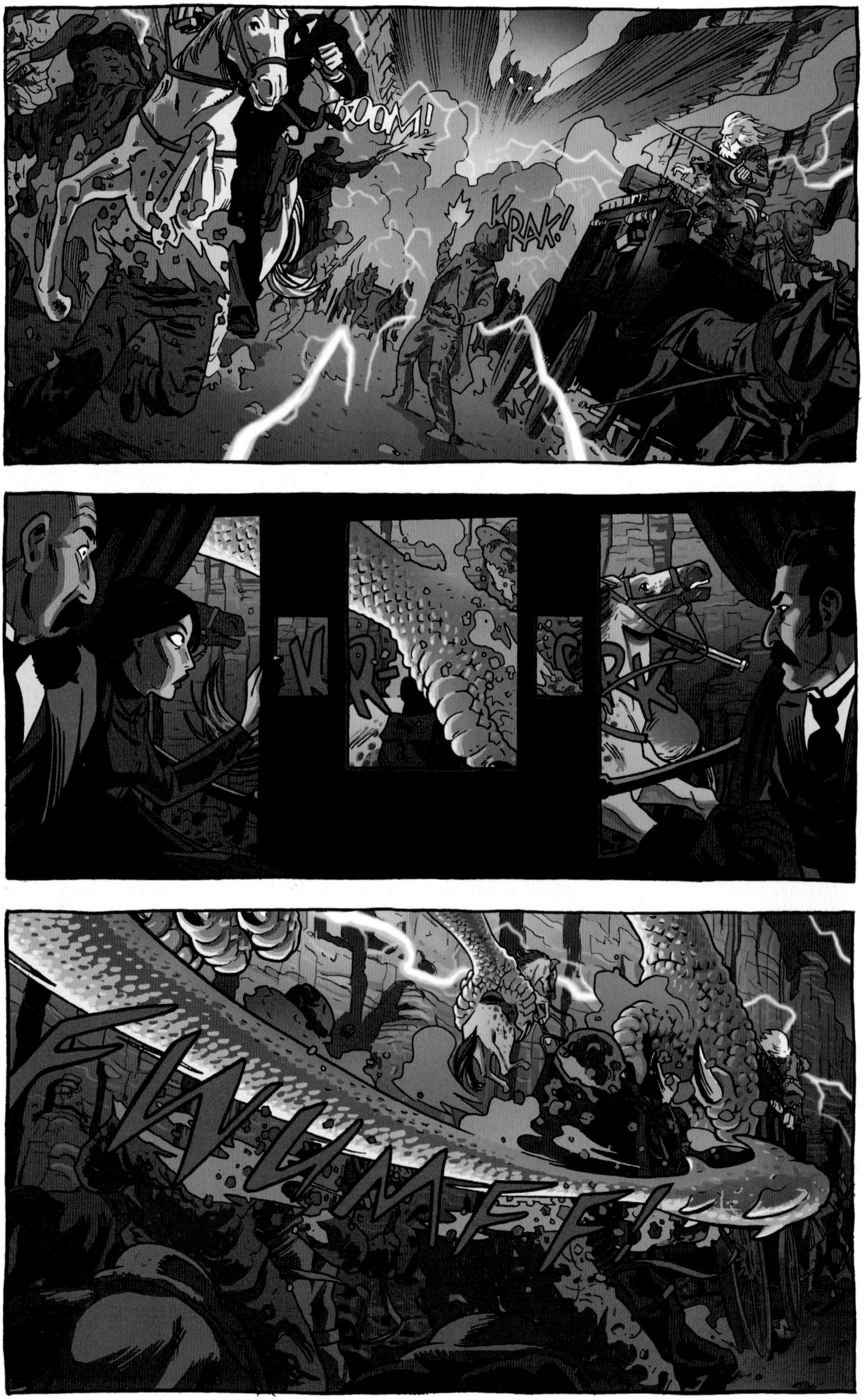
BOOOM!
KRAK!
FWUMFF!

I'm gonna do us all a favor, girl...

Can't see that what you need is a simple killing.

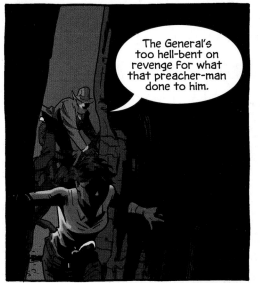

The General's too hell-bent on revenge for what that preacher-man done to him.

I aim to rectify that right—

Howdy, Bill.

Sinclair...

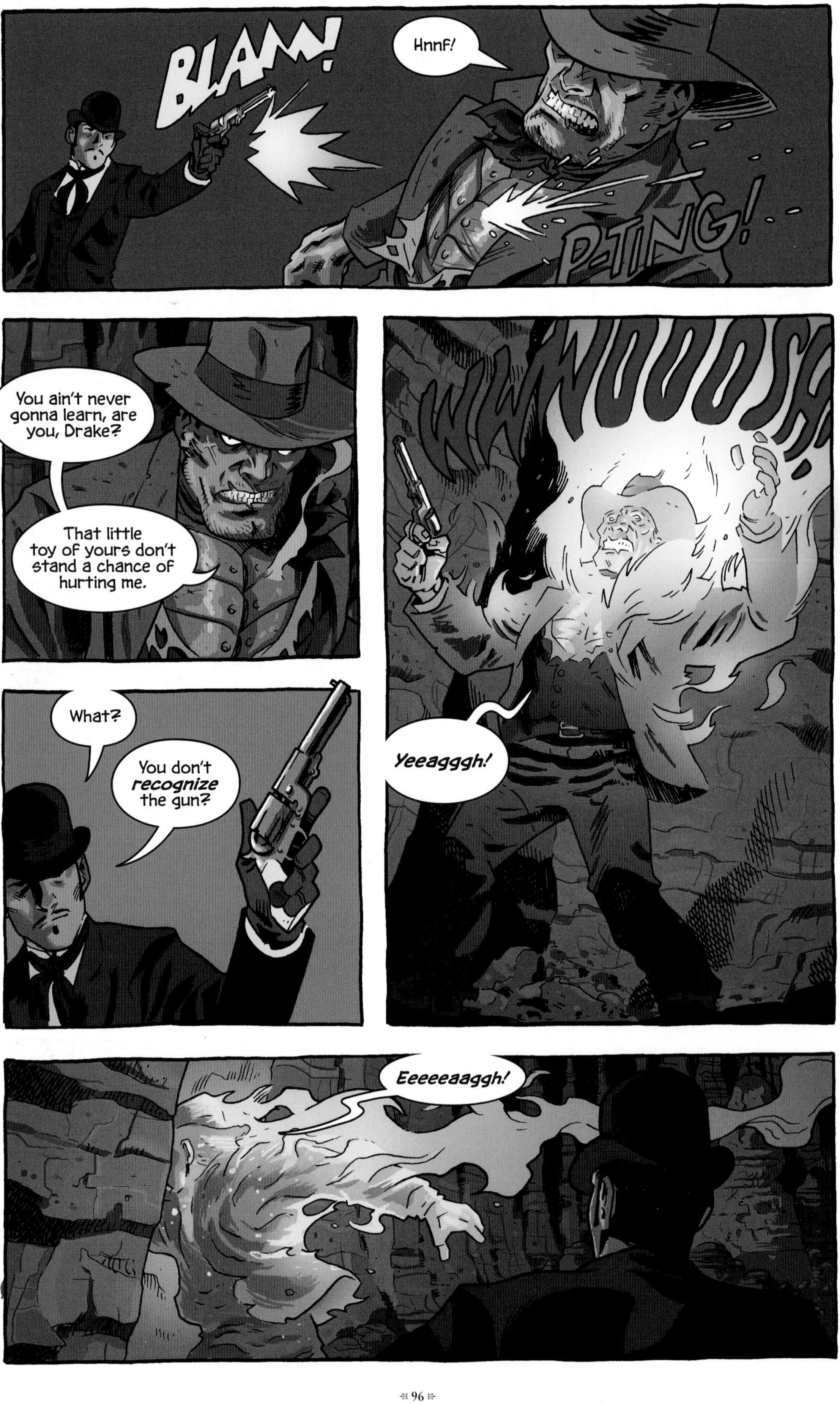
BLAM!
Hnnf!
P-TING!
You ain't never gonna learn, are you, Drake?
That little toy of yours don't stand a chance of hurting me.
What?
You don't *recognize* the gun?
WWWOOOSH!
*Yeeagggh!*
*Eeeeeaaggh!*

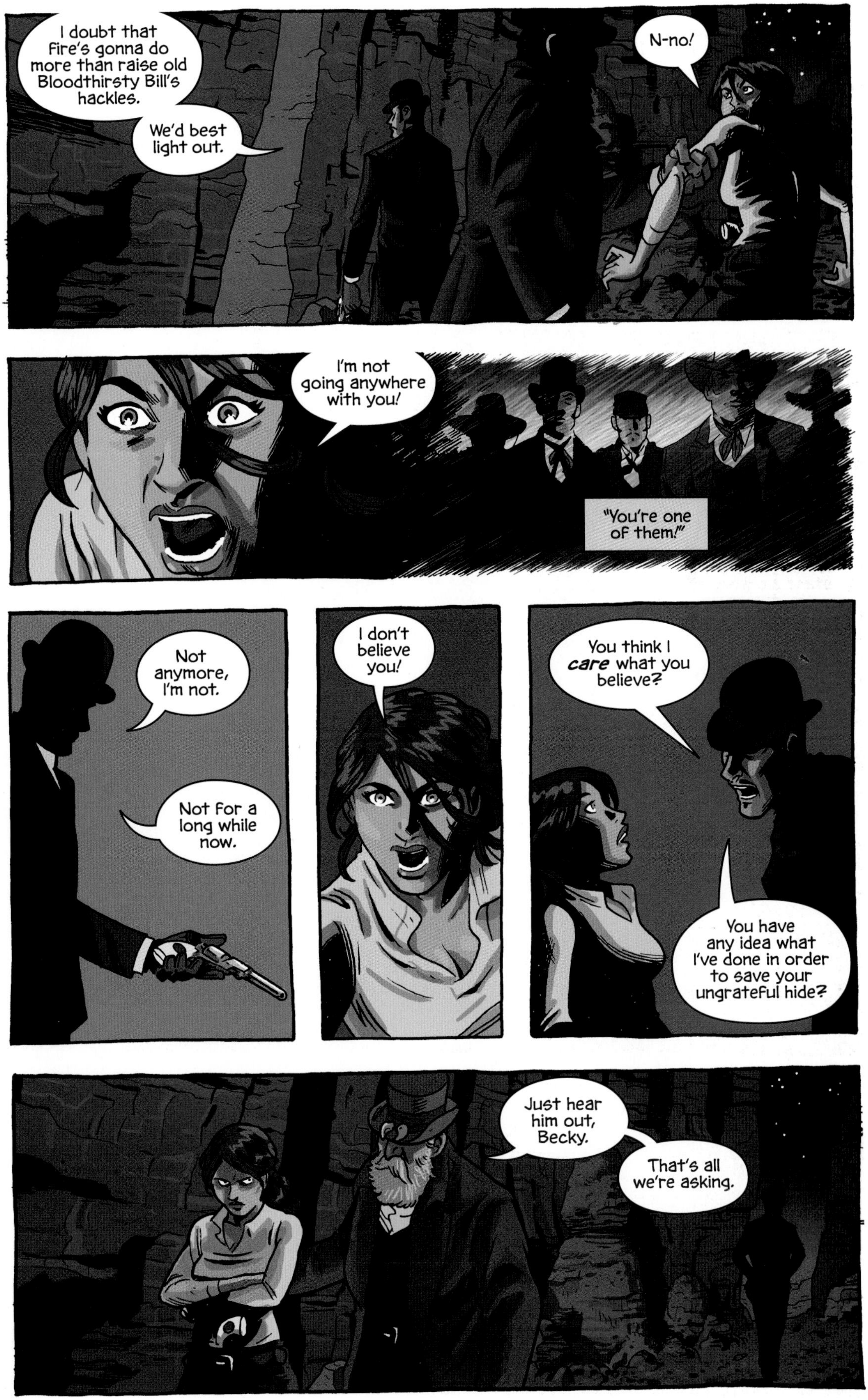

I doubt that fire's gonna do more than raise old Bloodthirsty Bill's hackles.
We'd best light out.
N-no!
I'm not going anywhere with you!
"You're one of them!"
Not anymore, I'm not.
Not for a long while now.
I don't believe you!
You think I *care* what you believe?
You have any idea what I've done in order to save your ungrateful hide?
Just hear him out, Becky.
That's all we're asking.

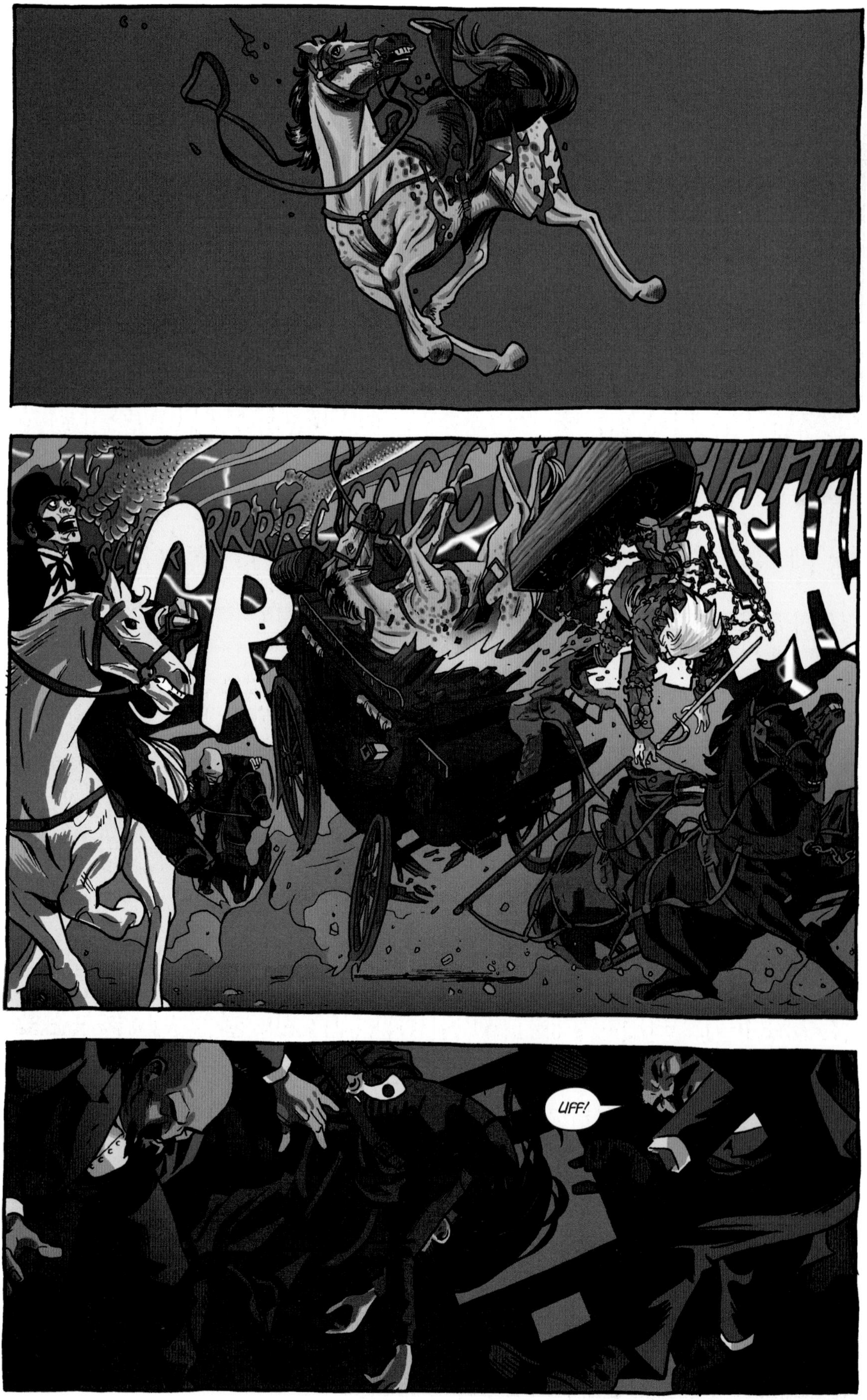
UFF!

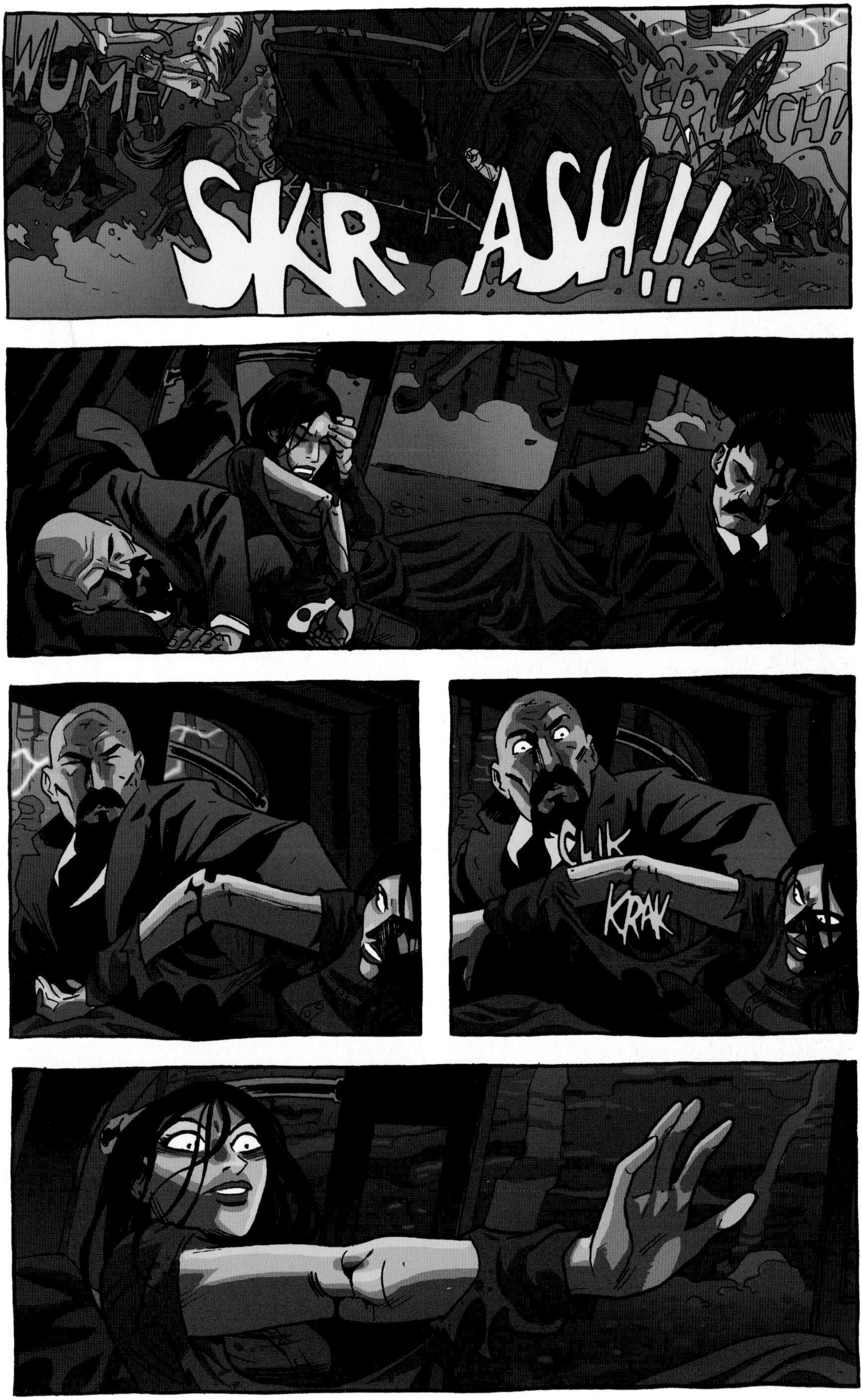
WUMF!
SKR-ASH!!
CRUNCH!
CLIK
KRAK

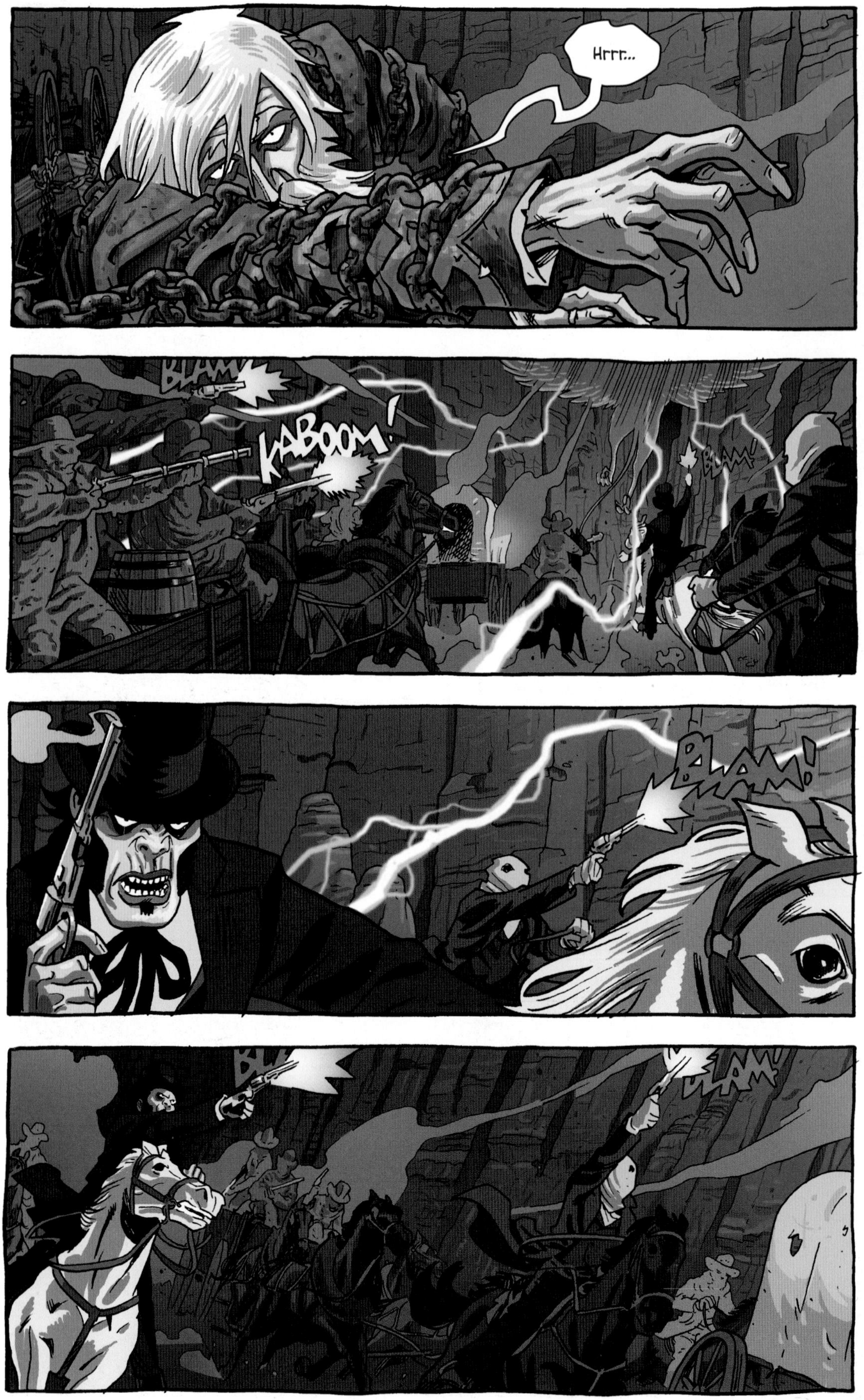
Hrrr...
BLAM
KABOOM!
BLAM!
BLAM!

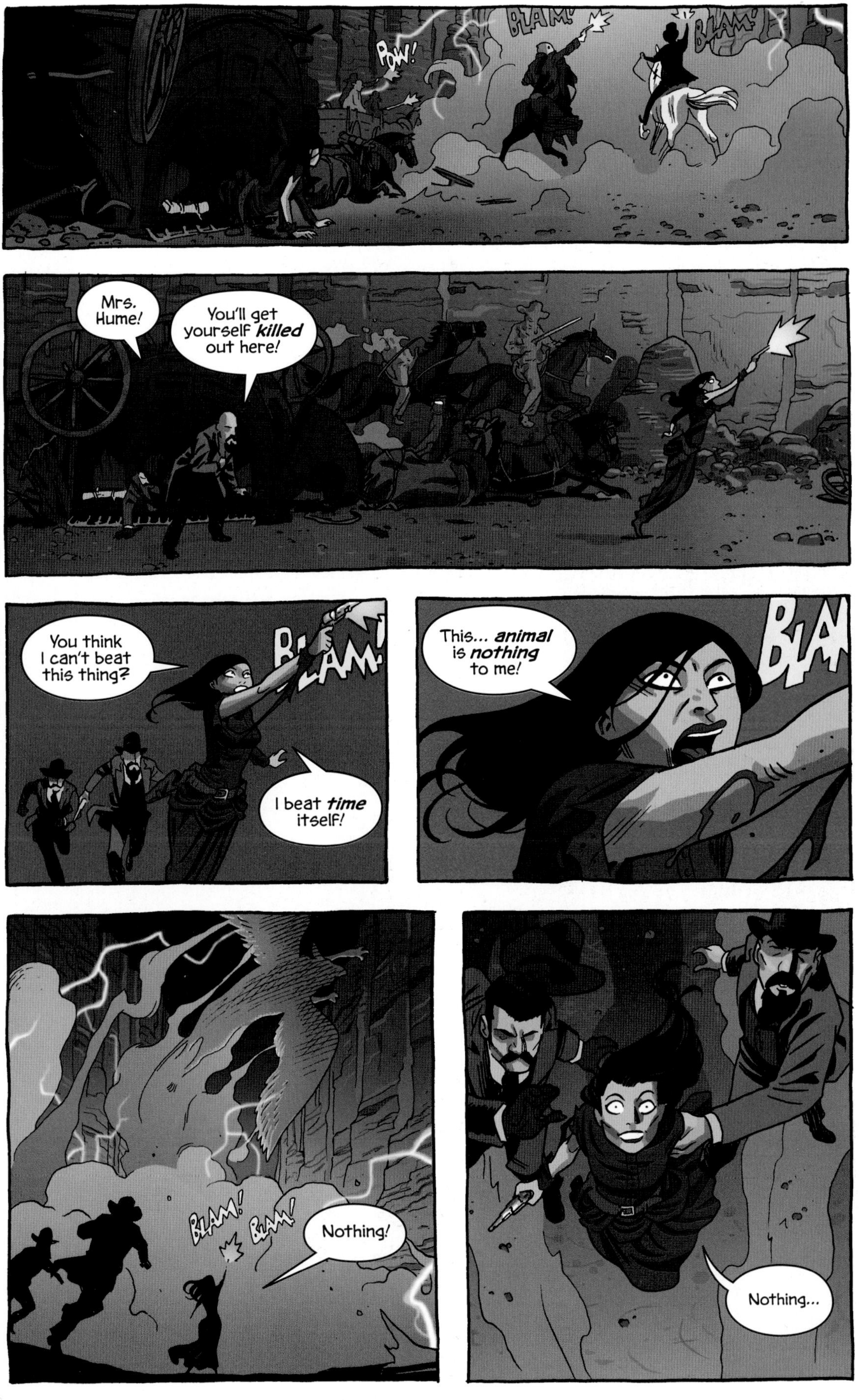
POW!
BLAM!
BLAM!
Mrs. Hume!
You'll get yourself *killed* out here!
You think I can't beat this thing?
BLAM!
I beat *time* itself!
This... *animal* is *nothing* to me!
BLAM
BLAM!
BLAM!
Nothing!
Nothing...

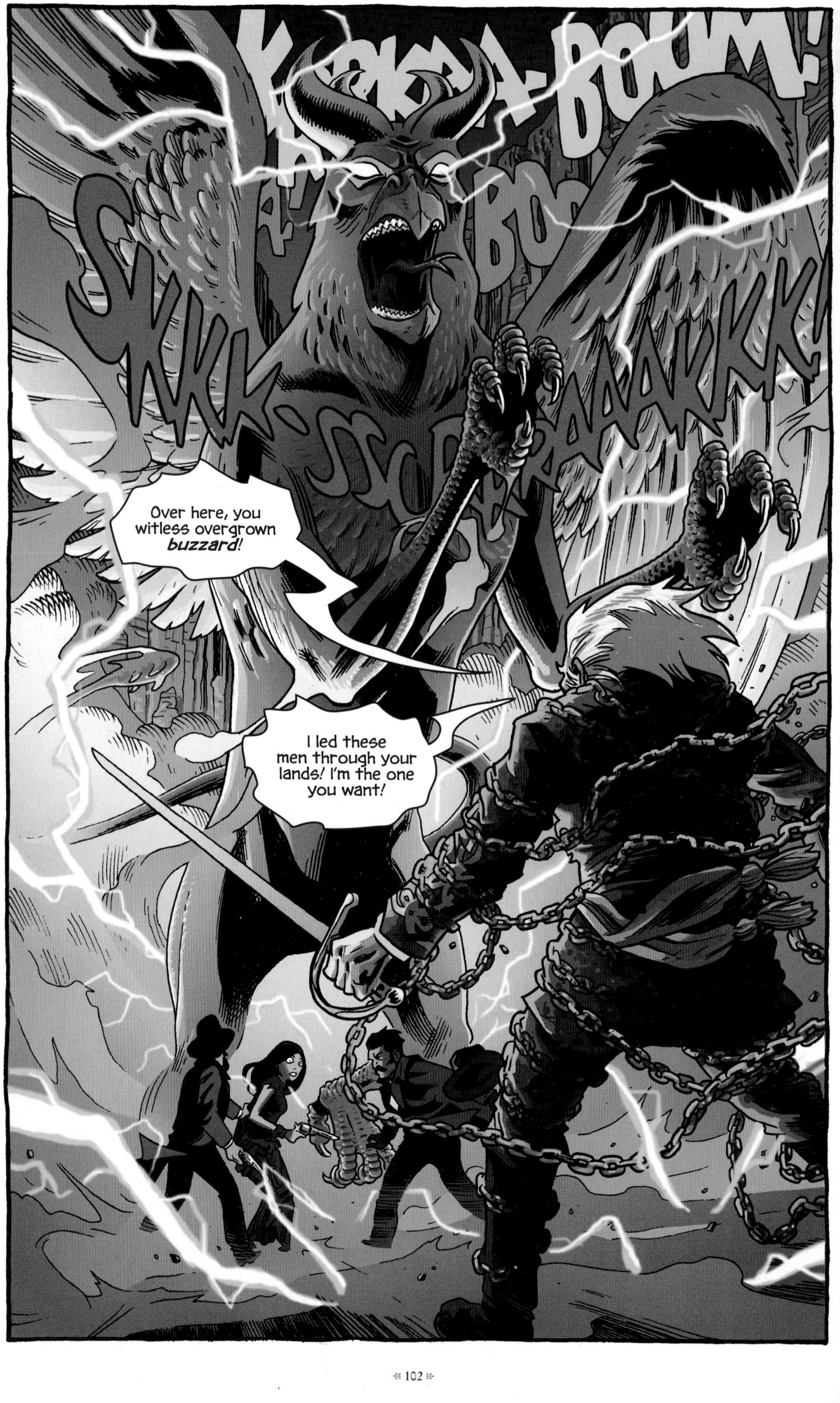
Over here, you witless overgrown *buzzard*!
I led these men through your lands! I'm the one you want!

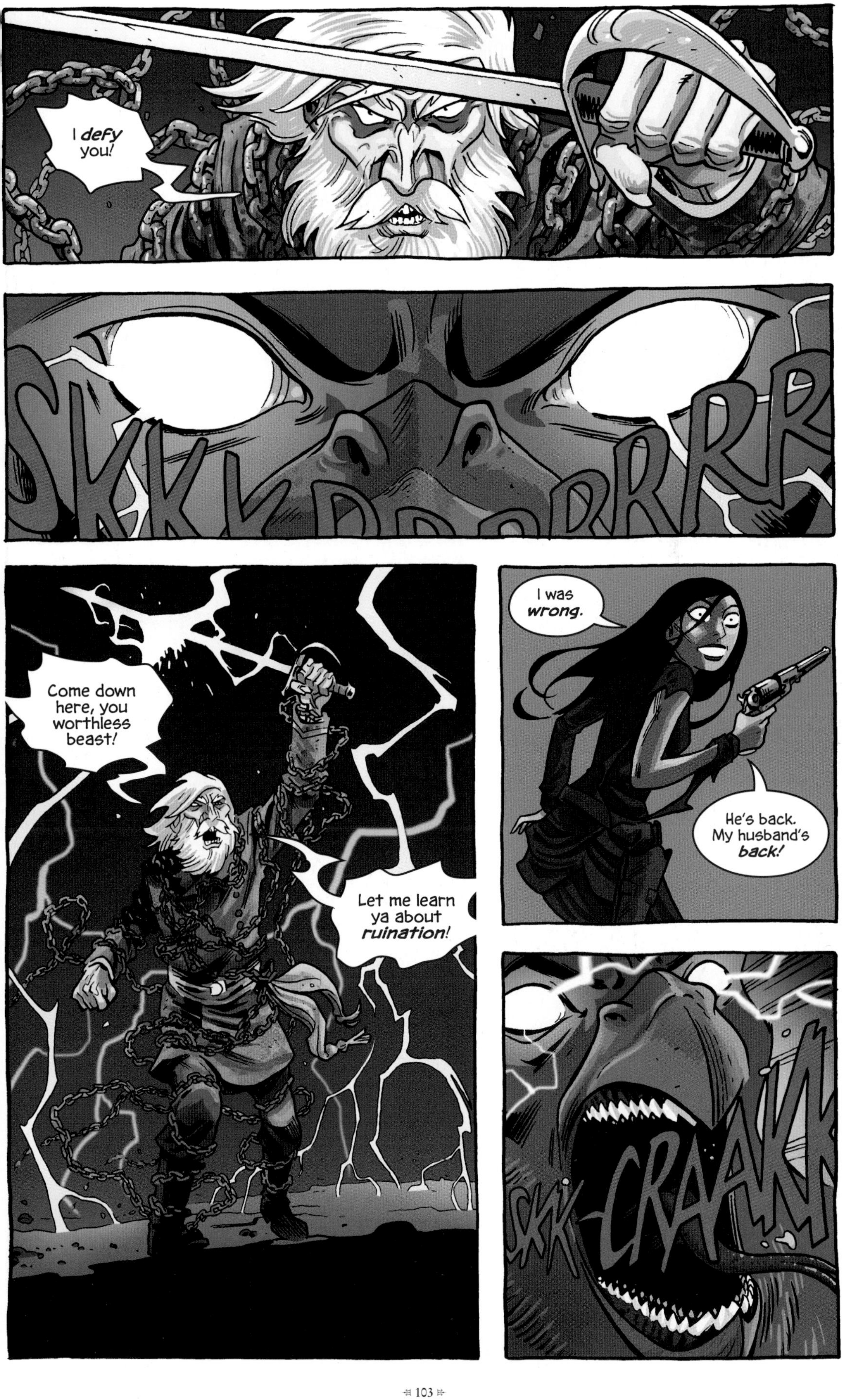

I *defy* you!
SKKKRRRRRRRR
Come down here, you worthless beast!
Let me learn ya about *ruination*!
I was *wrong*.
He's back. My husband's *back*!
SKK-CRAAKK

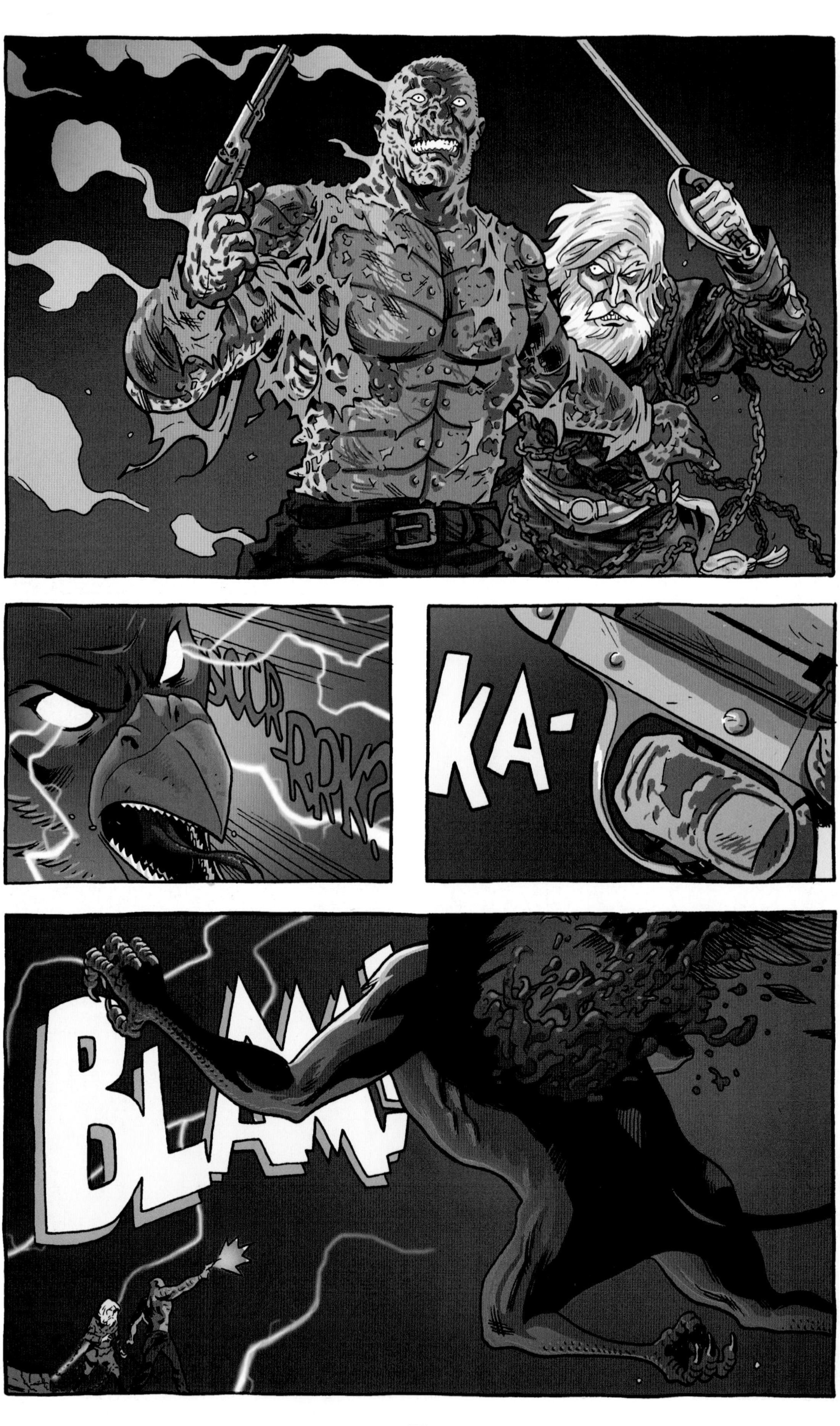
SCCR RRK?
KA-
BLA

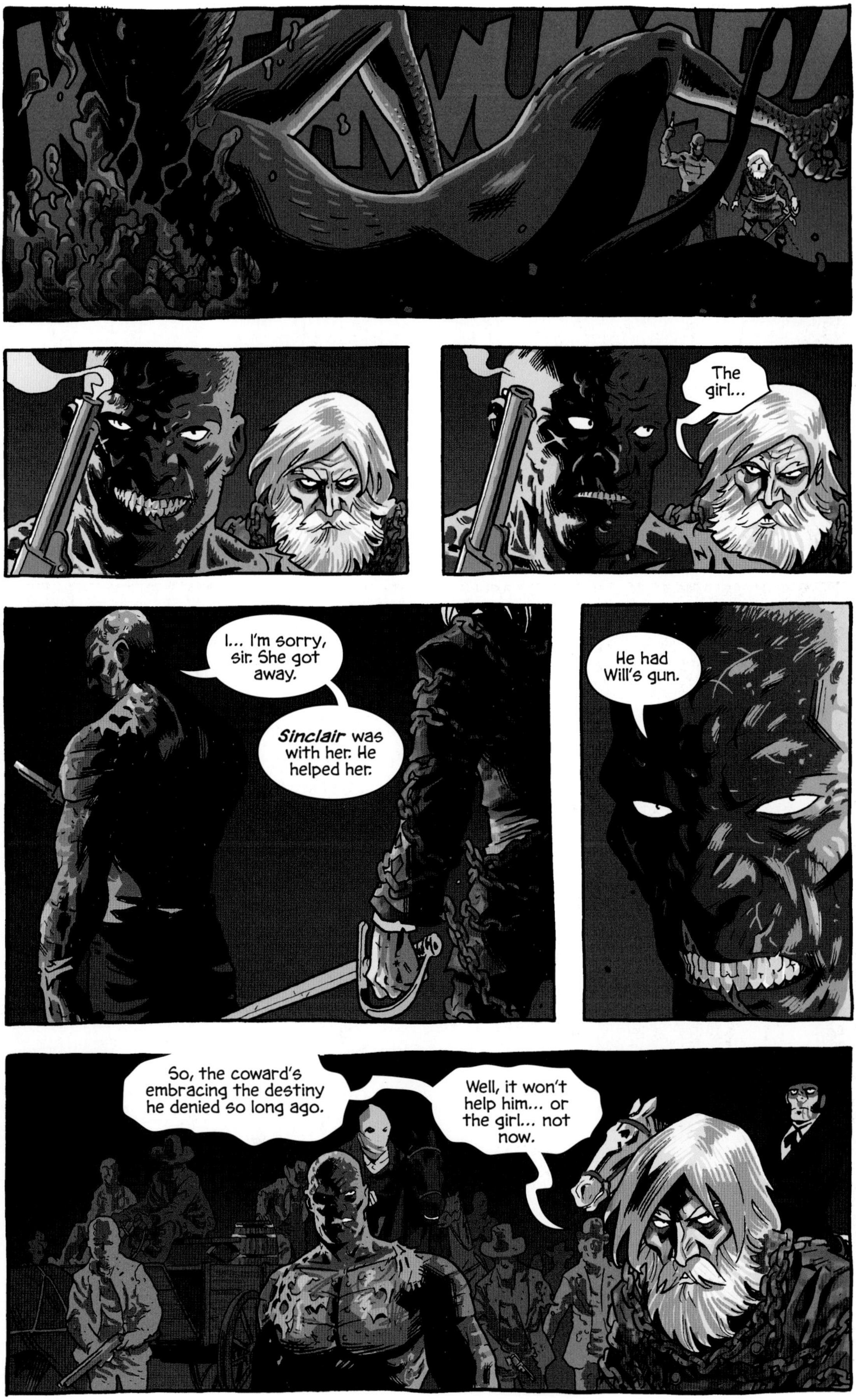
The girl...
I... I'm sorry, sir. She got away.
Sinclair was with her. He helped her.
He had Will's gun.
So, the coward's embracing the destiny he denied so long ago.
Well, it won't help him... or the girl... not now.

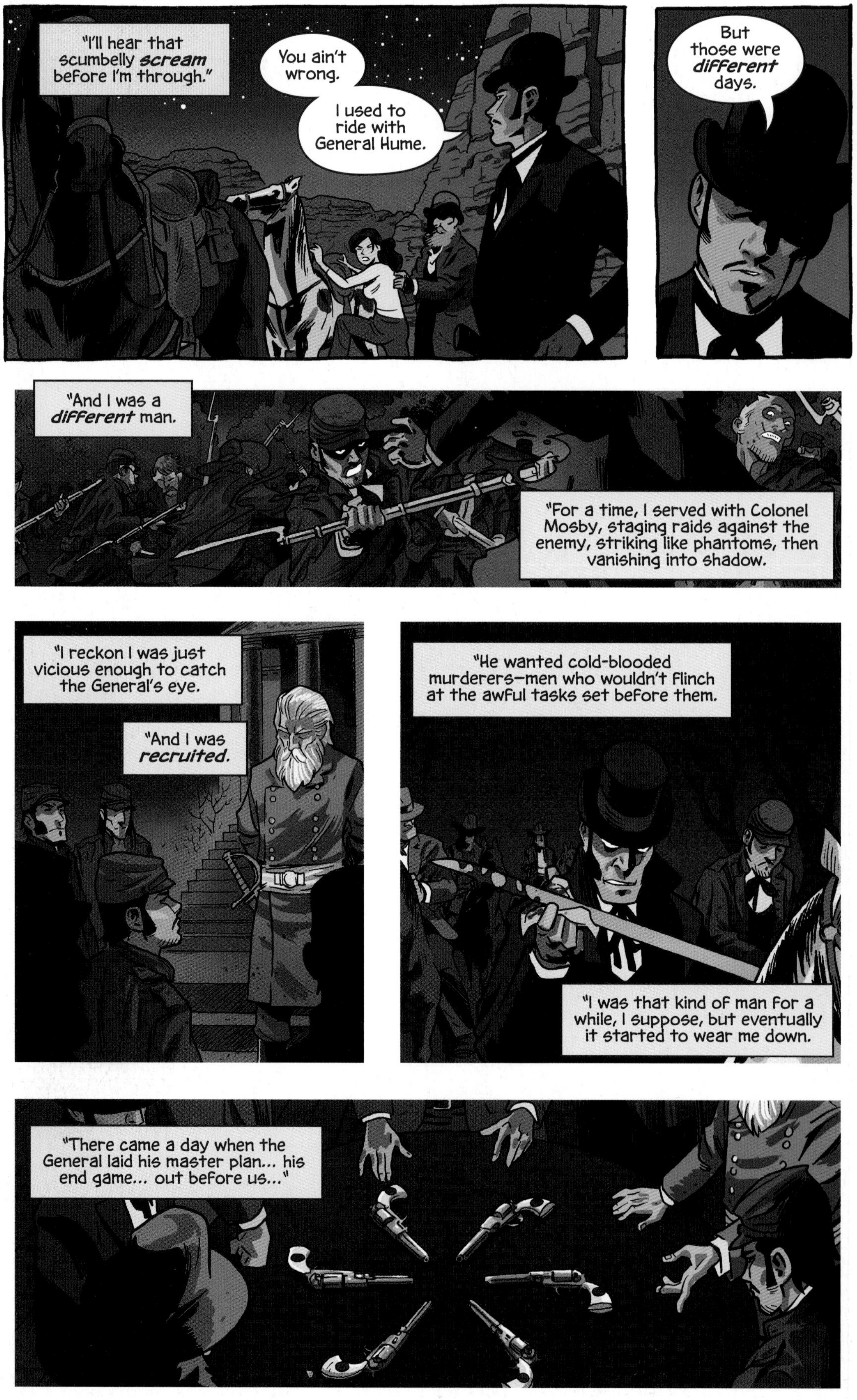
"I'll hear that scumbelly *scream* before I'm through."
You ain't wrong.
I used to ride with General Hume.
But those were *different* days.
"And I was a *different* man.
"For a time, I served with Colonel Mosby, staging raids against the enemy, striking like phantoms, then vanishing into shadow.
"I reckon I was just vicious enough to catch the General's eye.
"And I was *recruited*.
"He wanted cold-blooded murderers—men who wouldn't flinch at the awful tasks set before them.
"I was that kind of man for a while, I suppose, but eventually it started to wear me down.
"There came a day when the General laid his master plan... his end game... out before us..."

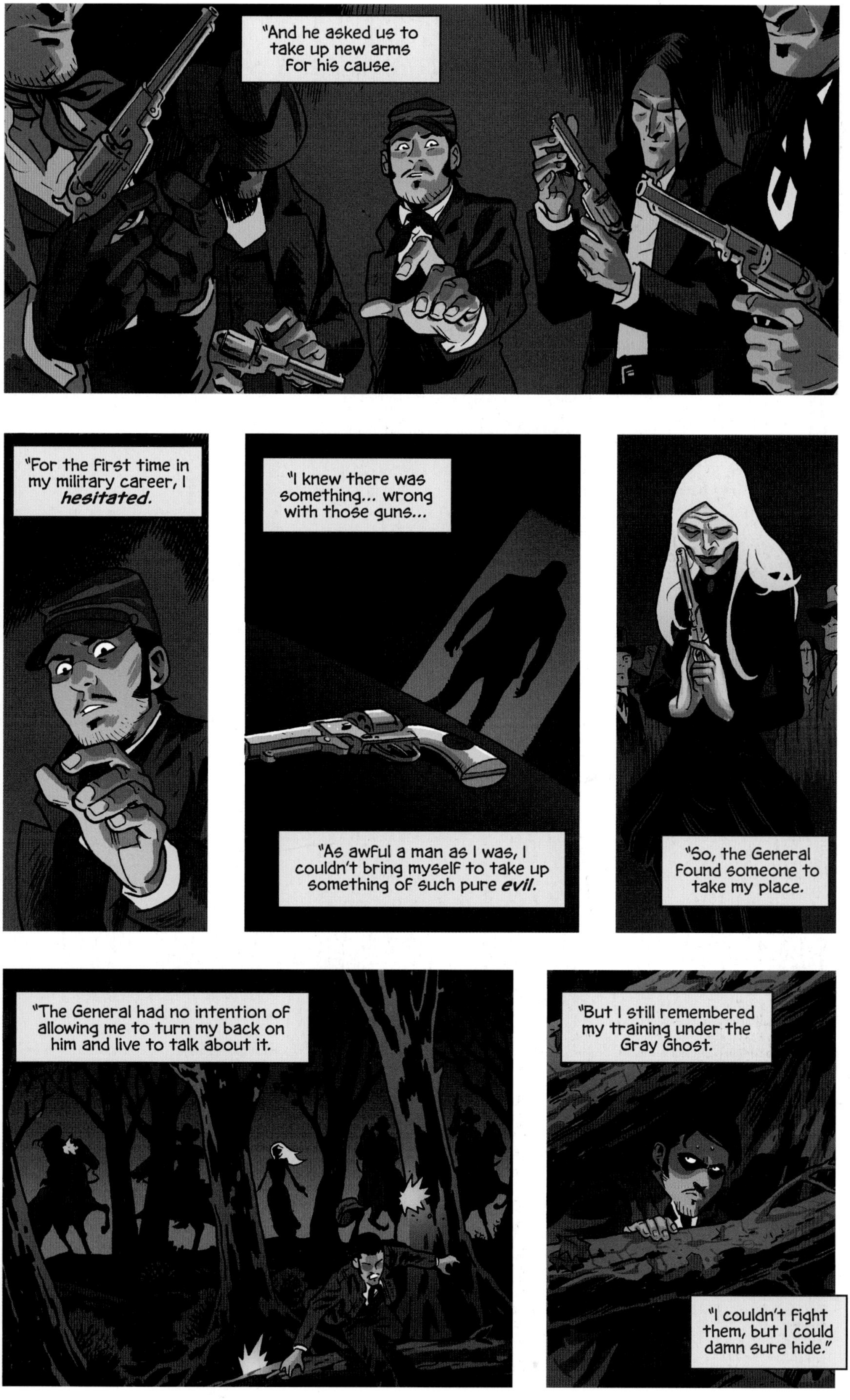
"And he asked us to take up new arms for his cause.
"For the first time in my military career, I *hesitated.*
"I knew there was something... wrong with those guns...
"As awful a man as I was, I couldn't bring myself to take up something of such pure *evil.*
"So, the General found someone to take my place.
"The General had no intention of allowing me to turn my back on him and live to talk about it.
"But I still remembered my training under the Gray Ghost.
"I couldn't fight them, but I could damn sure hide."

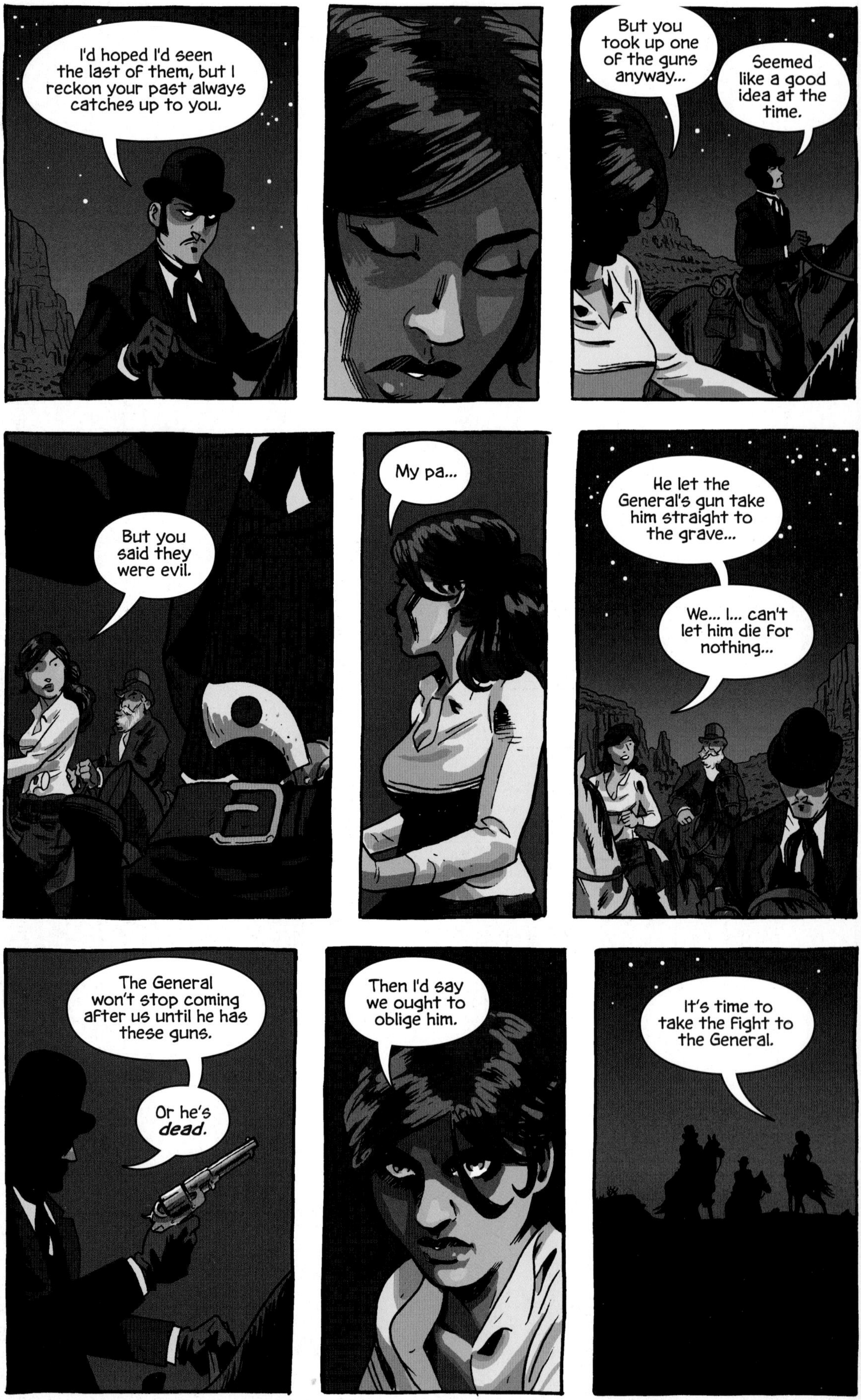
I'd hoped I'd seen the last of them, but I reckon your past always catches up to you.
But you took up one of the guns anyway...
Seemed like a good idea at the time.
But you said they were evil.
My pa...
He let the General's gun take him straight to the grave...
We... I... can't let him die for nothing...
The General won't stop coming after us until he has these guns.
Or he's *dead*.
Then I'd say we ought to oblige him.
It's time to take the fight to the General.

CHAPTER FIVE

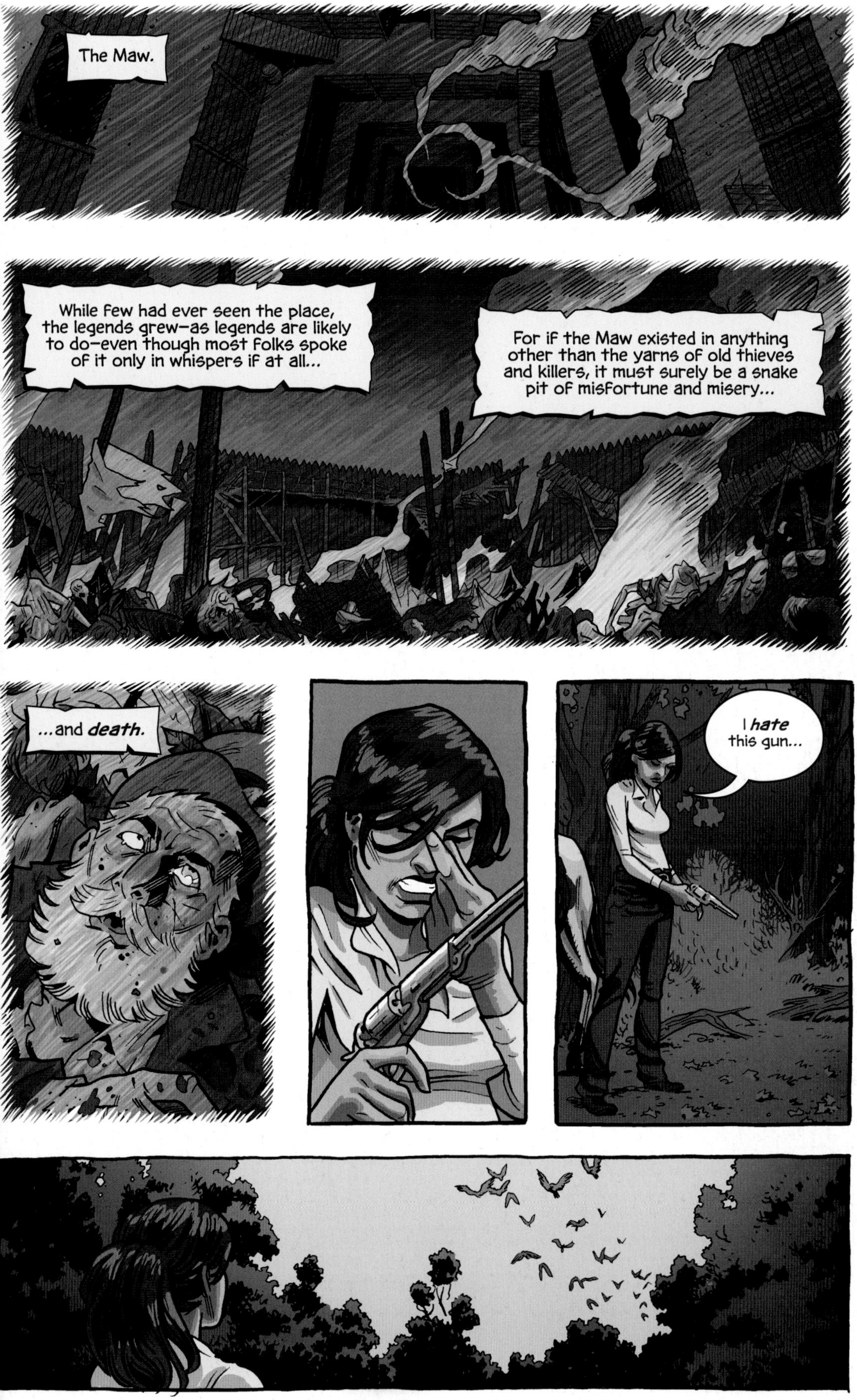
The Maw.
While few had ever seen the place, the legends grew—as legends are likely to do—even though most folks spoke of it only in whispers if at all...
For if the Maw existed in anything other than the yarns of old thieves and killers, it must surely be a snake pit of misfortune and misery...
...and *death*.
I *hate* this gun...

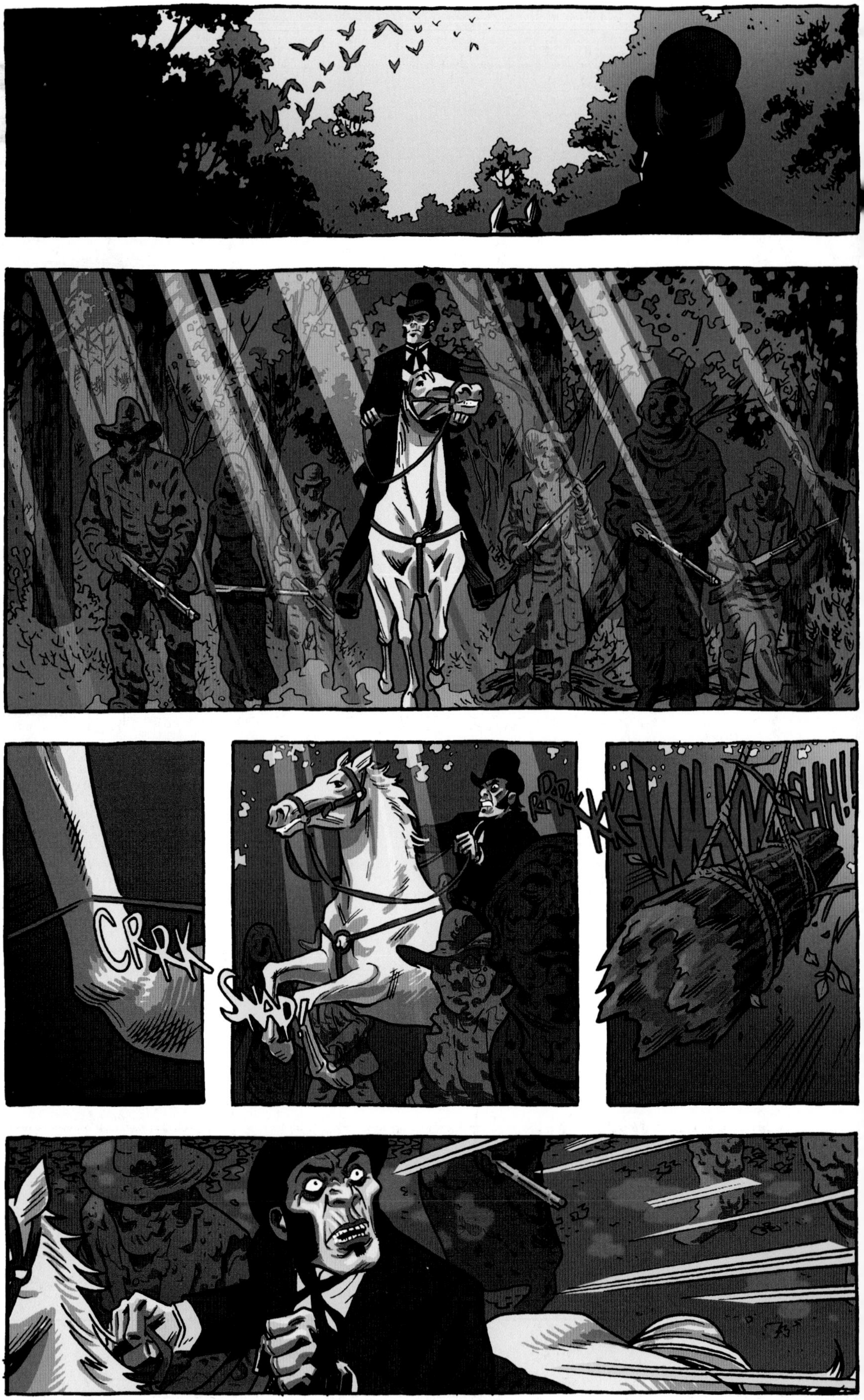
CRRK
SNAP!
RRRRKK

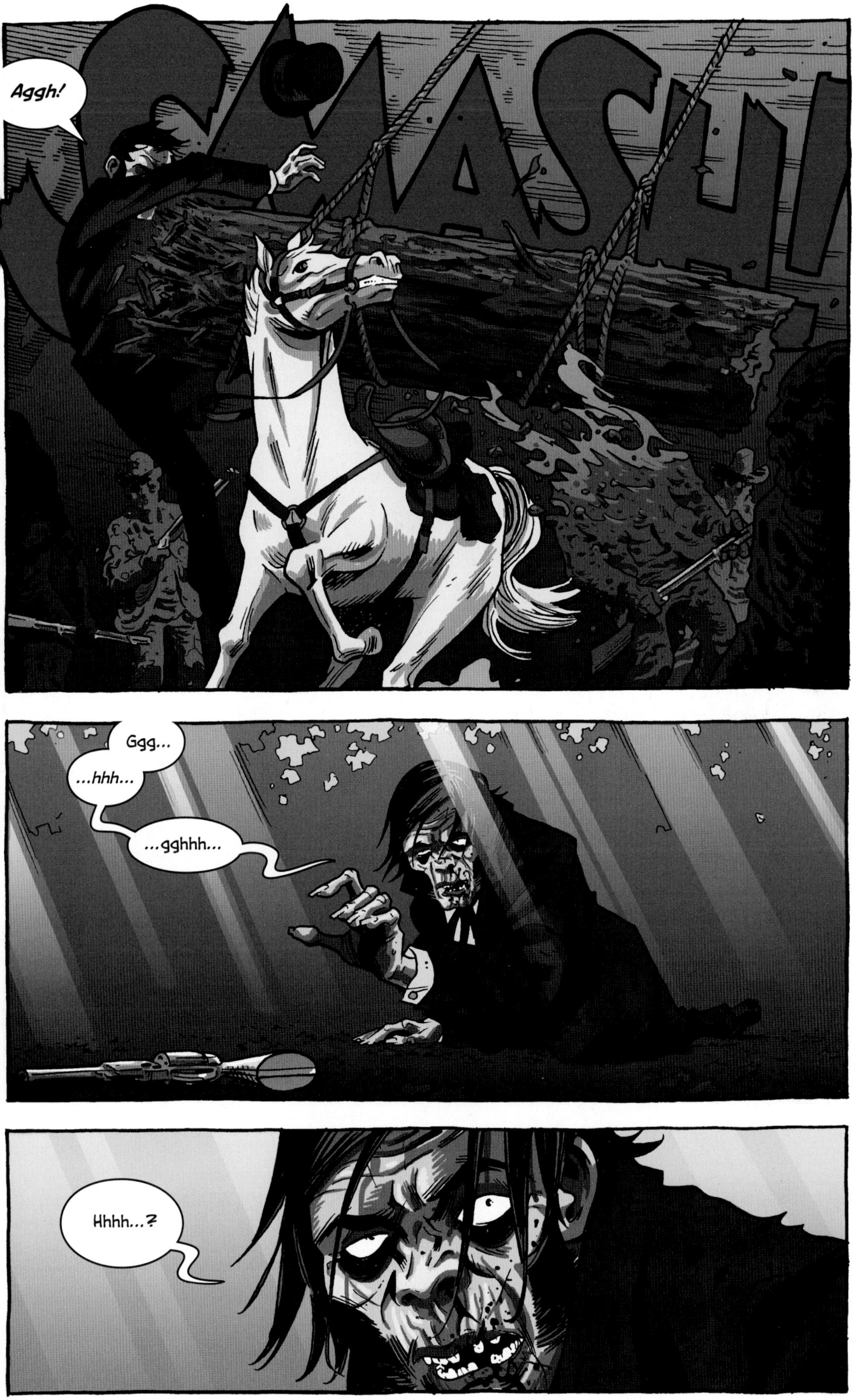
Agh!
SMASH!
Ggg...
...hhh...
...gghhh...
Hhhh...?

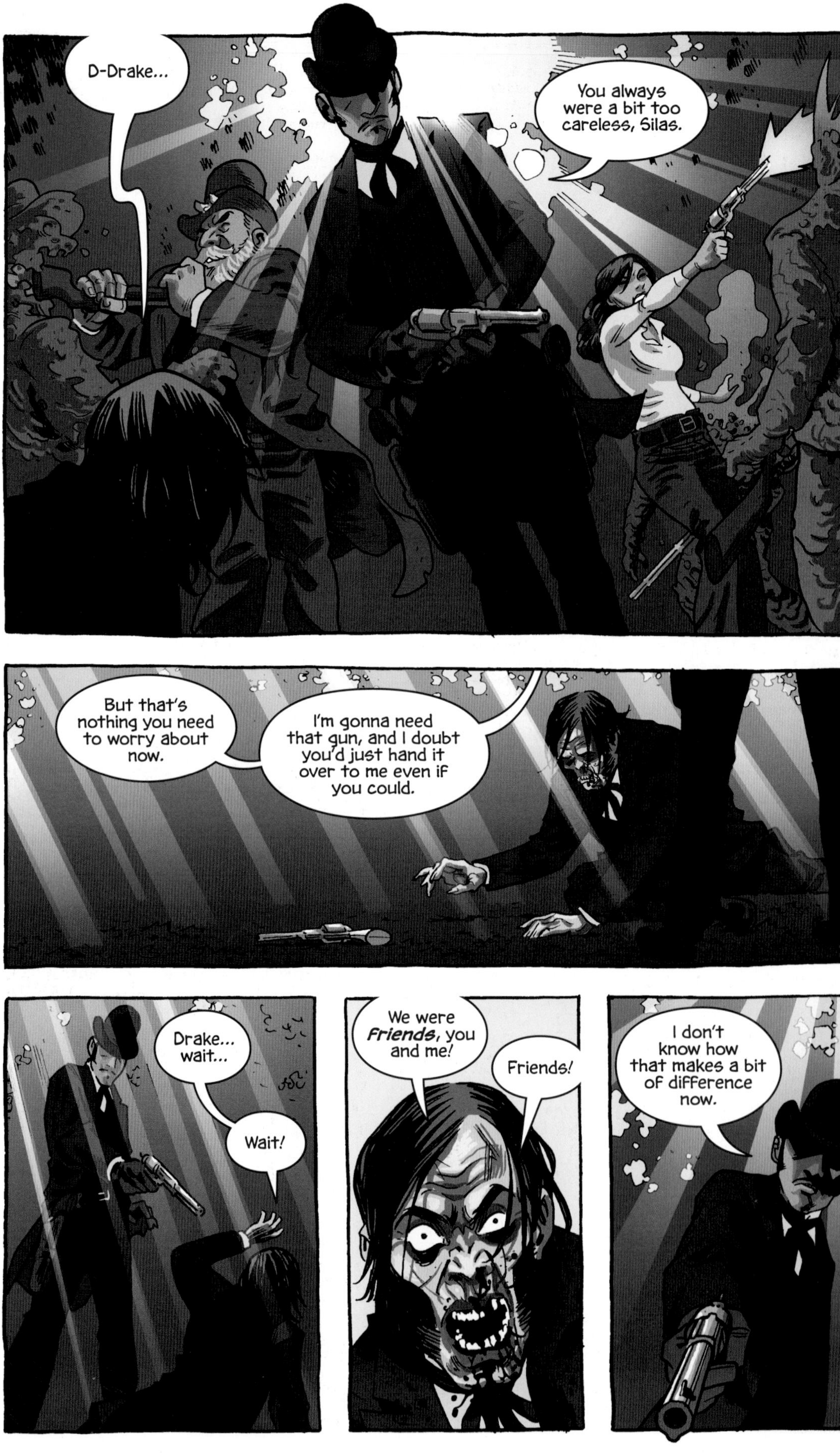
D-Drake...
You always were a bit too careless, Silas.
But that's nothing you need to worry about now.
I'm gonna need that gun, and I doubt you'd just hand it over to me even if you could.
Drake... wait...
Wait!
We were *Friends*, you and me!
Friends!
I don't know how that makes a bit of difference now.

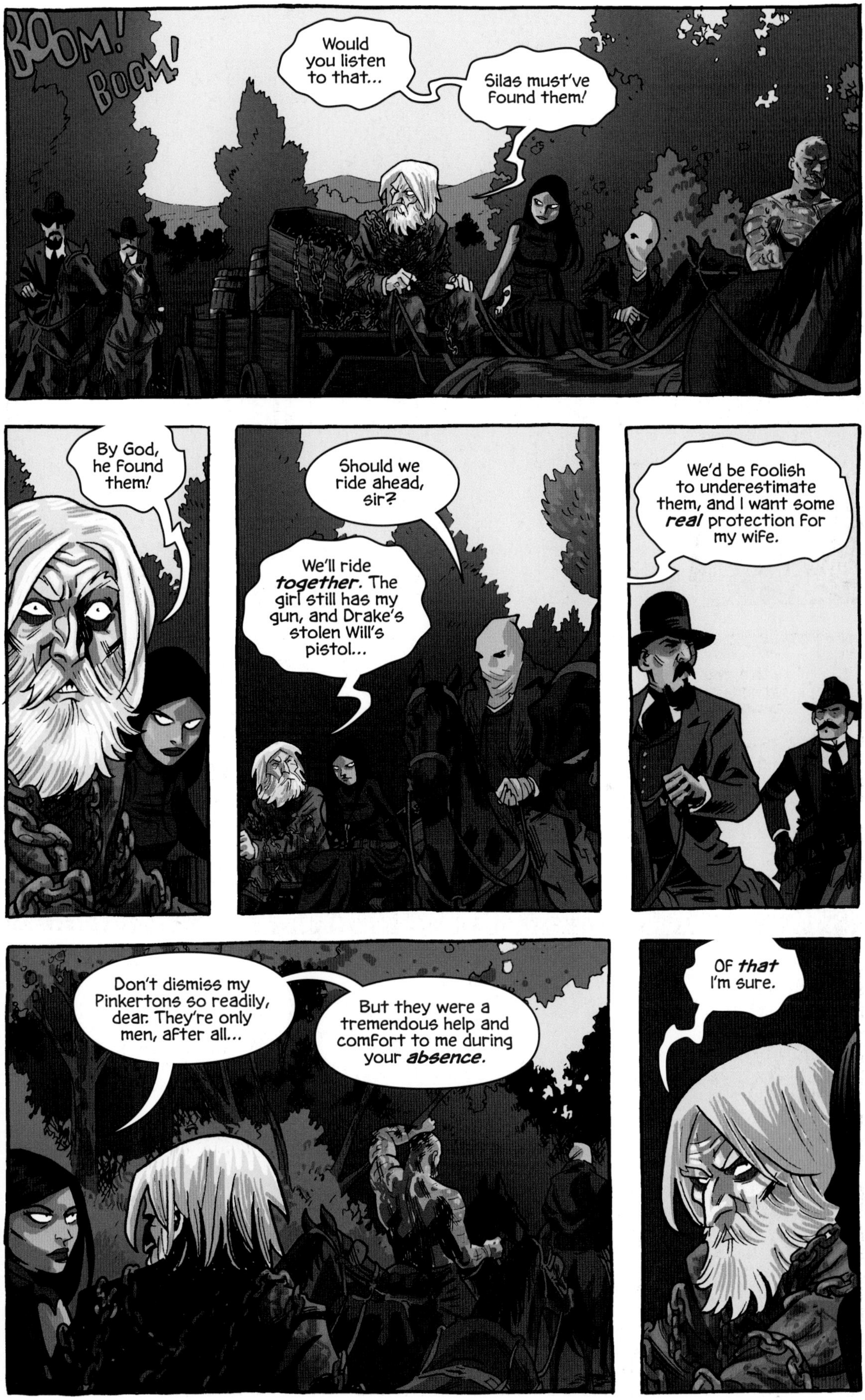
BOOM! BOOM!
Would you listen to that...
Silas must've found them!
By God, he found them!
Should we ride ahead, sir?
We'll ride *together*. The girl still has my gun, and Drake's stolen Will's pistol...
We'd be foolish to underestimate them, and I want some *real* protection for my wife.
Don't dismiss my Pinkertons so readily, dear. They're only men, after all...
But they were a tremendous help and comfort to me during your *absence*.
Of *that* I'm sure.

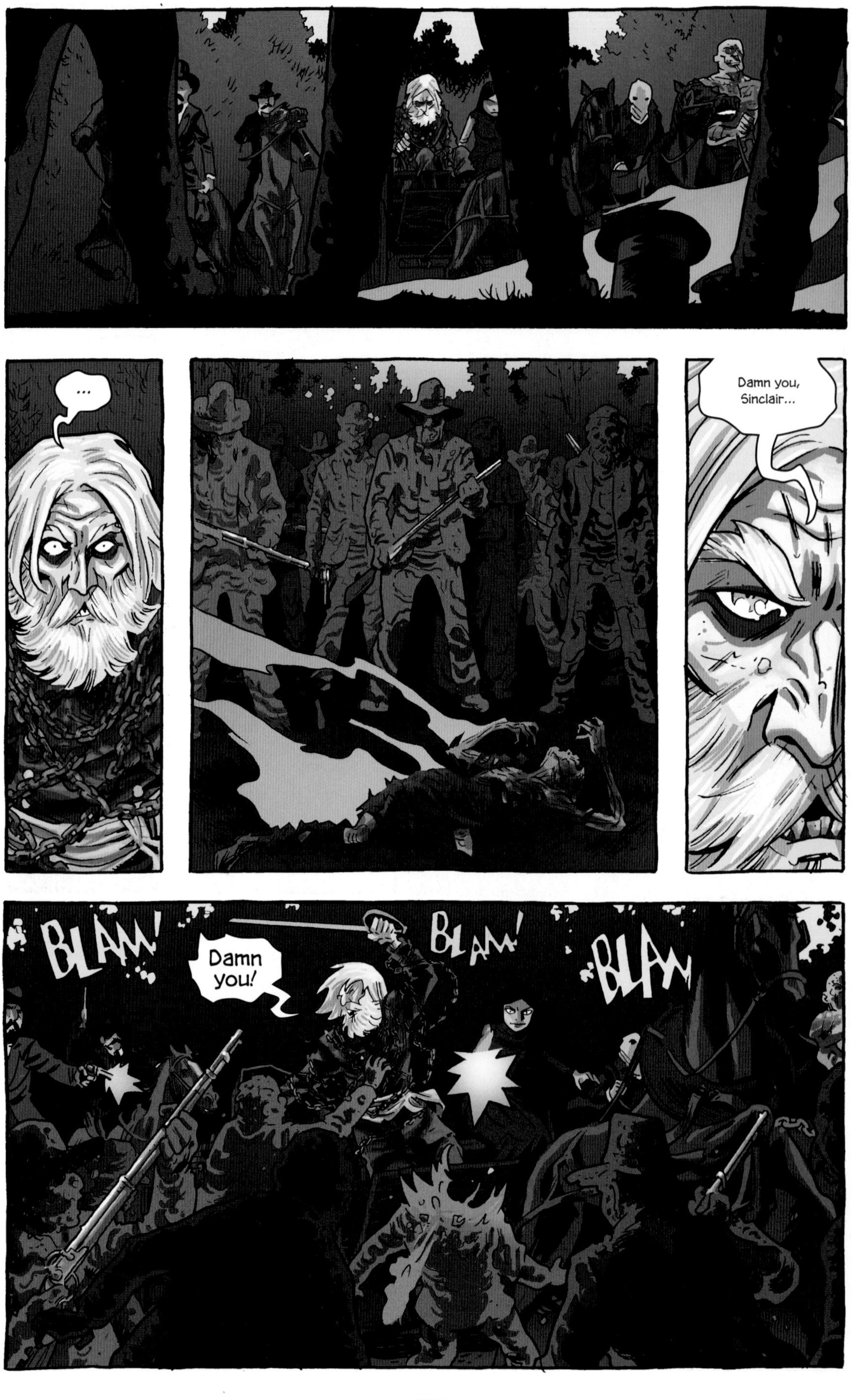
...
Damn you, Sinclair...
BLAM!
Damn you!
BLAM!
BLAM

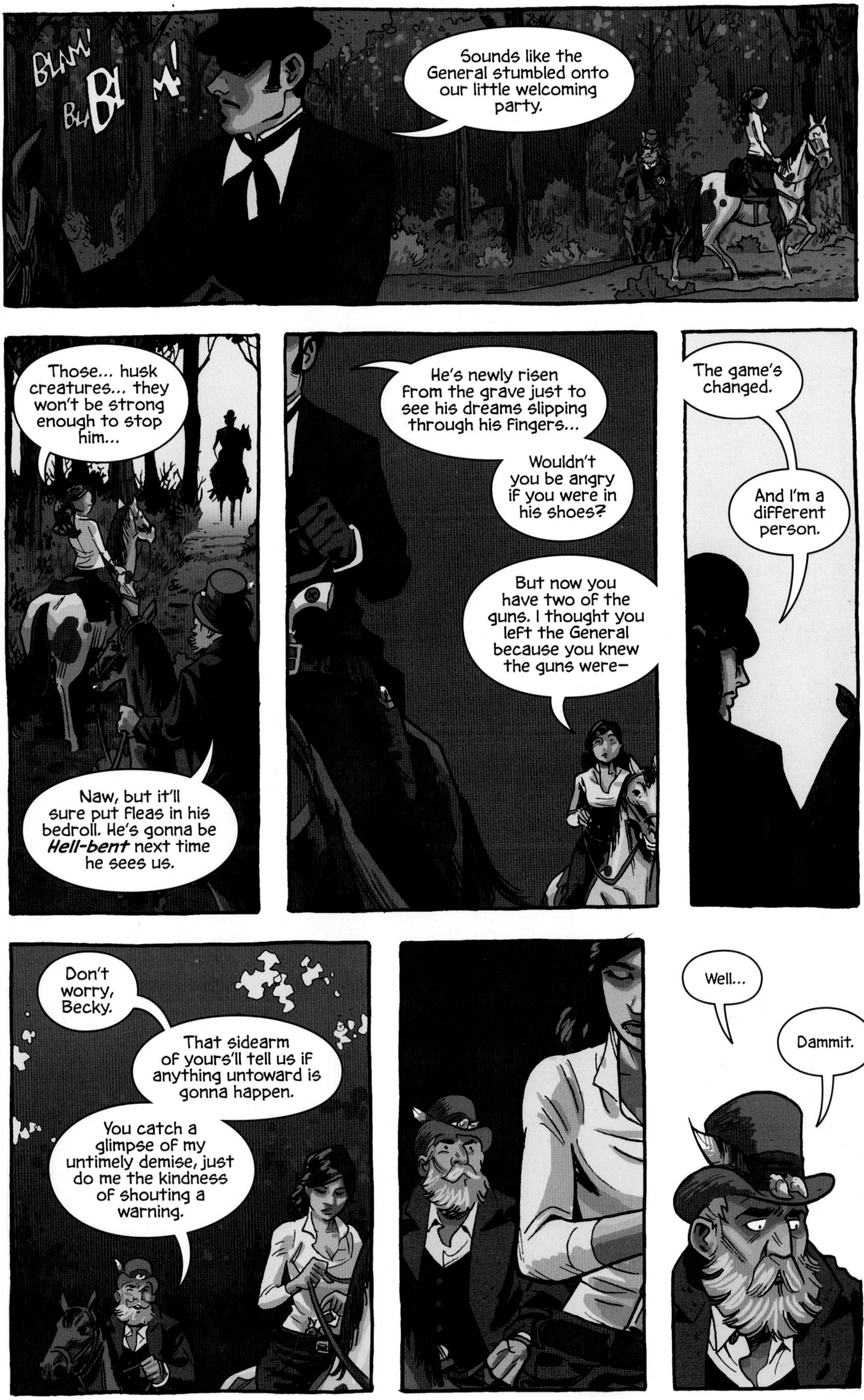
BLAM! BLABLAM!
Sounds like the General stumbled onto our little welcoming party.
Those... husk creatures... they won't be strong enough to stop him...
Naw, but it'll sure put fleas in his bedroll. He's gonna be *Hell-bent* next time he sees us.
He's newly risen from the grave just to see his dreams slipping through his fingers...
Wouldn't you be angry if you were in his shoes?
But now you have two of the guns. I thought you left the General because you knew the guns were—
The game's changed.
And I'm a different person.
Don't worry, Becky.
That sidearm of yours'll tell us if anything untoward is gonna happen.
You catch a glimpse of my untimely demise, just do me the kindness of shouting a warning.
Well...
Dammit.

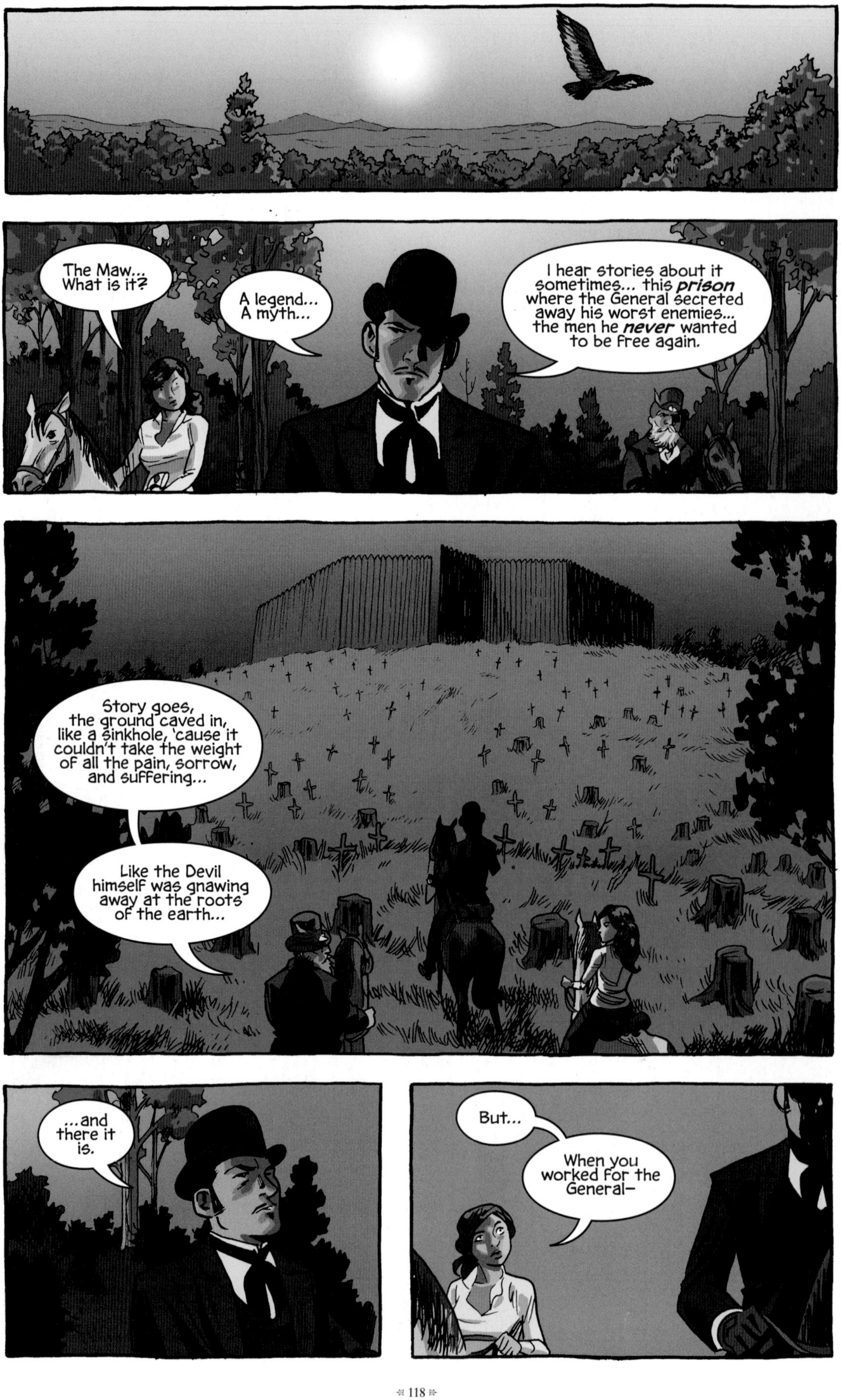

The Maw... What is it?
A legend... A myth...
I hear stories about it sometimes... this *prison* where the General secreted away his worst enemies... the men he *never* wanted to be free again.
Story goes, the ground caved in, like a sinkhole, 'cause it couldn't take the weight of all the pain, sorrow, and suffering...
Like the Devil himself was gnawing away at the roots of the earth...
...and there it is.
But...
When you worked for the General–

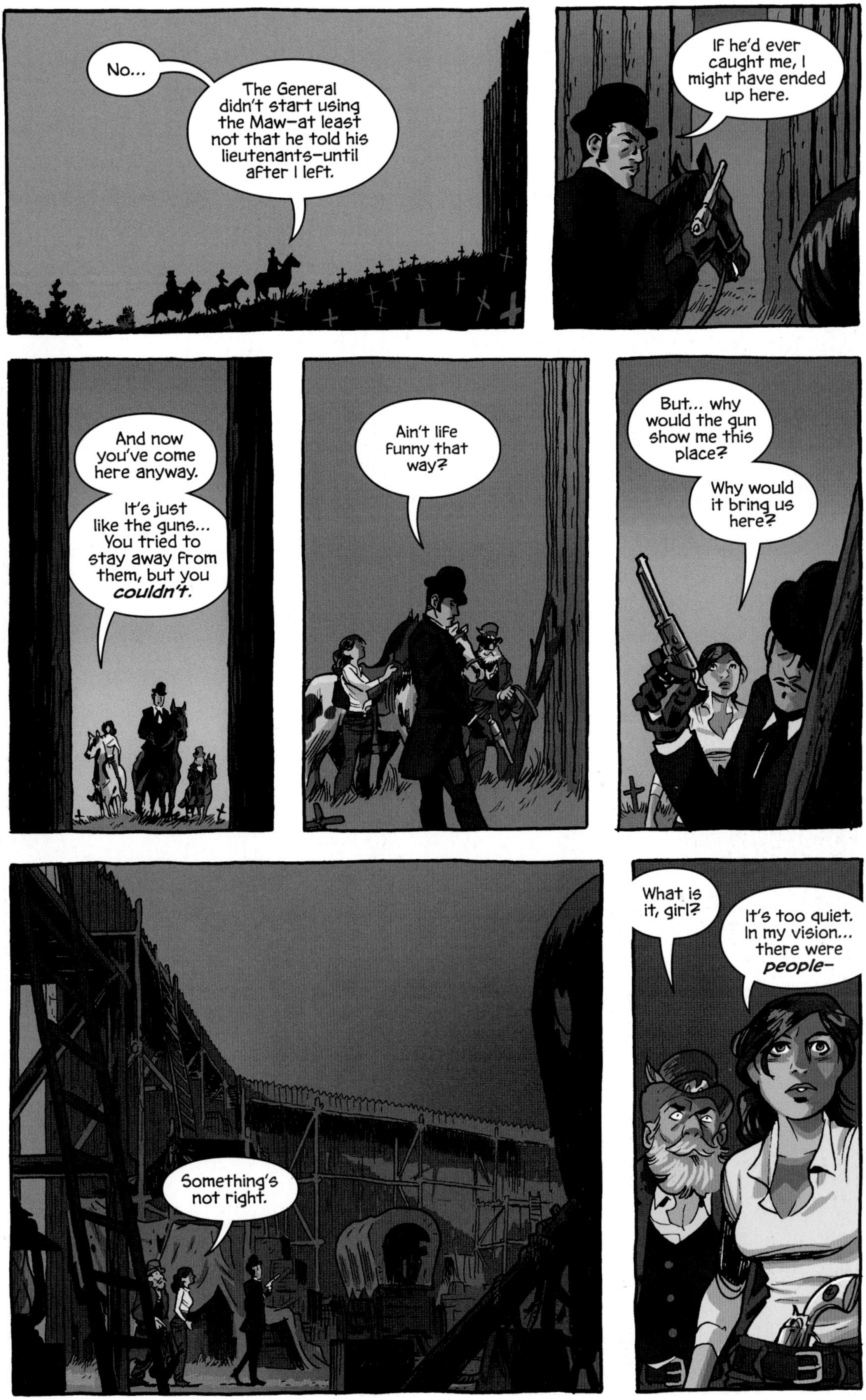

No...
The General didn't start using the Maw—at least not that he told his lieutenants—until after I left.
If he'd ever caught me, I might have ended up here.
And now you've come here anyway.
It's just like the guns... You tried to stay away from them, but you *couldn't*.
Ain't life funny that way?
But... why would the gun show me this place?
Why would it bring us here?
Something's not right.
What is it, girl?
It's too quiet. In my vision... there were *people*—

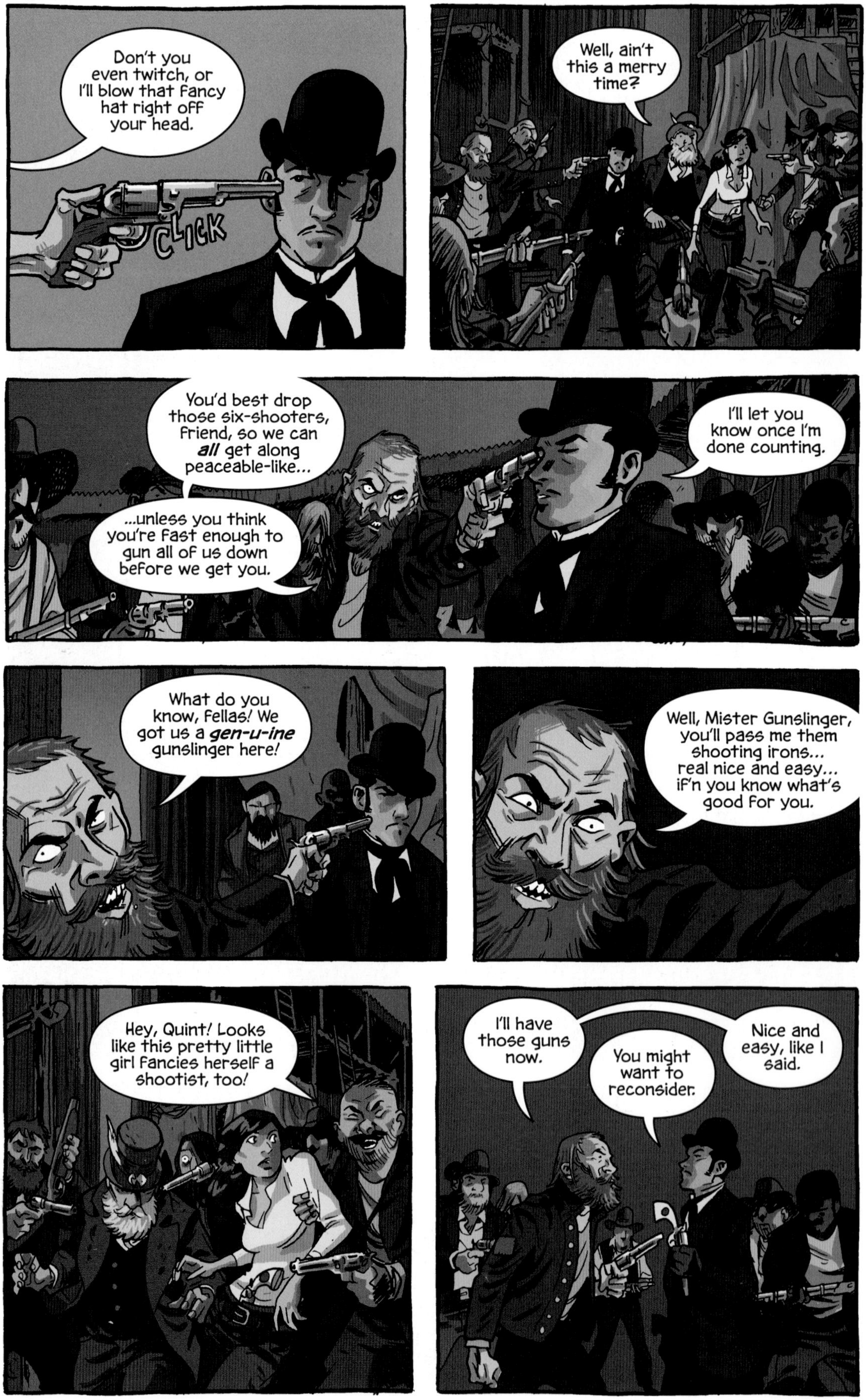

Don't you even twitch, or I'll blow that fancy hat right off your head.
CLICK
Well, ain't this a merry time?
You'd best drop those six-shooters, friend, so we can *all* get along peaceable-like...
...unless you think you're fast enough to gun all of us down before we get you.
I'll let you know once I'm done counting.
What do you know, fellas! We got us a *gen-u-ine* gunslinger here!
Well, Mister Gunslinger, you'll pass me them shooting irons... real nice and easy... if'n you know what's good for you.
Hey, Quint! Looks like this pretty little girl fancies herself a shootist, too!
I'll have those guns now.
Nice and easy, like I said.
You might want to reconsider.

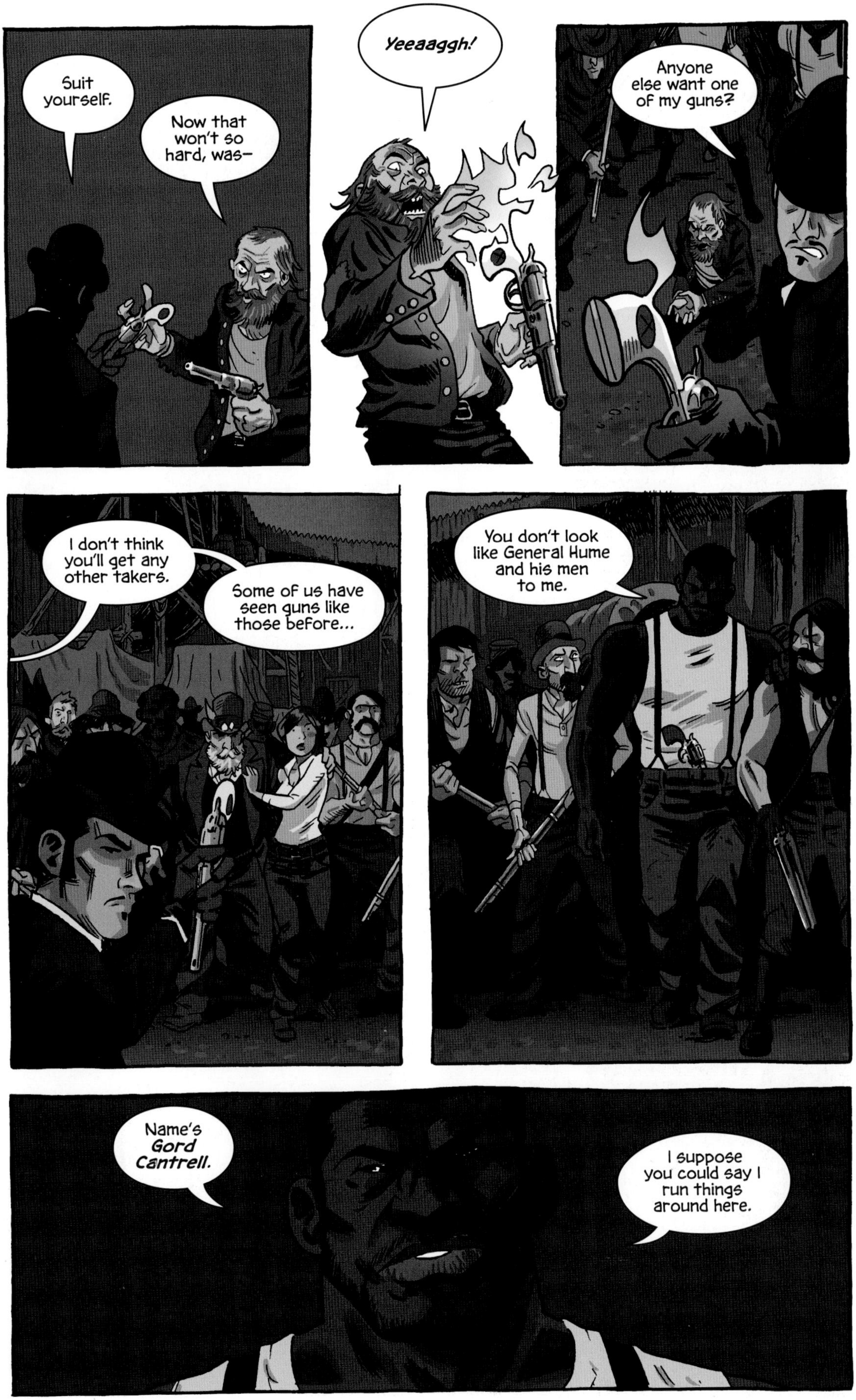

Suit yourself.
Now that won't so hard, was–
Yeeaaggh!
Anyone else want one of my guns?
I don't think you'll get any other takers.
Some of us have seen guns like those before...
You don't look like General Hume and his men to me.
Name's *Gord Cantrell.*
I suppose you could say I run things around here.

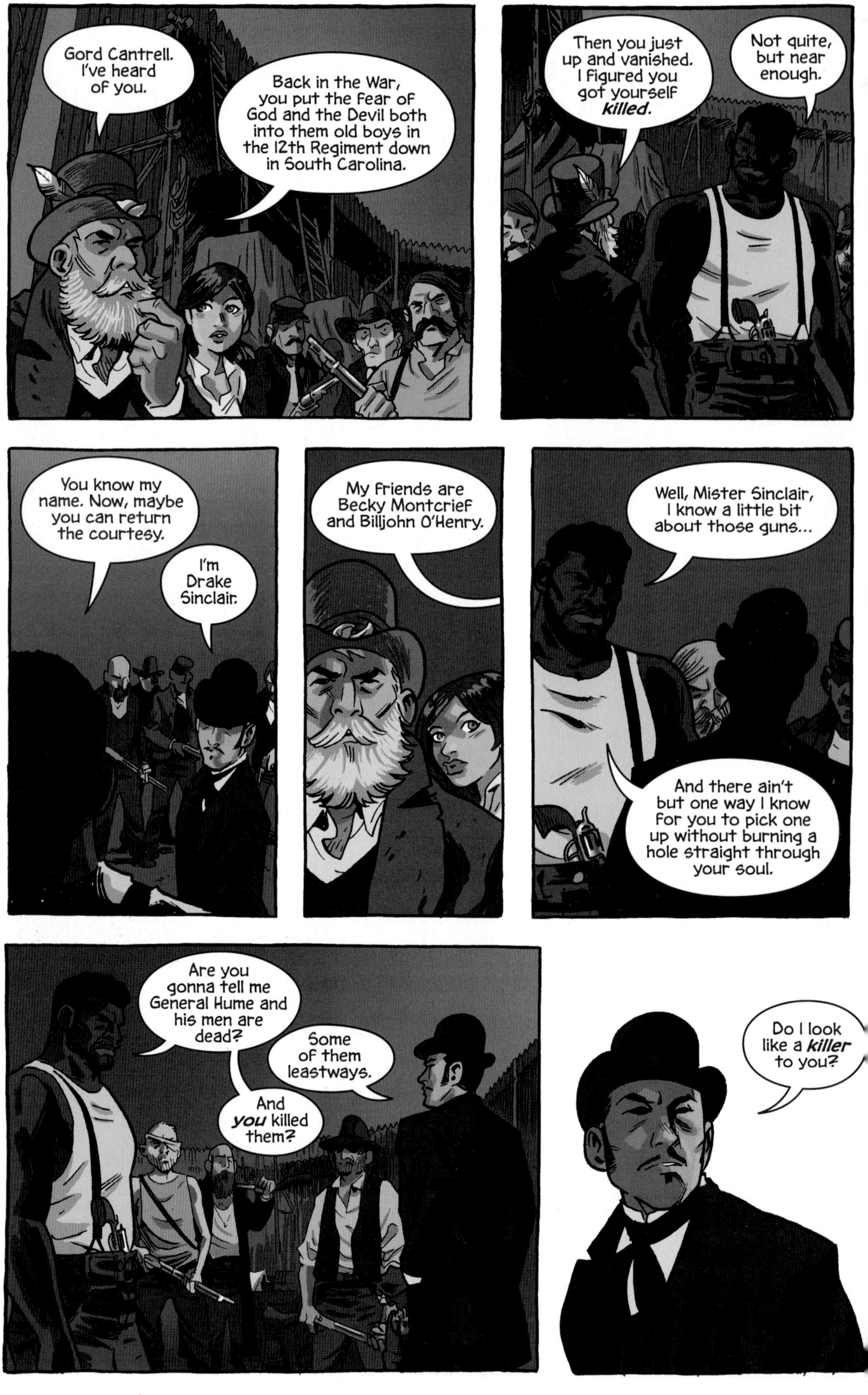

Gord Cantrell. I've heard of you.
Back in the War, you put the Fear of God and the Devil both into them old boys in the 12th Regiment down in South Carolina.
Then you just up and vanished. I figured you got yourself ***killed.***
Not quite, but near enough.
You know my name. Now, maybe you can return the courtesy.
I'm Drake Sinclair.
My friends are Becky Montcrief and Billjohn O'Henry.
Well, Mister Sinclair, I know a little bit about those guns...
And there ain't but one way I know for you to pick one up without burning a hole straight through your soul.
Are you gonna tell me General Hume and his men are dead?
Some of them leastways.
And ***you*** killed them?
Do I look like a ***killer*** to you?

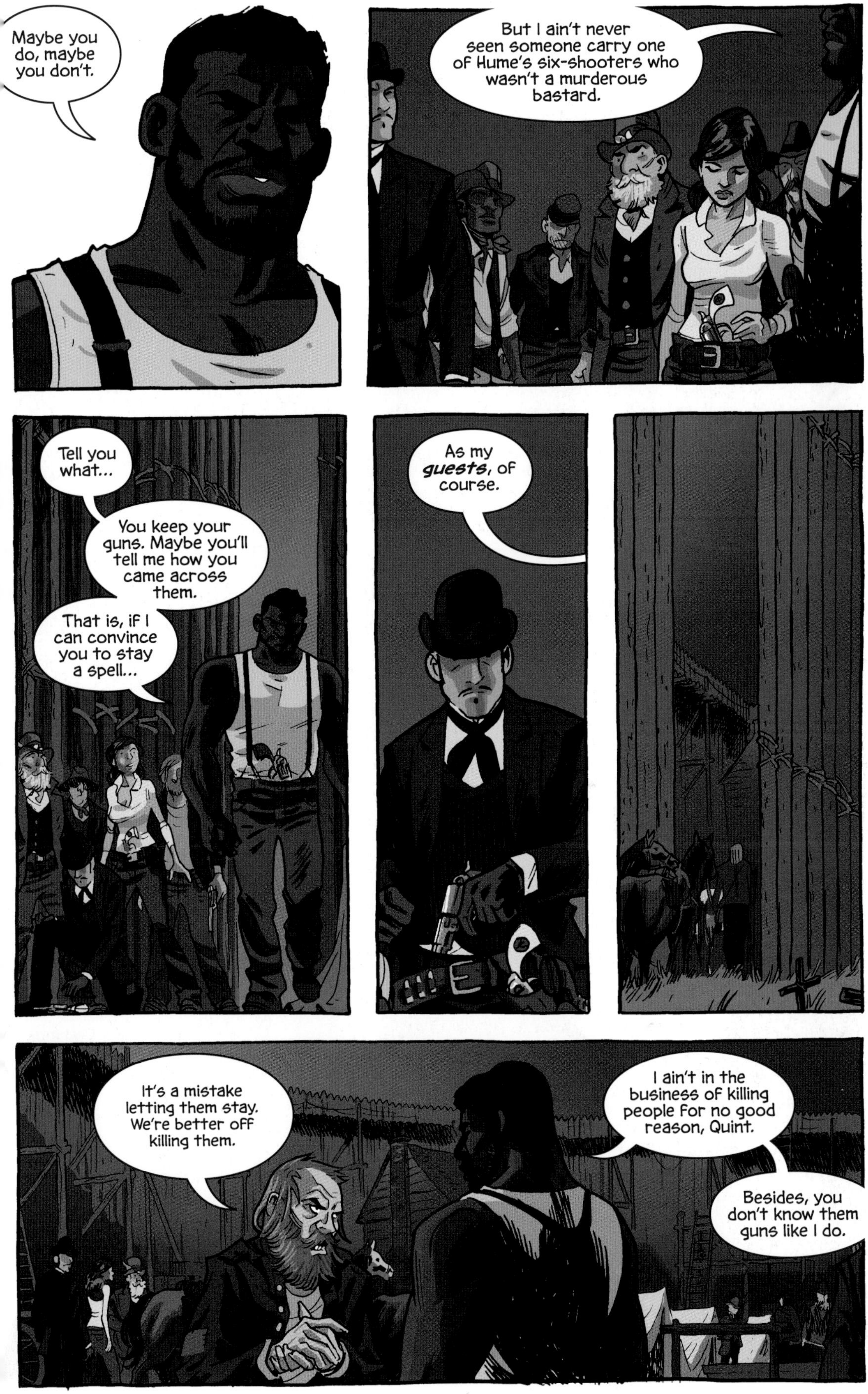

Maybe you do, maybe you don't.
But I ain't never seen someone carry one of Hume's six-shooters who wasn't a murderous bastard.
Tell you what...
You keep your guns. Maybe you'll tell me how you came across them.
That is, if I can convince you to stay a spell...
As my *guests*, of course.
It's a mistake letting them stay. We're better off killing them.
I ain't in the business of killing people for no good reason, Quint.
Besides, you don't know them guns like I do.

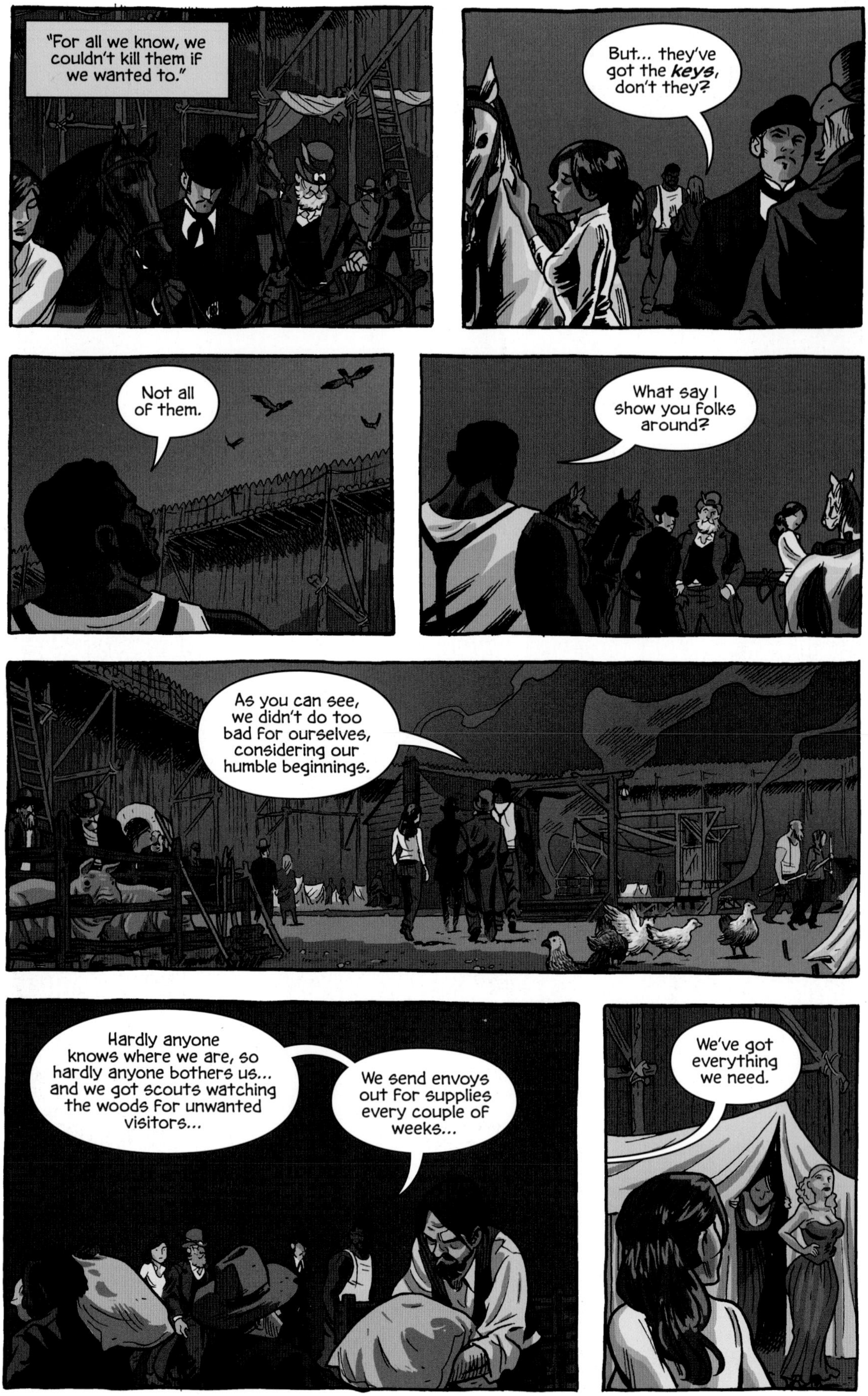
"For all we know, we couldn't kill them if we wanted to."
But... they've got the *keys*, don't they?
Not all of them.
What say I show you folks around?
As you can see, we didn't do too bad for ourselves, considering our humble beginnings.
Hardly anyone knows where we are, so hardly anyone bothers us... and we got scouts watching the woods for unwanted visitors...
We send envoys out for supplies every couple of weeks...
We've got everything we need.

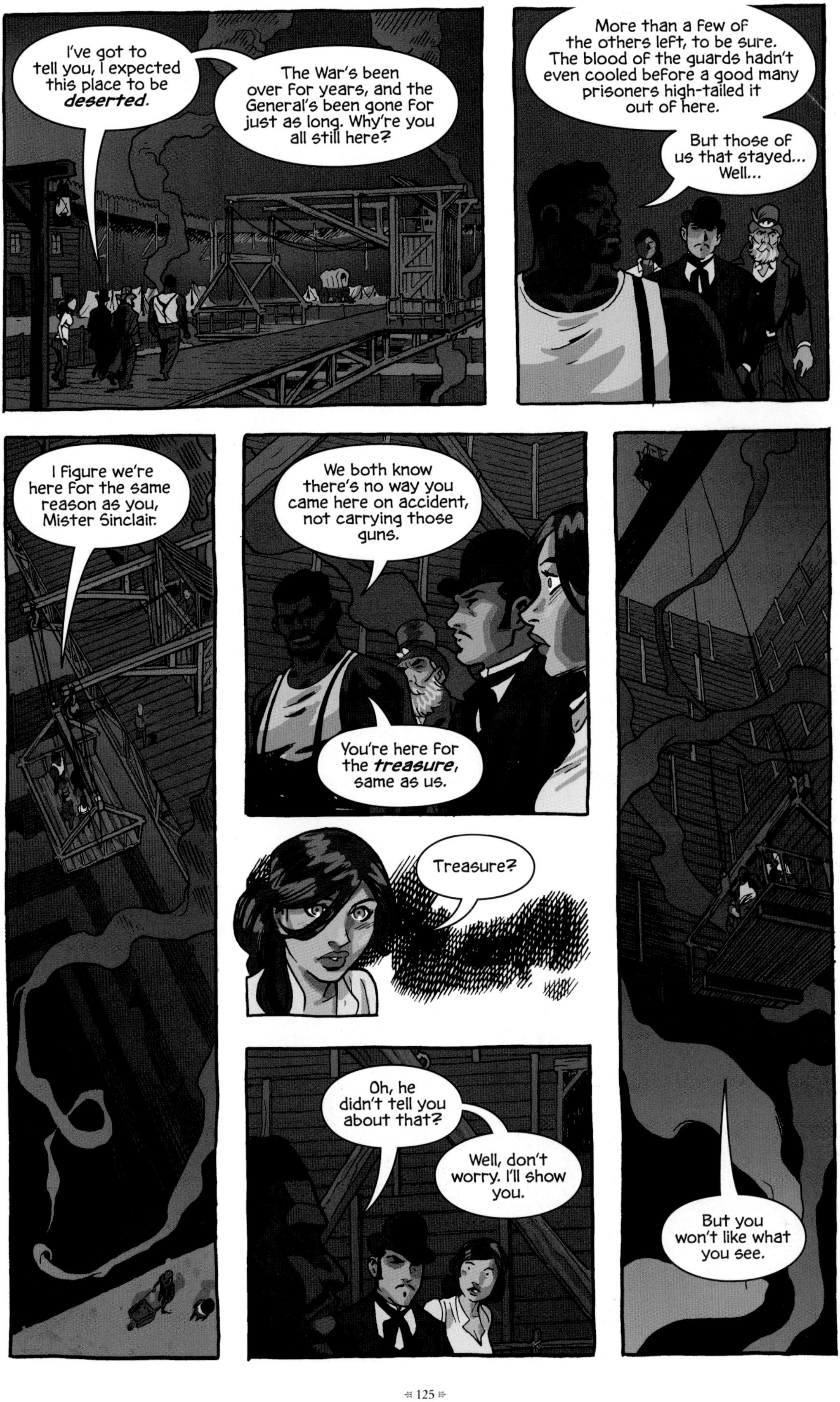
I've got to tell you, I expected this place to be *deserted*.
The War's been over for years, and the General's been gone for just as long. Why're you all still here?
More than a few of the others left, to be sure. The blood of the guards hadn't even cooled before a good many prisoners high-tailed it out of here.
But those of us that stayed... Well...
I figure we're here for the same reason as you, Mister Sinclair.
We both know there's no way you came here on accident, not carrying those guns.
You're here for the *treasure*, same as us.
Treasure?
Oh, he didn't tell you about that?
Well, don't worry. I'll show you.
But you won't like what you see.

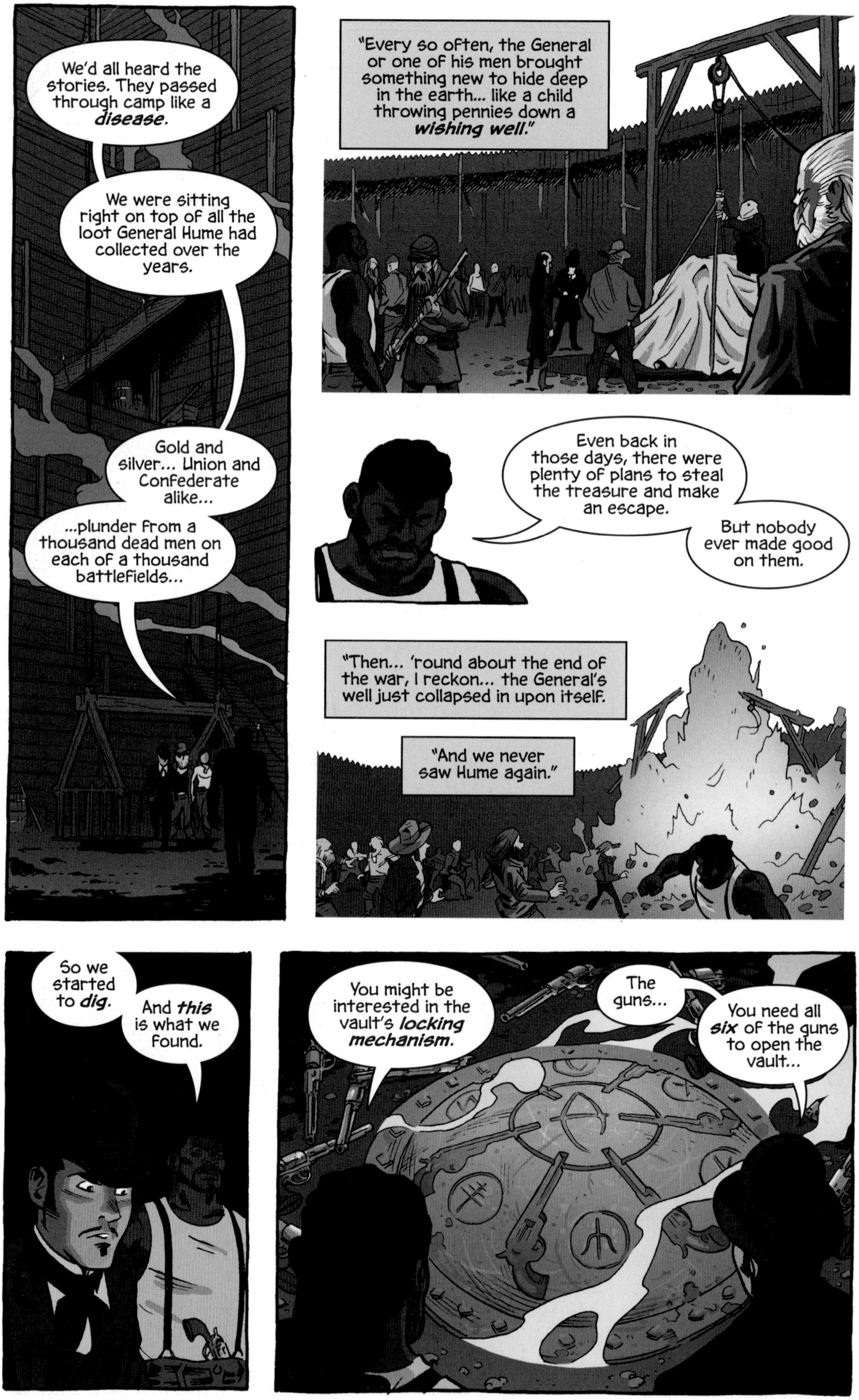

We'd all heard the stories. They passed through camp like a *disease.*
We were sitting right on top of all the loot General Hume had collected over the years.
Gold and silver... Union and Confederate alike...
...plunder from a thousand dead men on each of a thousand battlefields...
"Every so often, the General or one of his men brought something new to hide deep in the earth... like a child throwing pennies down a *wishing well.*"
Even back in those days, there were plenty of plans to steal the treasure and make an escape.
But nobody ever made good on them.
"Then... 'round about the end of the war, I reckon... the General's well just collapsed in upon itself.
"And we never saw Hume again."
So we started to *dig.*
And *this* is what we found.
You might be interested in the vault's *locking mechanism.*
The guns...
You need all *six* of the guns to open the vault...

Damn...

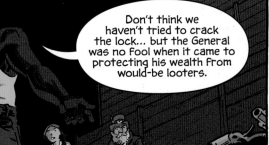

Don't think we haven't tried to crack the lock... but the General was no fool when it came to protecting his wealth from would-be looters.

Is that what this is about?

Money?!

After everything that's happened... everything we've been through... you're just here because of *buried treasure*?!

Would you have helped me get away from Missy Hume if it wasn't for—

...

What's wrong, girl?

This is wrong...

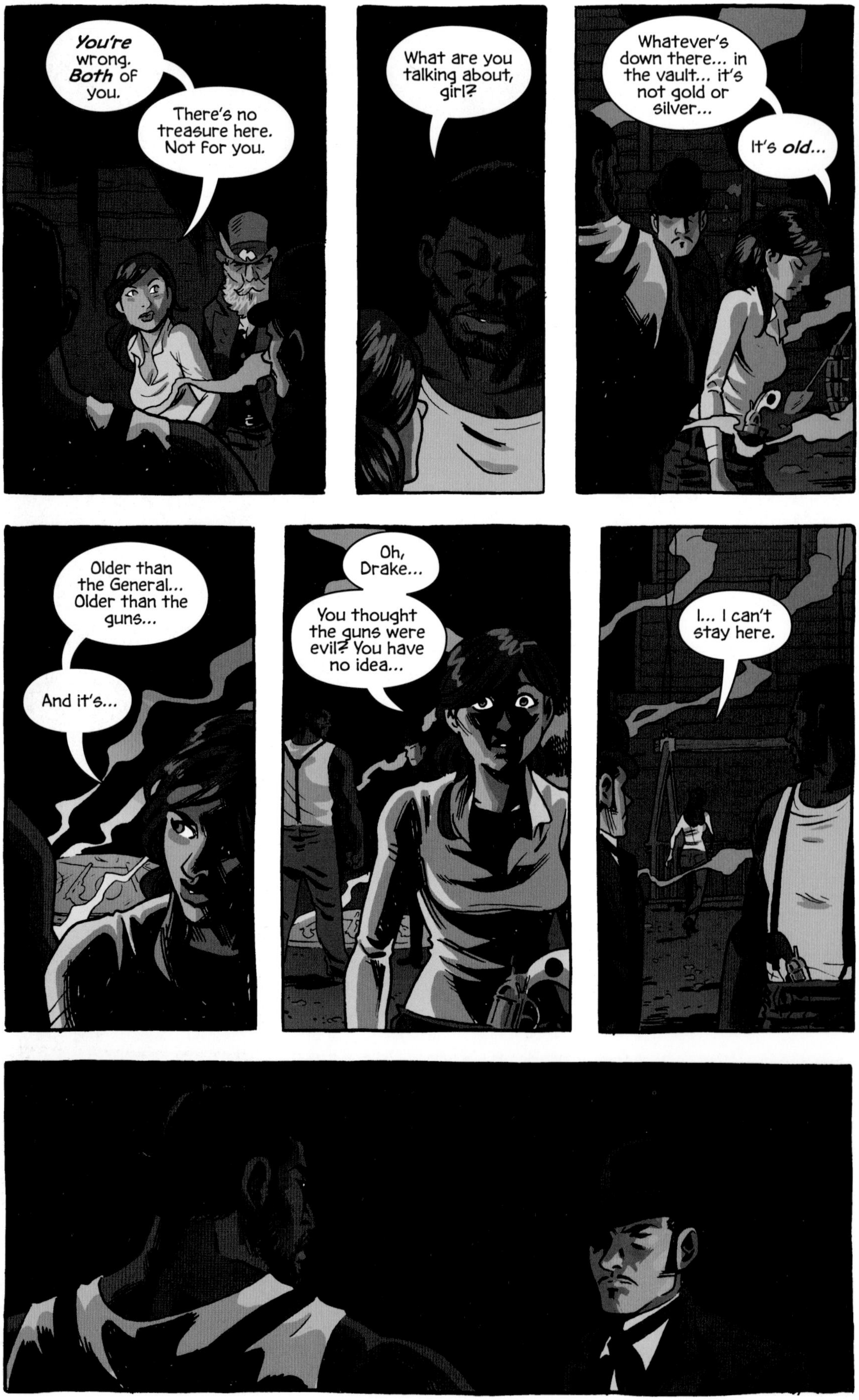
*You're* wrong. *Both* of you.
There's no treasure here. Not for you.
What are you talking about, girl?
Whatever's down there... in the vault... it's not gold or silver...
It's *old*...
Older than the General... Older than the guns...
And it's...
Oh, Drake...
You thought the guns were evil? You have no idea...
I... I can't stay here.

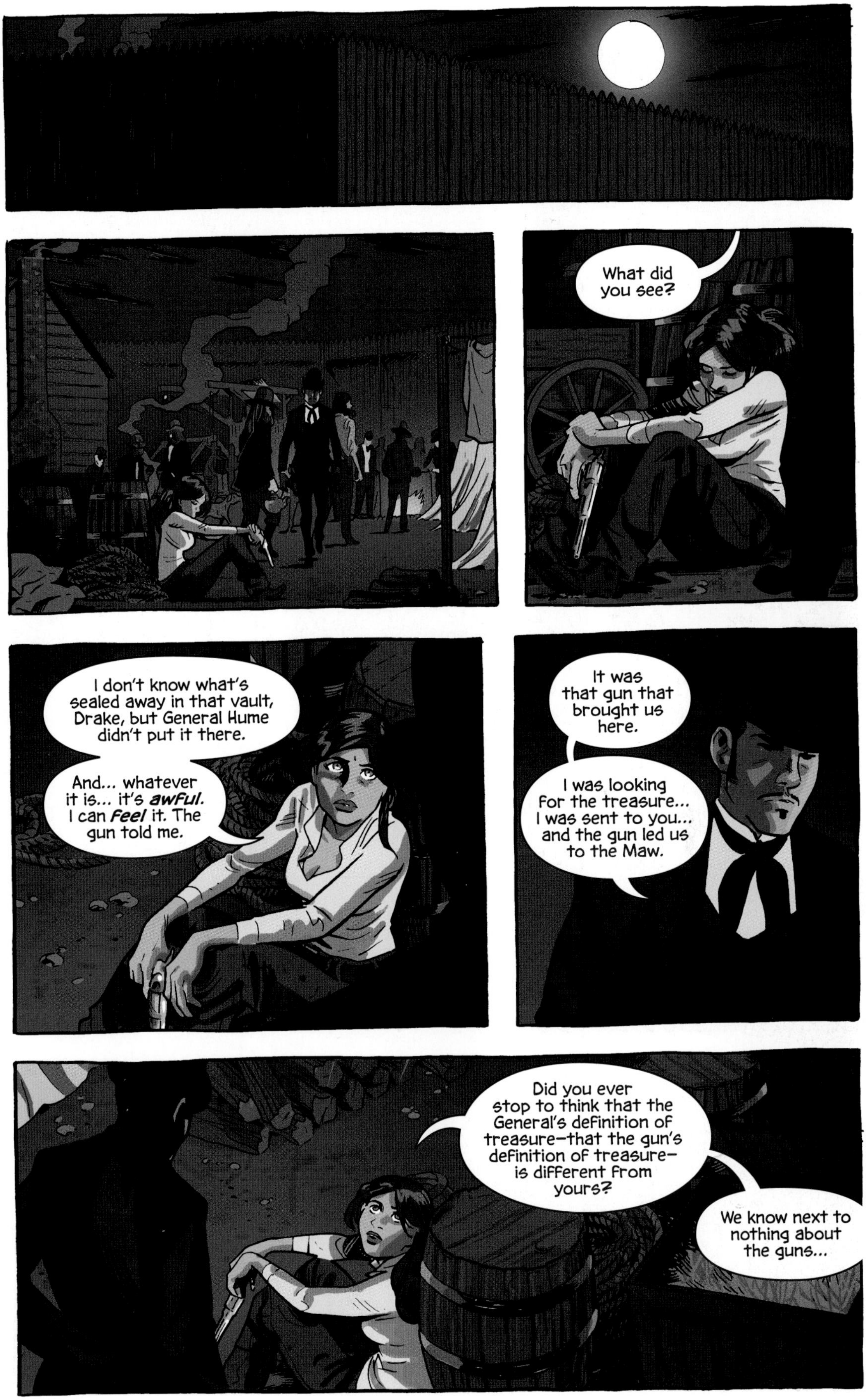
What did you see?
I don't know what's sealed away in that vault, Drake, but General Hume didn't put it there.
And... whatever it is... it's *awful.* I can *feel* it. The gun told me.
It was that gun that brought us here.
I was looking for the treasure... I was sent to you... and the gun led us to the Maw.
Did you ever stop to think that the General's definition of treasure—that the gun's definition of treasure—is different from yours?
We know next to nothing about the guns...

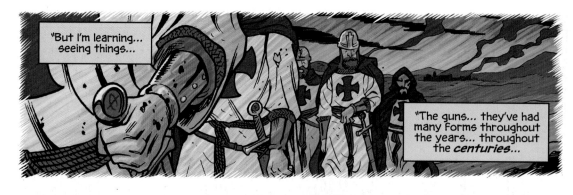

"But I'm learning... seeing things...

"The guns... they've had many forms throughout the years... throughout the *centuries*...

"They've been around for longer than you can imagine."

My *pa* died protecting this gun...

And seeing how the gun's just some... *key* for greedy men, I'd say he died protecting it from the likes of *you*.

Don't lecture me on the differences between righteousness and avarice, girl.

You think I can't taste the difference?

I *knew* your stepfather.

It was me that helped him sneak into the General's camp at Bitter Ridge.

What—

BONG!

BONG!

BONG!

What's that?

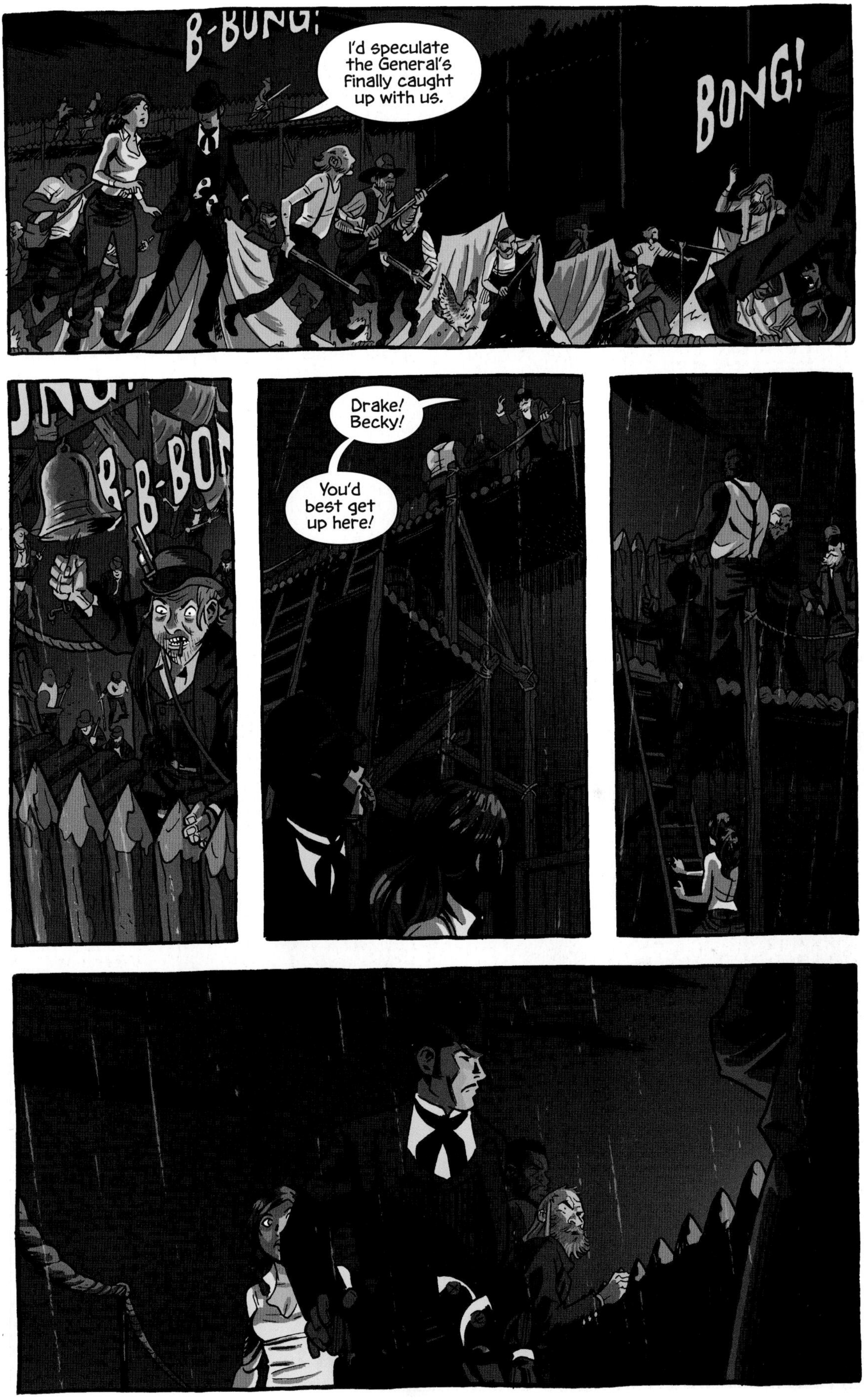

B-BUNG!
I'd speculate the General's finally caught up with us.
BONG!
B-B-BO
Drake! Becky!
You'd best get up here!

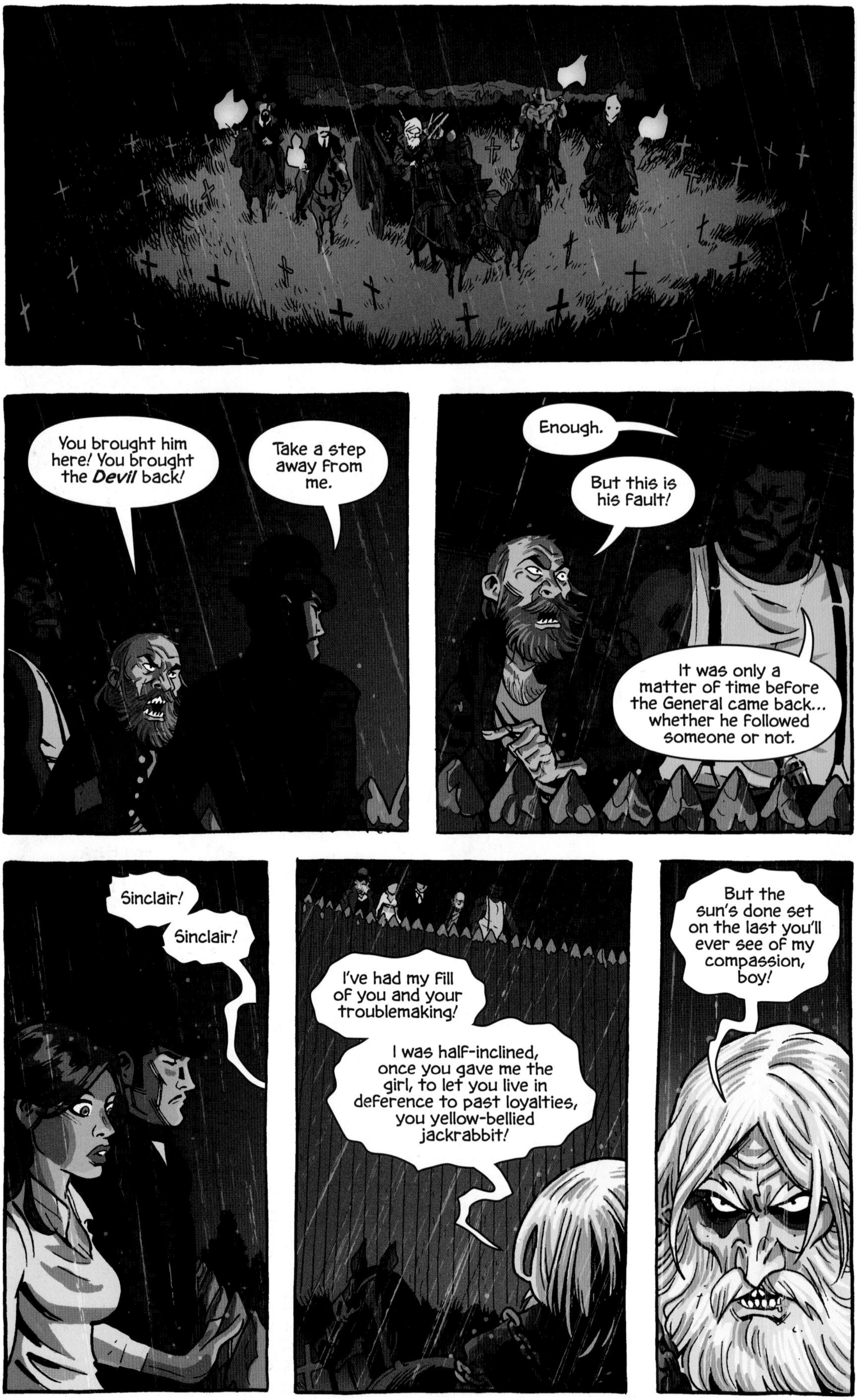
You brought him here! You brought the *Devil* back!
Take a step away from me.
Enough.
But this is his fault!
It was only a matter of time before the General came back... whether he followed someone or not.
Sinclair!
Sinclair!
I've had my fill of you and your troublemaking!
I was half-inclined, once you gave me the girl, to let you live in deference to past loyalties, you yellow-bellied jackrabbit!
But the sun's done set on the last you'll ever see of my compassion, boy!

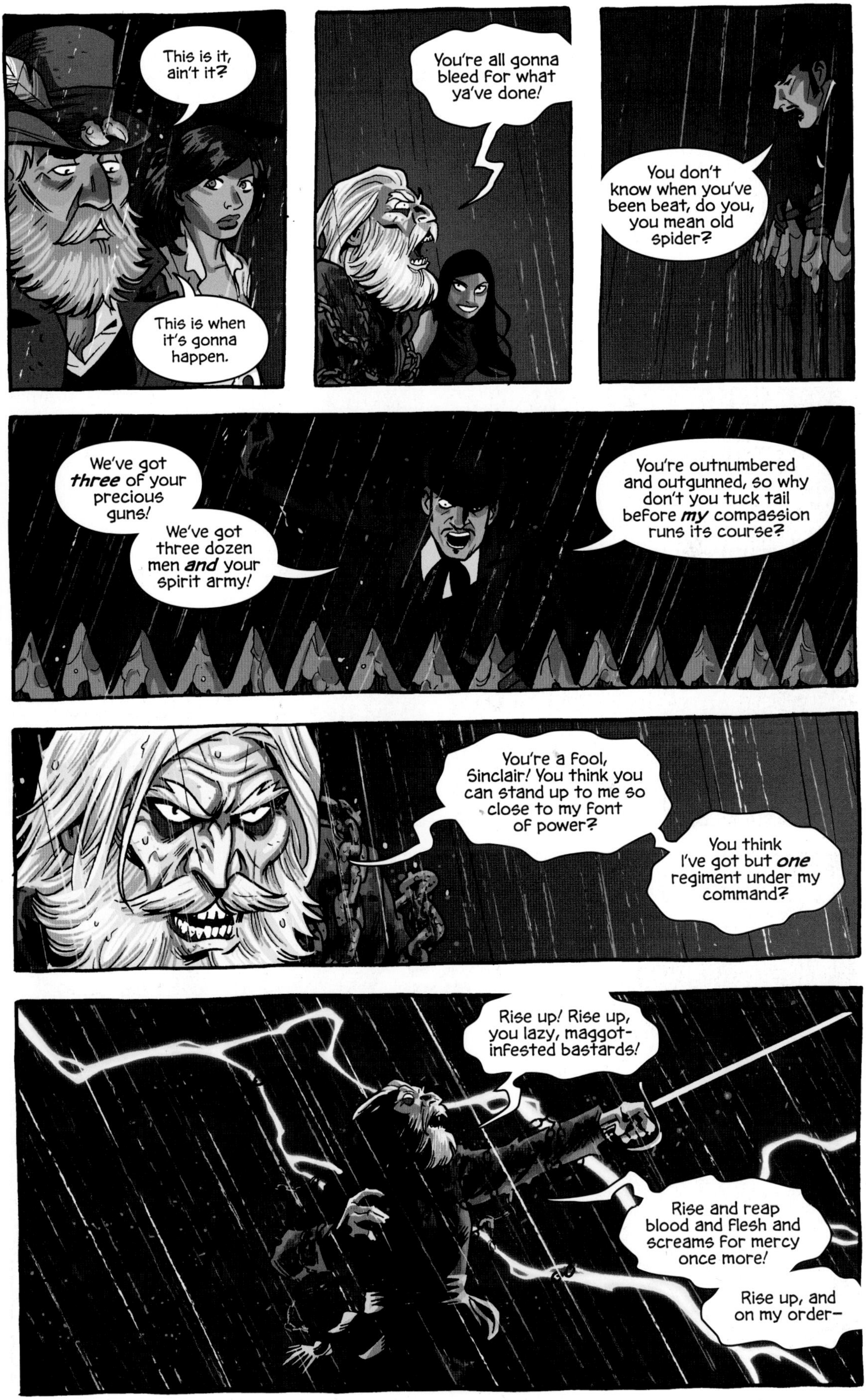

This is it, ain't it?
This is when it's gonna happen.
You're all gonna bleed for what ya've done!
You don't know when you've been beat, do you, you mean old spider?
We've got *three* of your precious guns!
We've got three dozen men *and* your spirit army!
You're outnumbered and outgunned, so why don't you tuck tail before *my* compassion runs its course?
You're a fool, Sinclair! You think you can stand up to me so close to my font of power?
You think I've got but *one* regiment under my command?
Rise up! Rise up, you lazy, maggot-infested bastards!
Rise and reap blood and flesh and screams for mercy once more!
Rise up, and on my order—

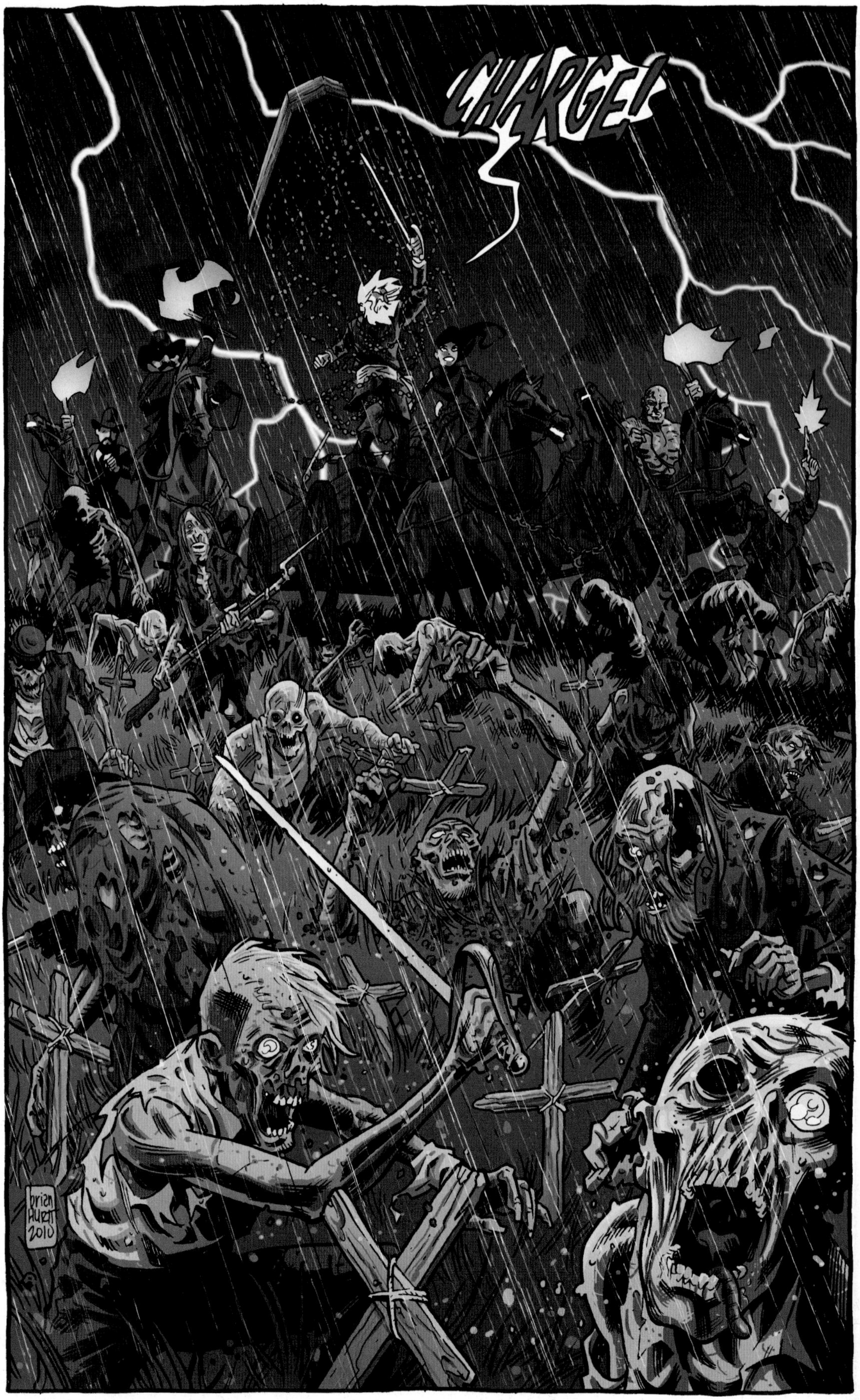
CHARGE!
brian HURTT 2010

# CHAPTER
# SIX

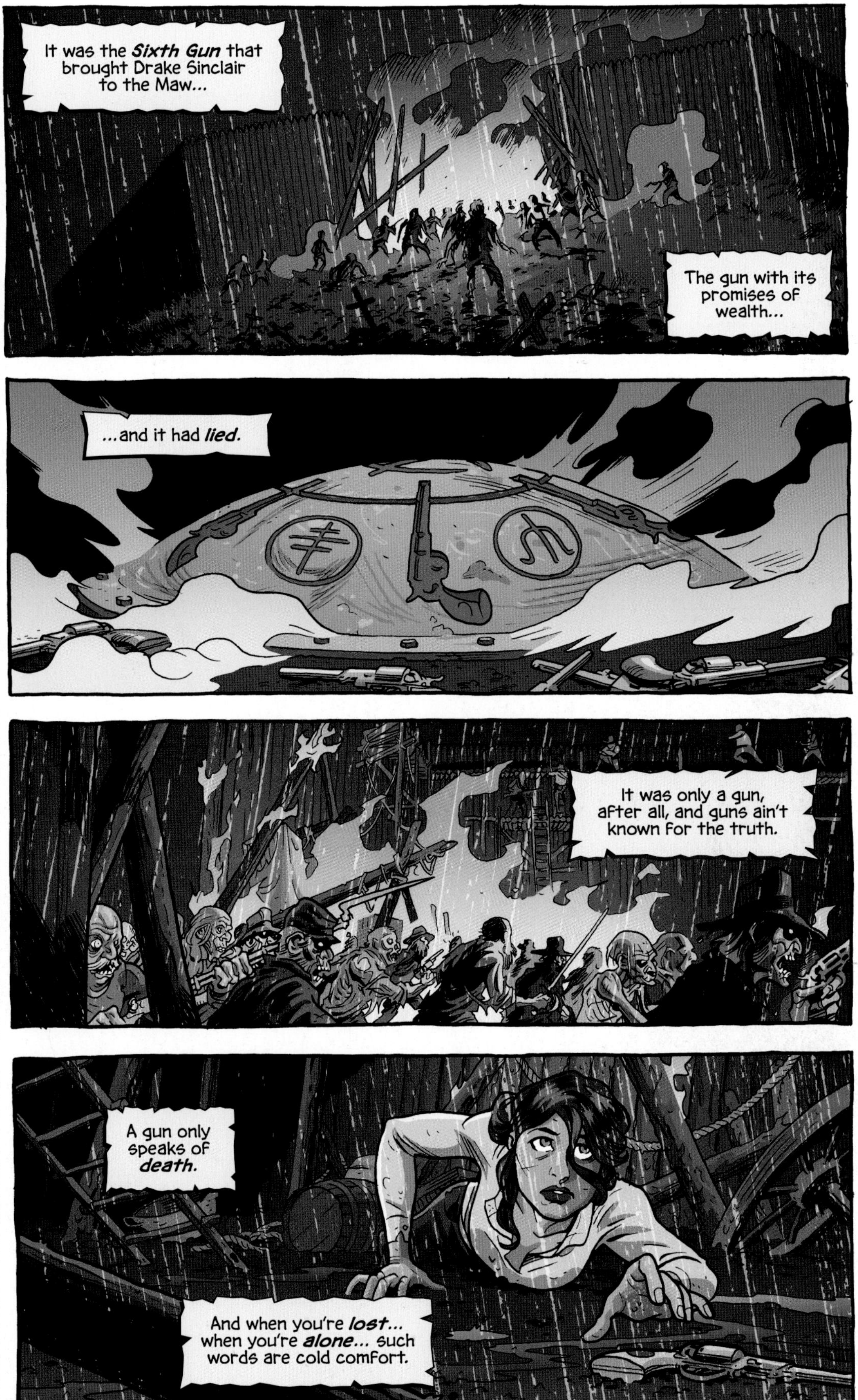
It was the *Sixth Gun* that brought Drake Sinclair to the Maw...
The gun with its promises of wealth...
...and it had *lied.*
It was only a gun, after all, and guns ain't known for the truth.
A gun only speaks of *death.*
And when you're *lost*... when you're *alone*... such words are cold comfort.

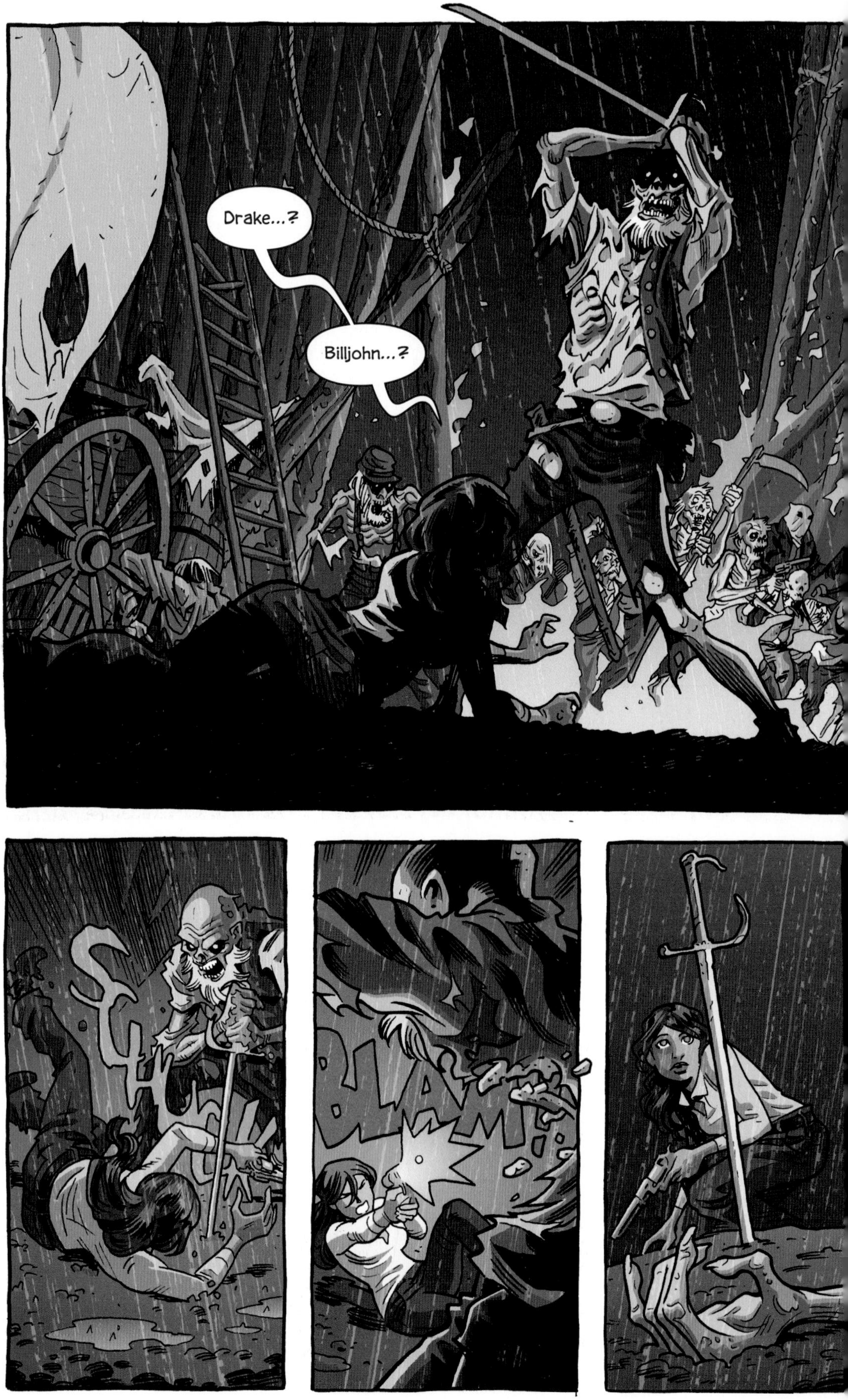
Drake...?
Billjohn...?
BLAM!

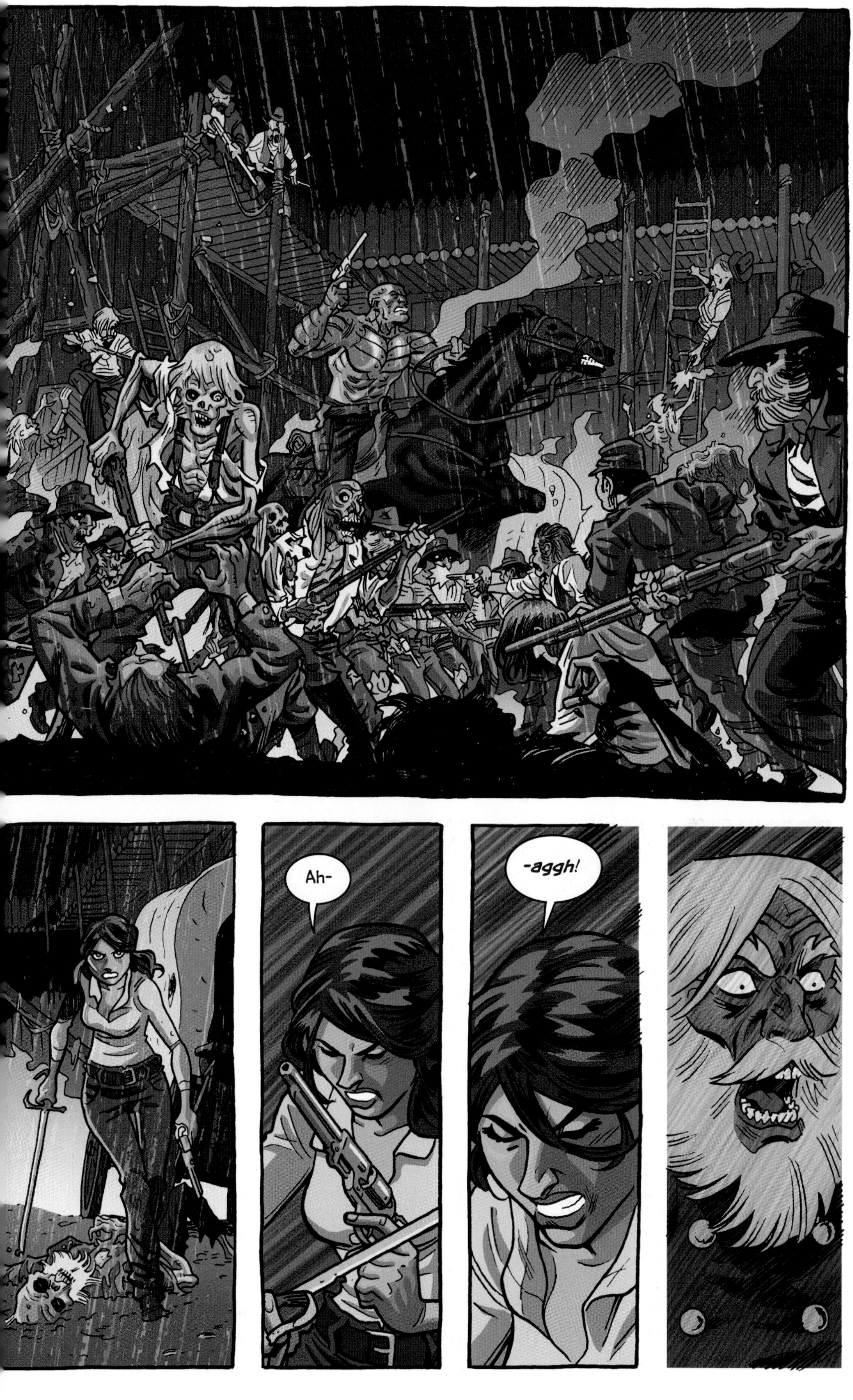
Ah-
-aggh!

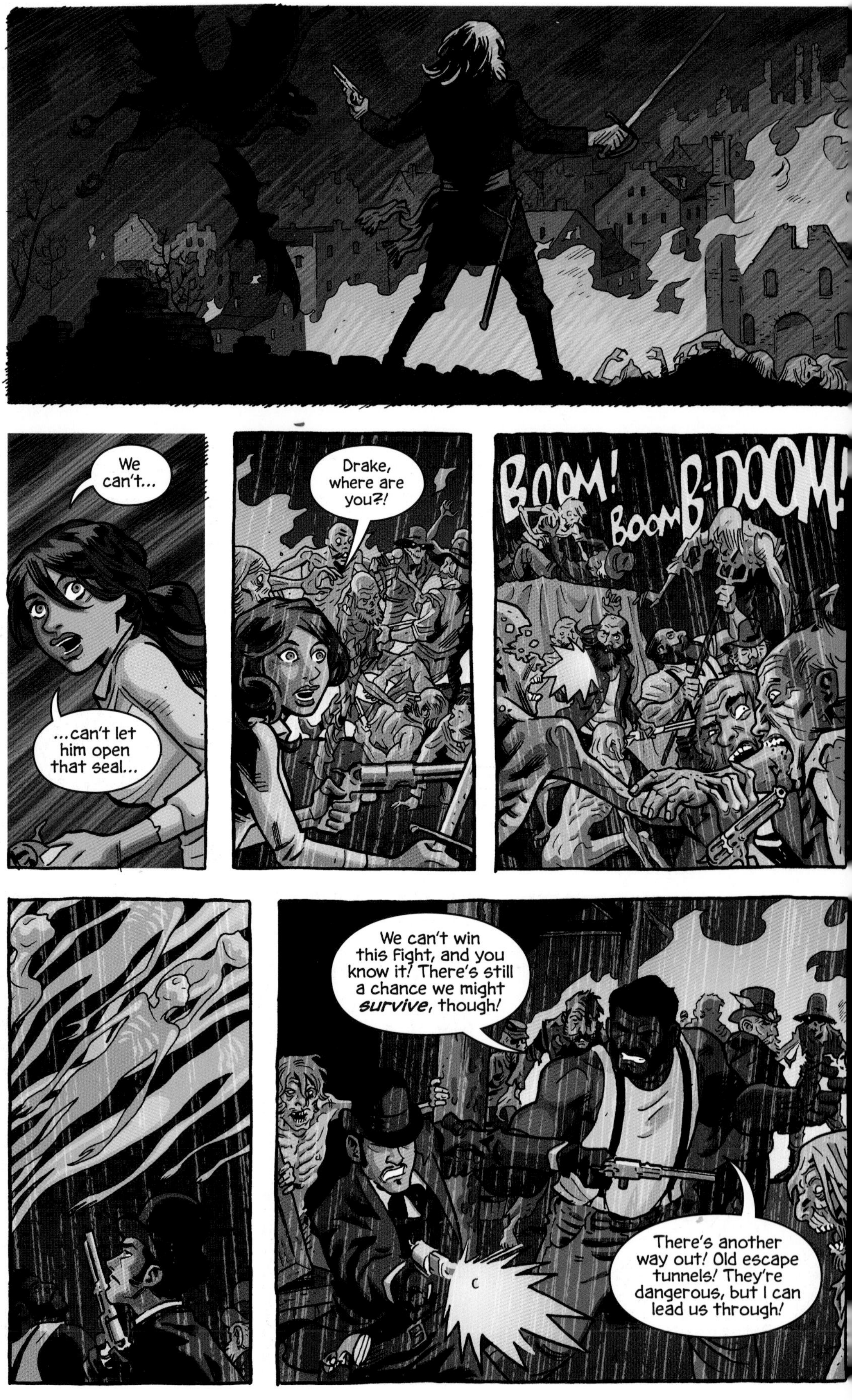
We can't...
...can't let him open that seal...
Drake, where are you?!
BOOM! BOOM B-DOOM!
We can't win this fight, and you know it! There's still a chance we might *survive*, though!
There's another way out! Old escape tunnels! They're dangerous, but I can lead us through!

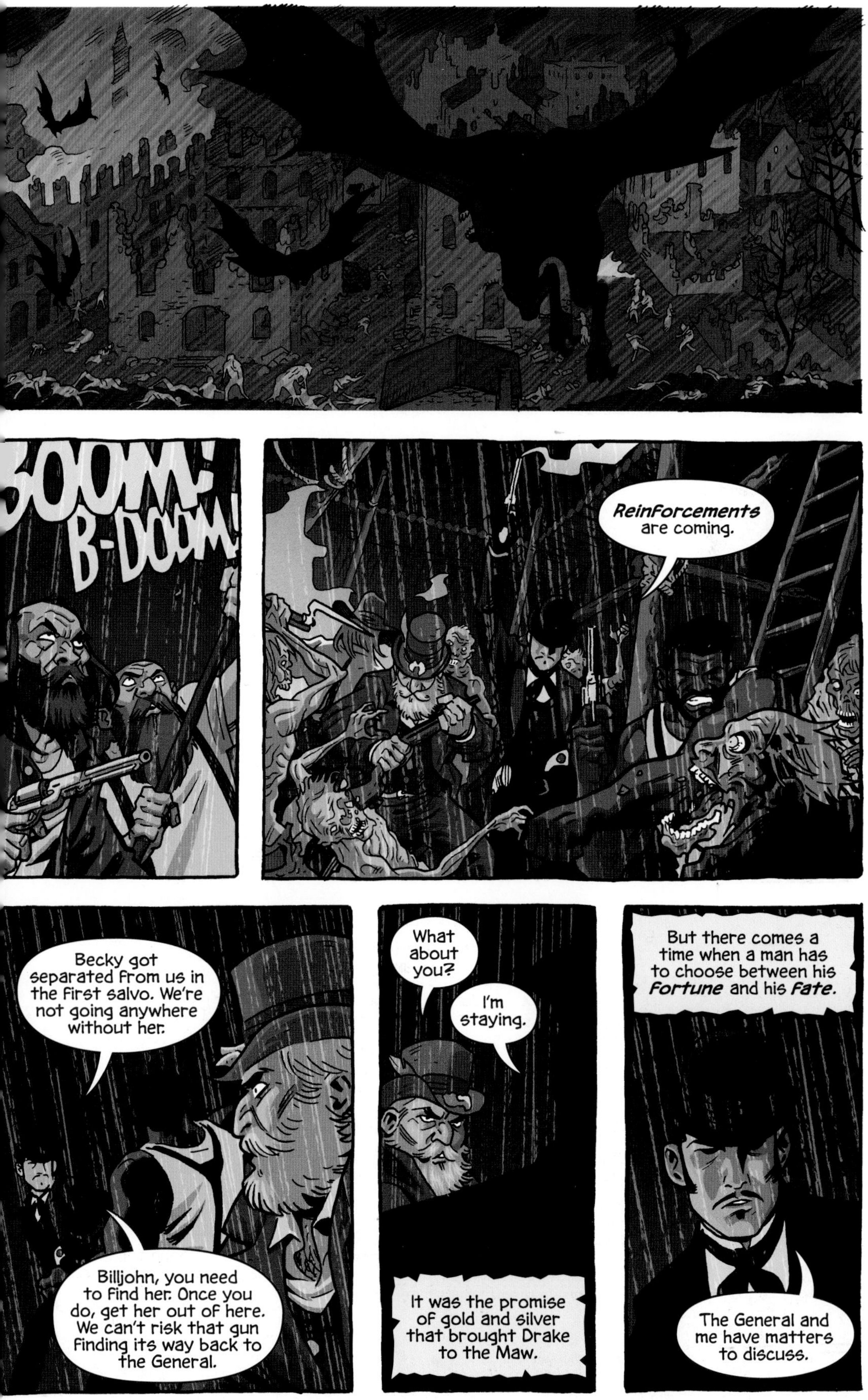
BOOM!
B-DOOM!
Reinforcements are coming.
Becky got separated from us in the first salvo. We're not going anywhere without her.
Billjohn, you need to find her. Once you do, get her out of here. We can't risk that gun finding its way back to the General.
What about you?
I'm staying.
It was the promise of gold and silver that brought Drake to the Maw.
But there comes a time when a man has to choose between his Fortune and his Fate.
The General and me have matters to discuss.

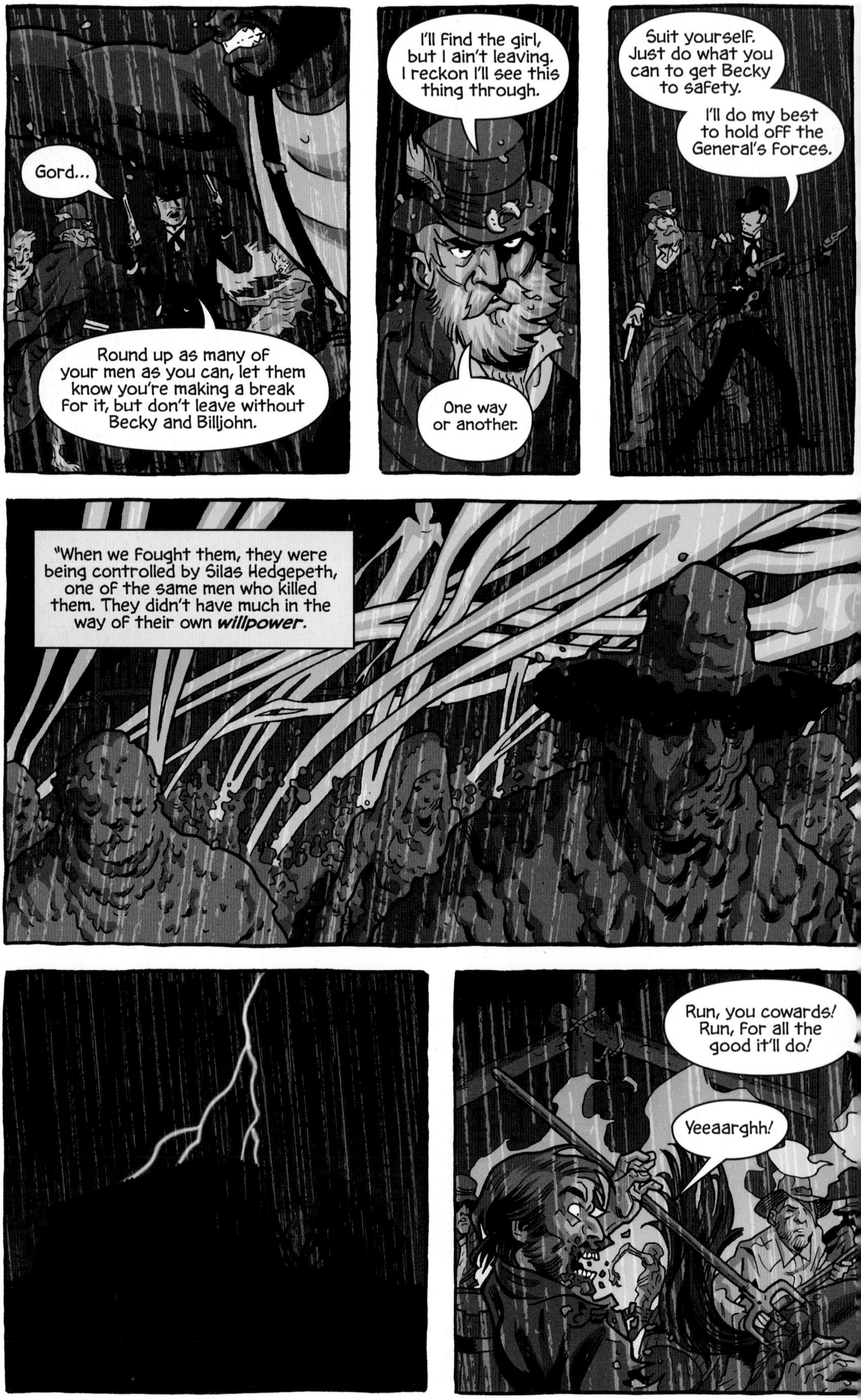
Gord...
Round up as many of your men as you can, let them know you're making a break for it, but don't leave without Becky and Billjohn.
I'll find the girl, but I ain't leaving. I reckon I'll see this thing through.
One way or another.
Suit yourself. Just do what you can to get Becky to safety.
I'll do my best to hold off the General's forces.
"When we fought them, they were being controlled by Silas Hedgepeth, one of the same men who killed them. They didn't have much in the way of their own *willpower*.
Run, you cowards! Run, for all the good it'll do!
Yeeaarghh!

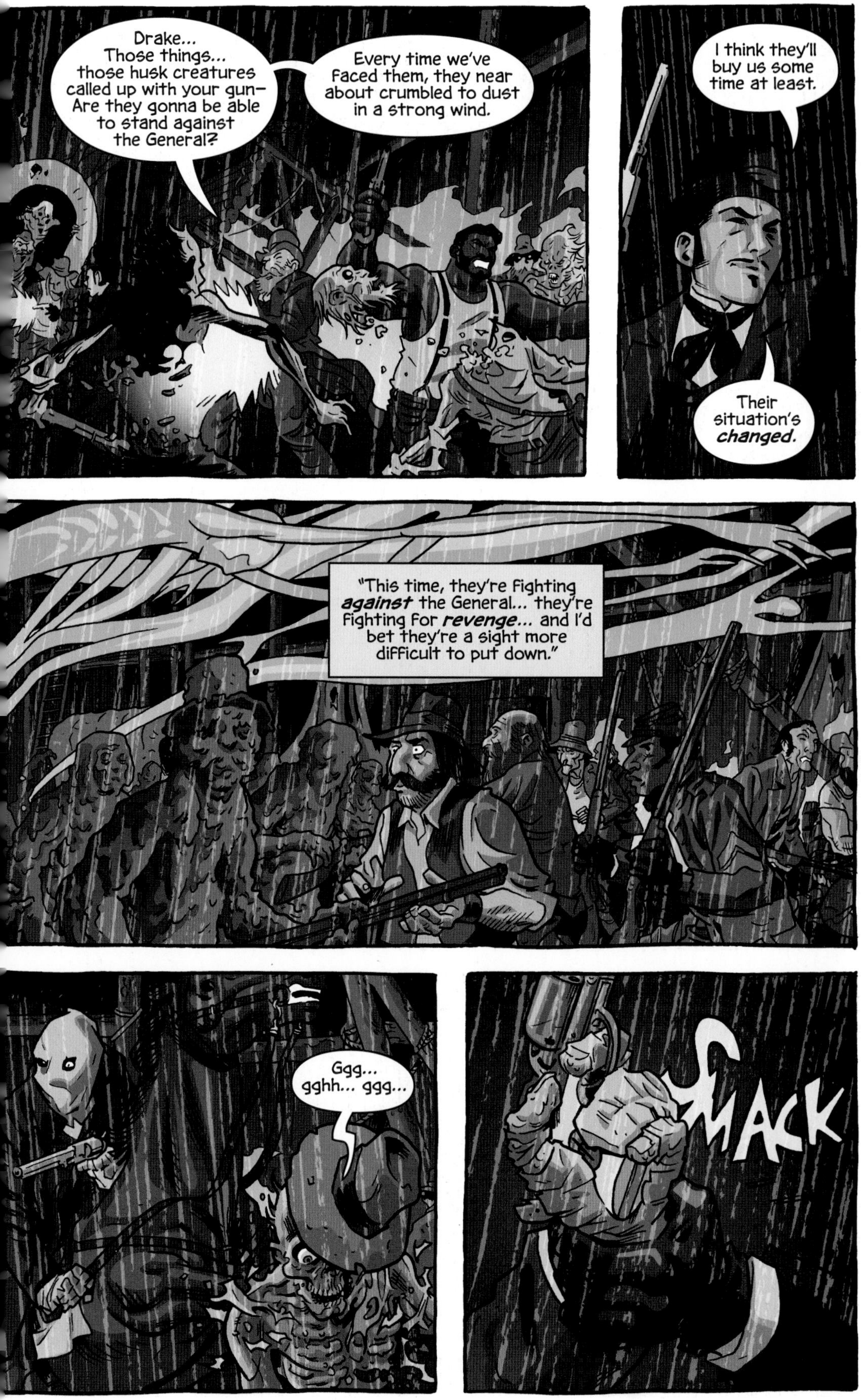
Drake... Those things... those husk creatures called up with your gun– Are they gonna be able to stand against the General?
Every time we've faced them, they near about crumbled to dust in a strong wind.
I think they'll buy us some time at least.
Their situation's ***changed.***
"This time, they're fighting ***against*** the General... they're fighting for ***revenge...*** and I'd bet they're a sight more difficult to put down."
Ggg... gghh... ggg...
SMACK

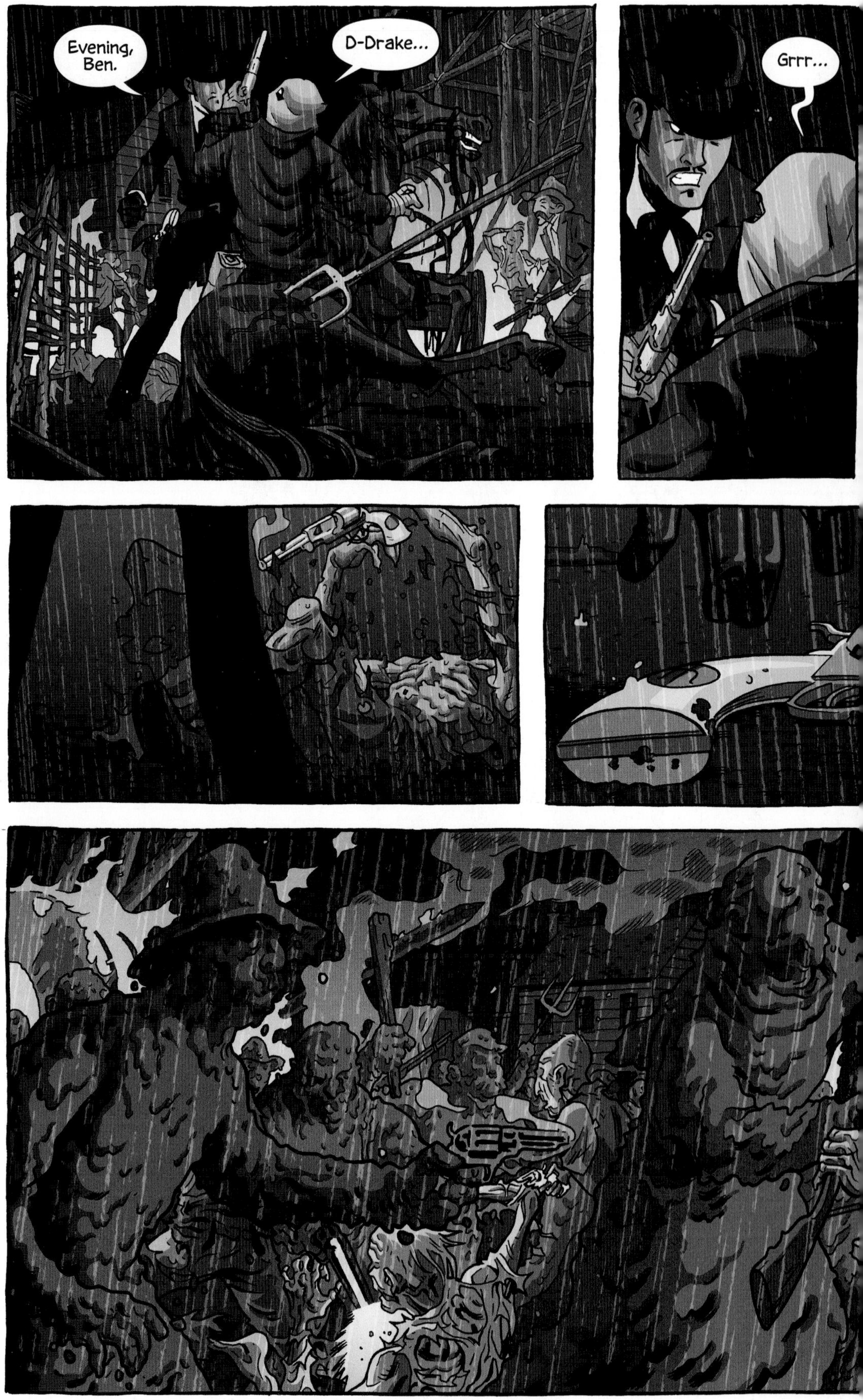
Evening, Ben.
D-Drake...
Grrr...

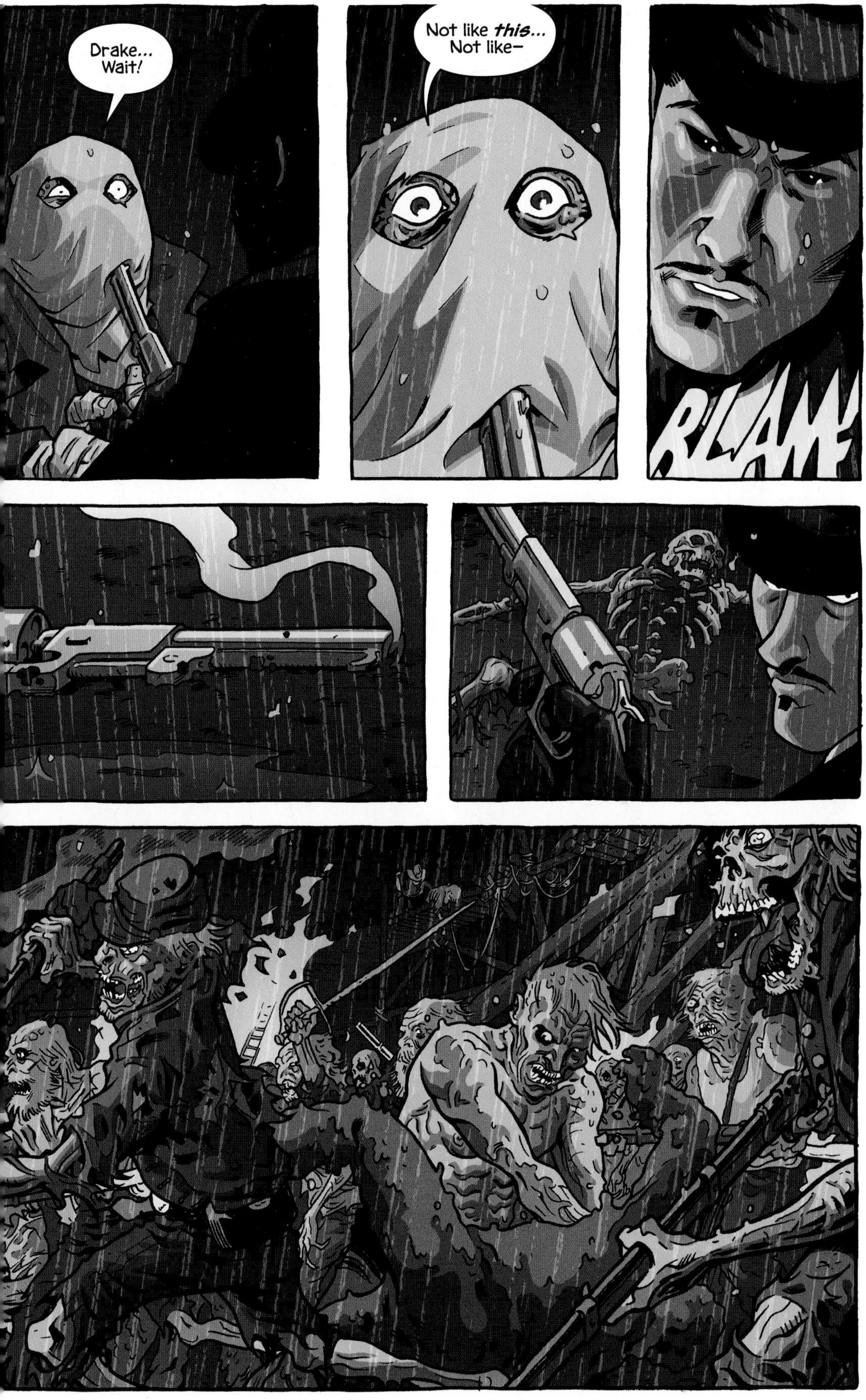
Drake...
Wait!
Not like this...
Not like–
BLAM

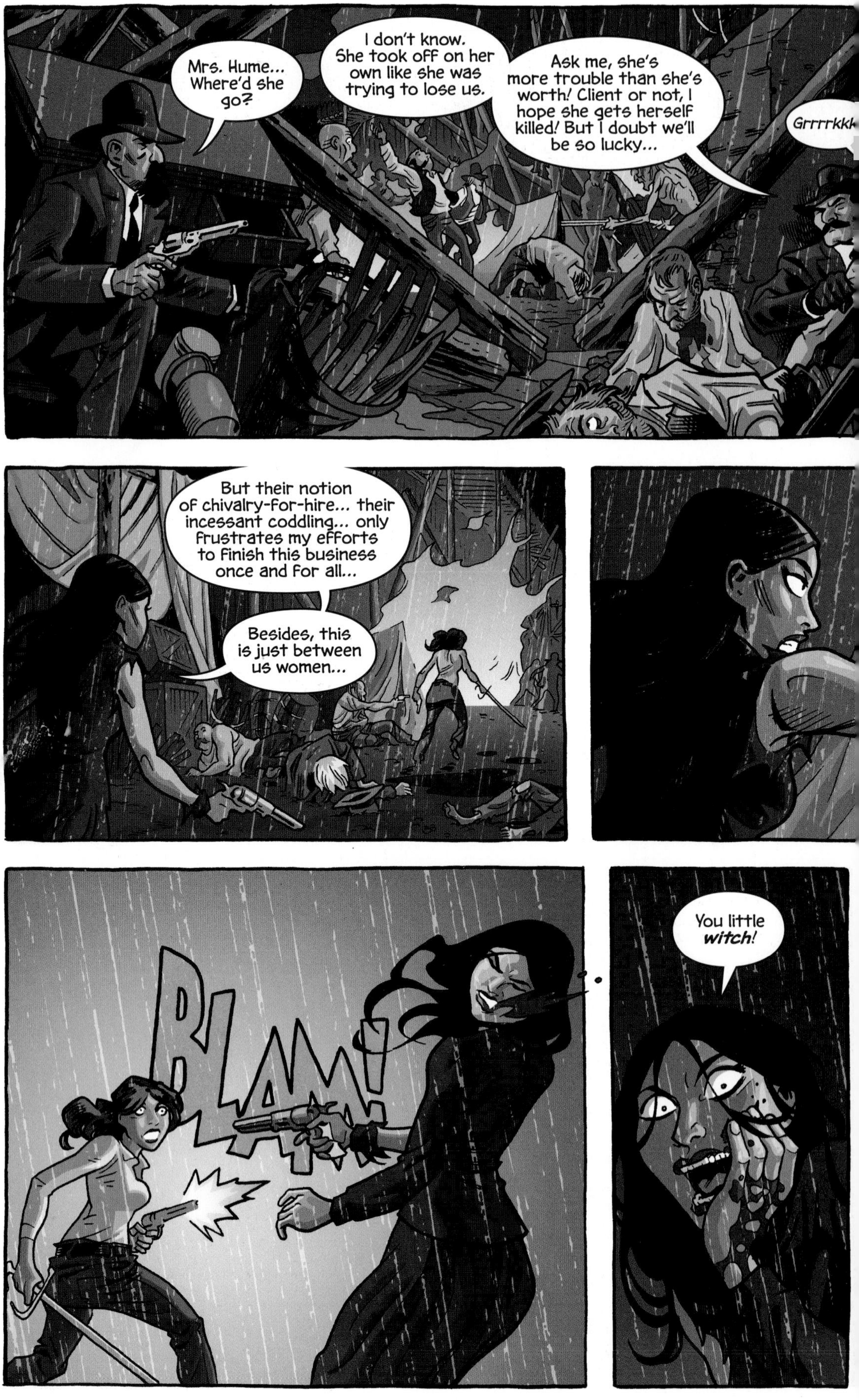
Mrs. Hume... Where'd she go?
I don't know. She took off on her own like she was trying to lose us.
Ask me, she's more trouble than she's worth! Client or not, I hope she gets herself killed! But I doubt we'll be so lucky...
Grrrrkkk
But their notion of chivalry-for-hire... their incessant coddling... only frustrates my efforts to finish this business once and for all...
Besides, this is just between us women...
BLAM!
You little *witch!*

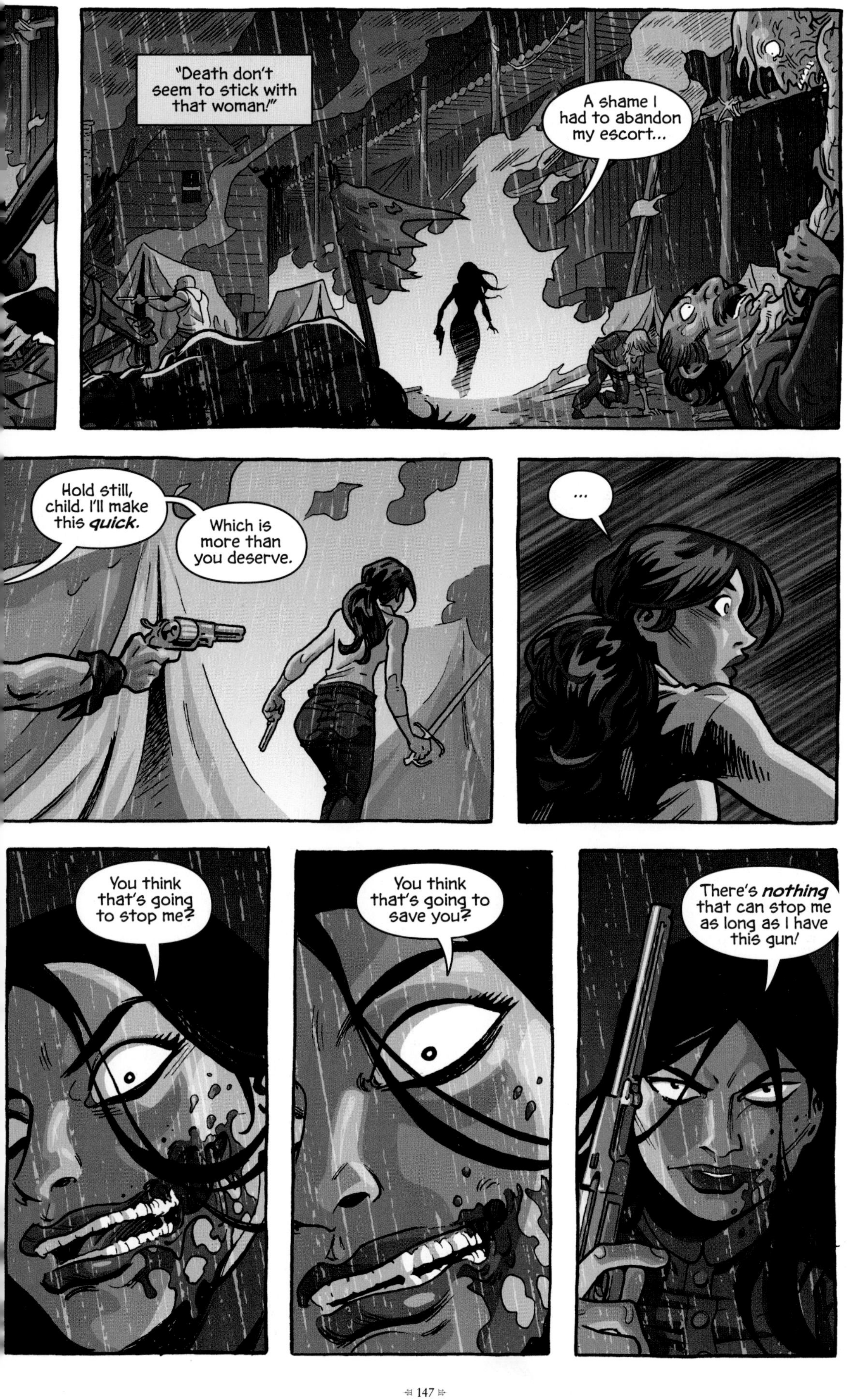
"Death don't seem to stick with that woman!"
A shame I had to abandon my escort...
Hold still, child. I'll make this *quick.*
Which is more than you deserve.
...
You think that's going to stop me?
You think that's going to save you?
There's *nothing* that can stop me as long as I have this gun!

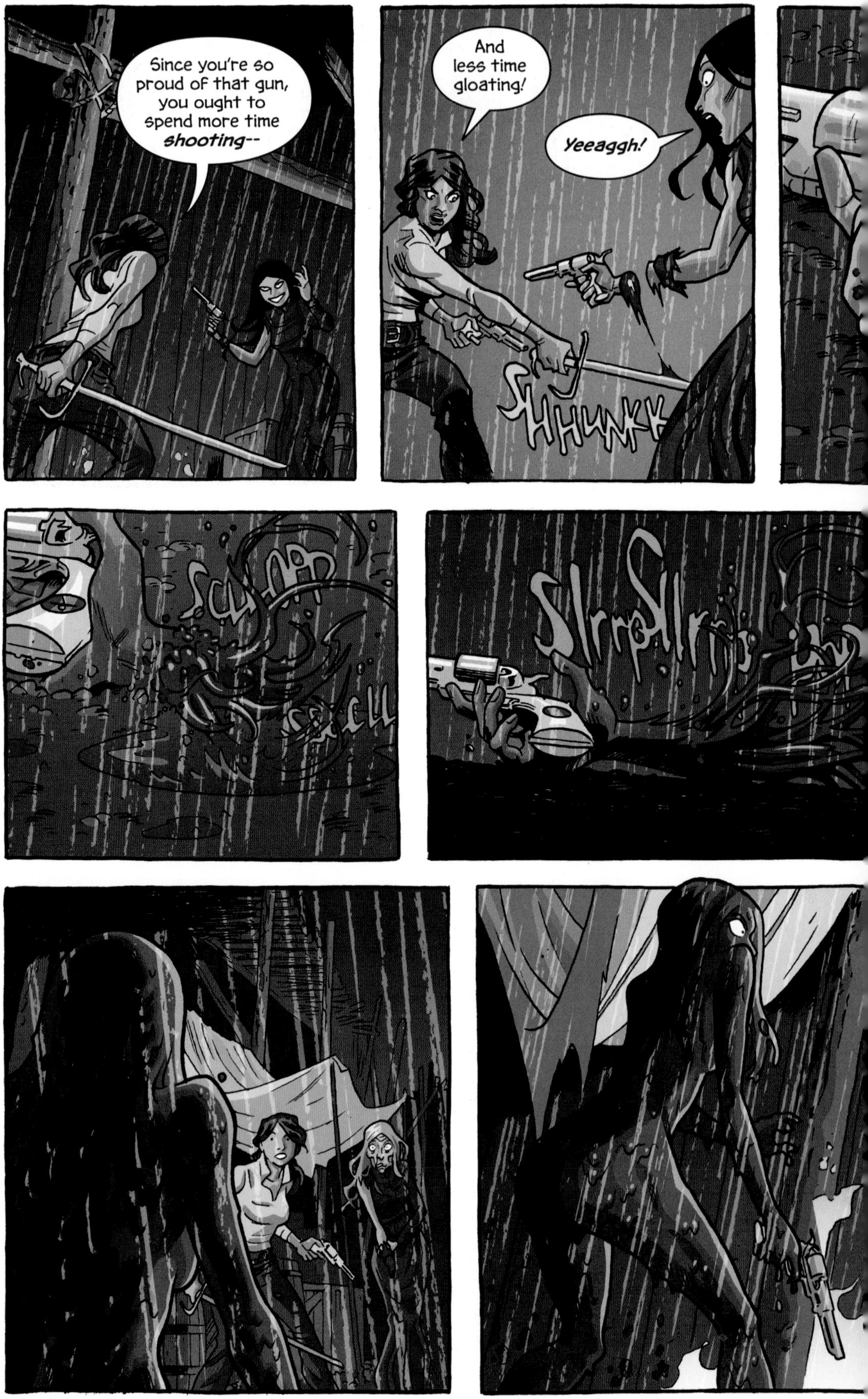

Since you're so proud of that gun, you ought to spend more time *shooting--*
And less time gloating!
*Yeeaggh!*
SHHUNK

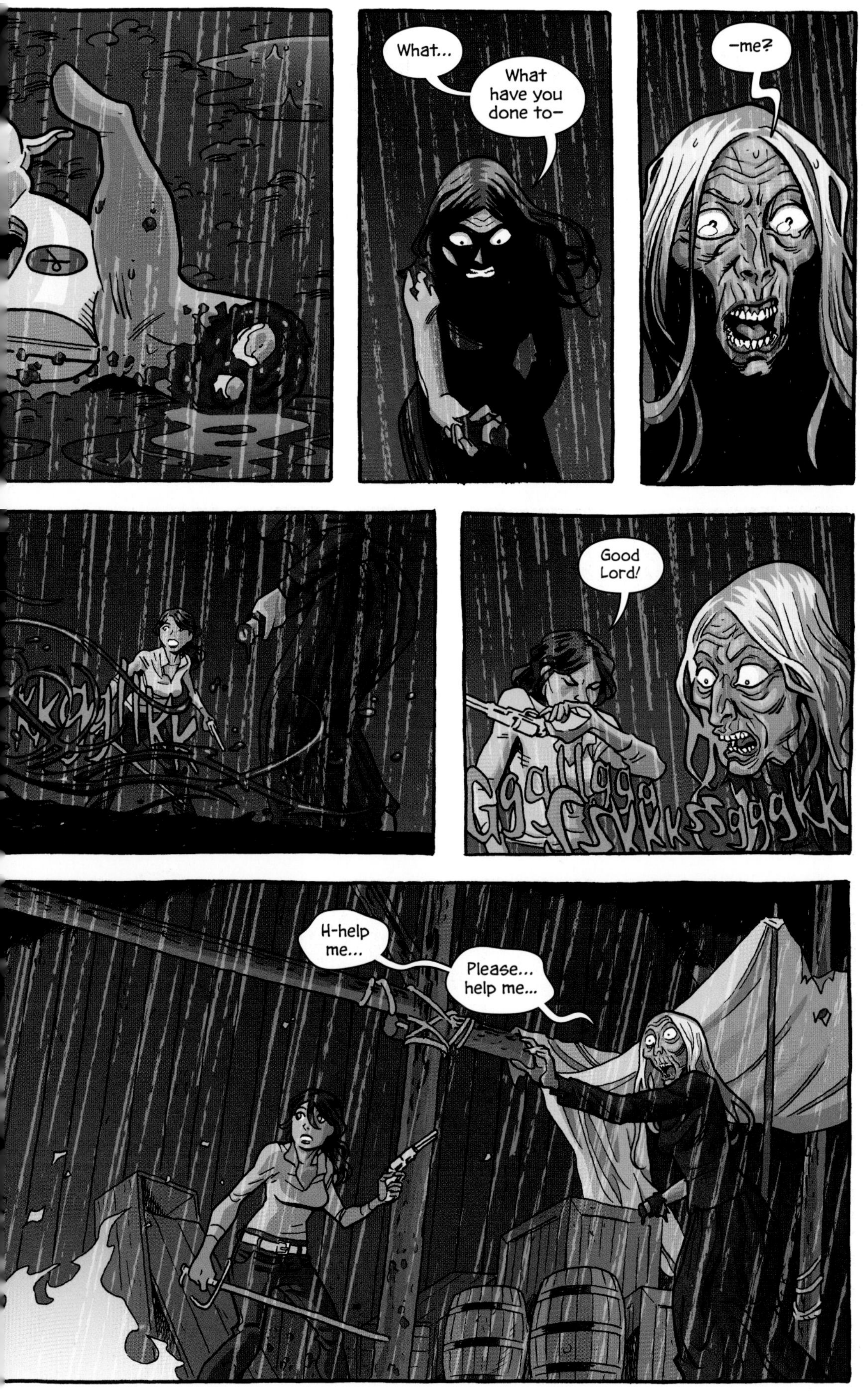
What...
What have you done to—
—me?
Good Lord!
H-help me...
Please... help me...

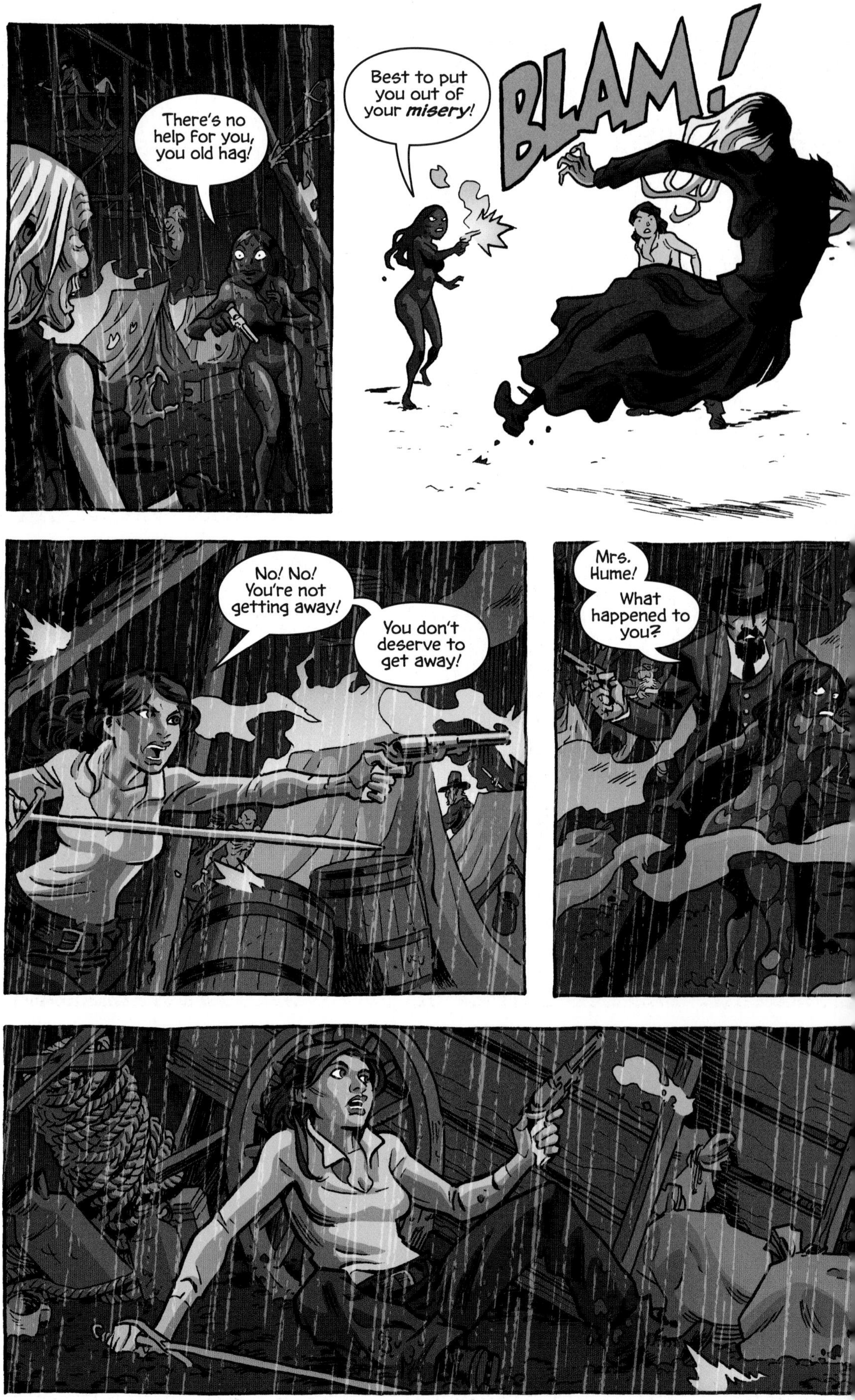
There's no help for you, you old hag!
Best to put you out of your *misery*!
BLAM!
No! No! You're not getting away!
You don't deserve to get away!
Mrs. Hume!
What happened to you?

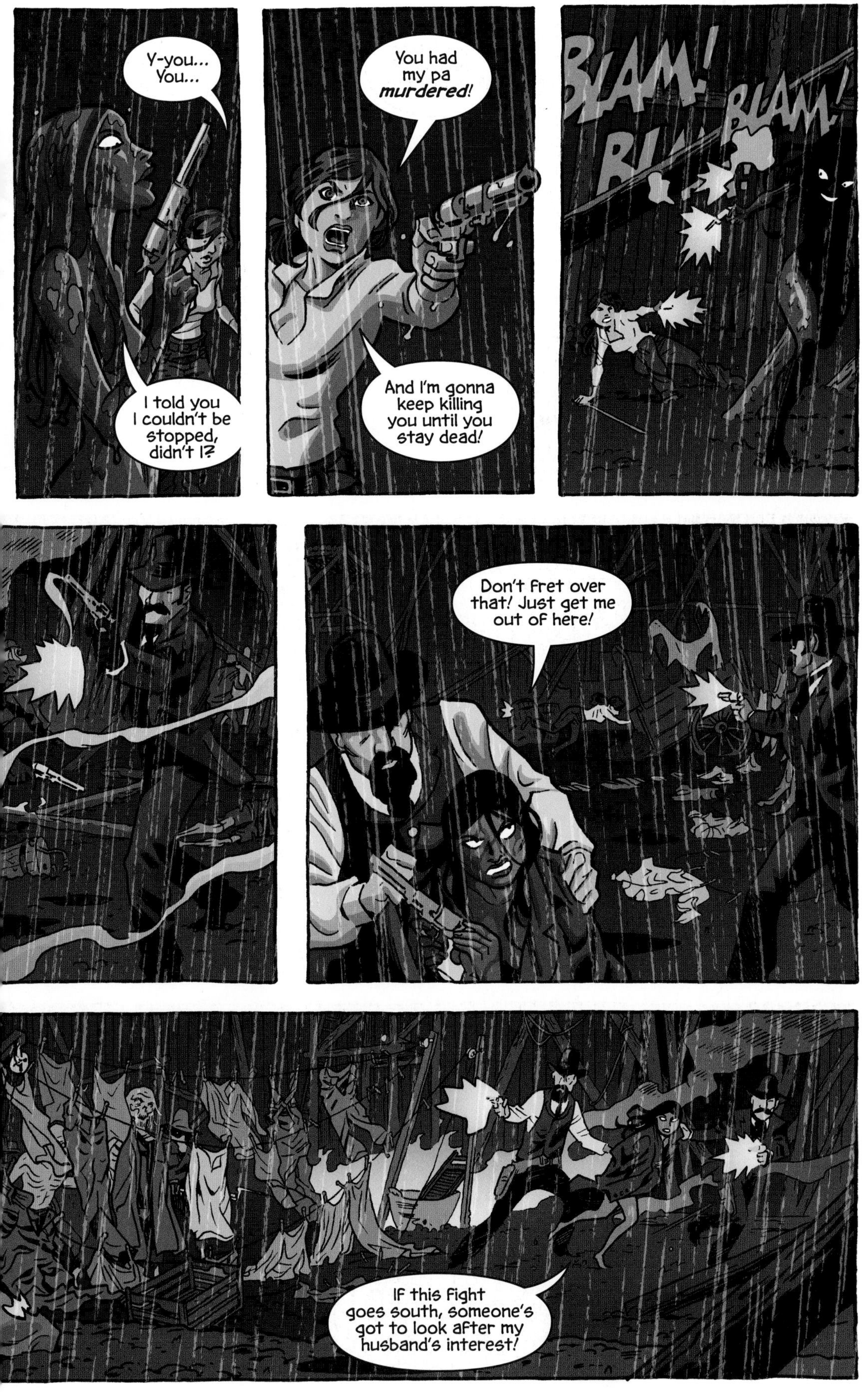
Y-you... You...
I told you I couldn't be stopped, didn't I?
You had my pa *murdered!*
And I'm gonna keep killing you until you stay dead!
BLAM! BLAM! BLAM!
Don't fret over that! Just get me out of here!
If this fight goes south, someone's got to look after my husband's interest!

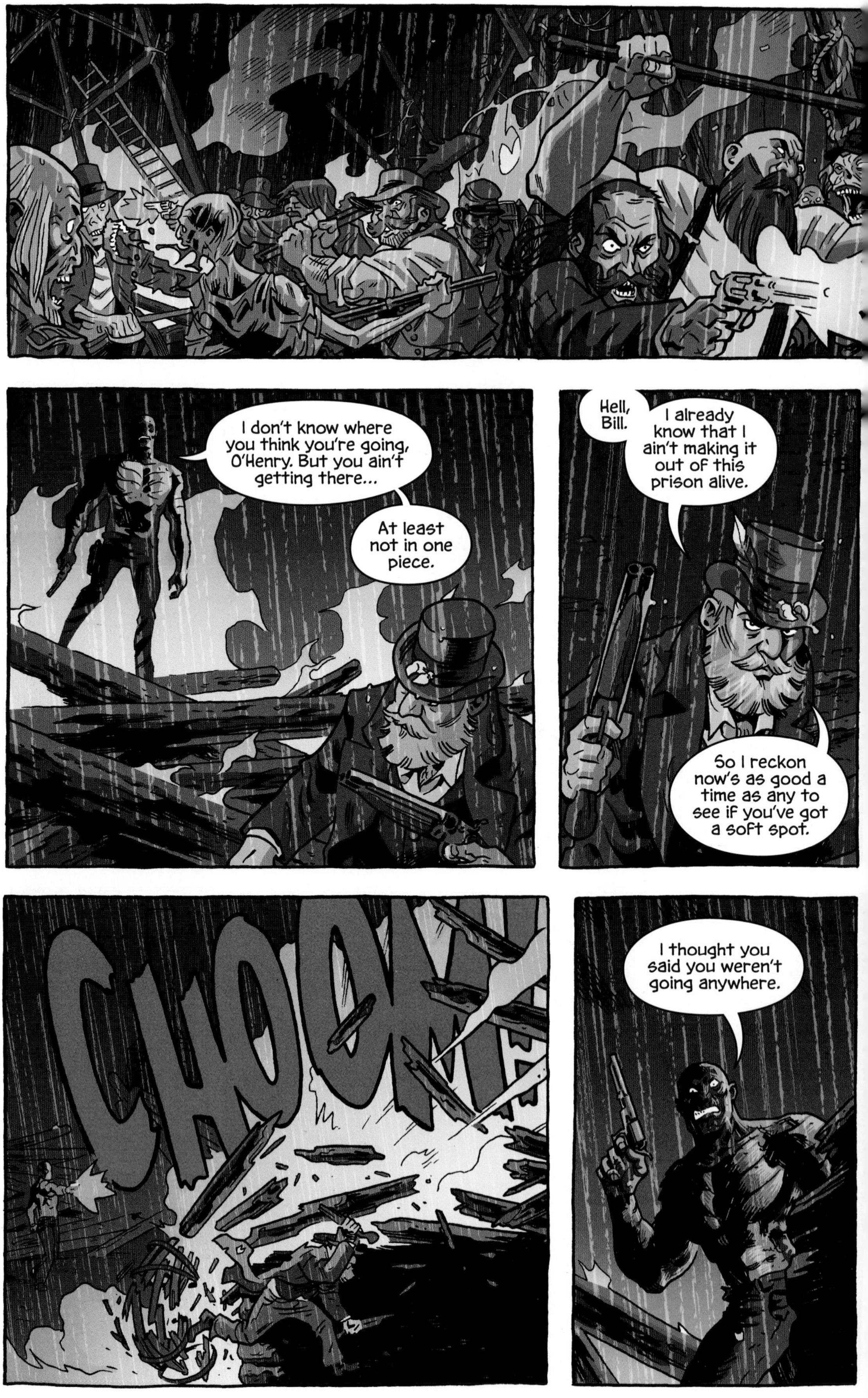

I don't know where you think you're going, O'Henry. But you ain't getting there...
At least not in one piece.
Hell, Bill.
I already know that I ain't making it out of this prison alive.
So I reckon now's as good a time as any to see if you've got a soft spot.
CHOOM
I thought you said you weren't going anywhere.

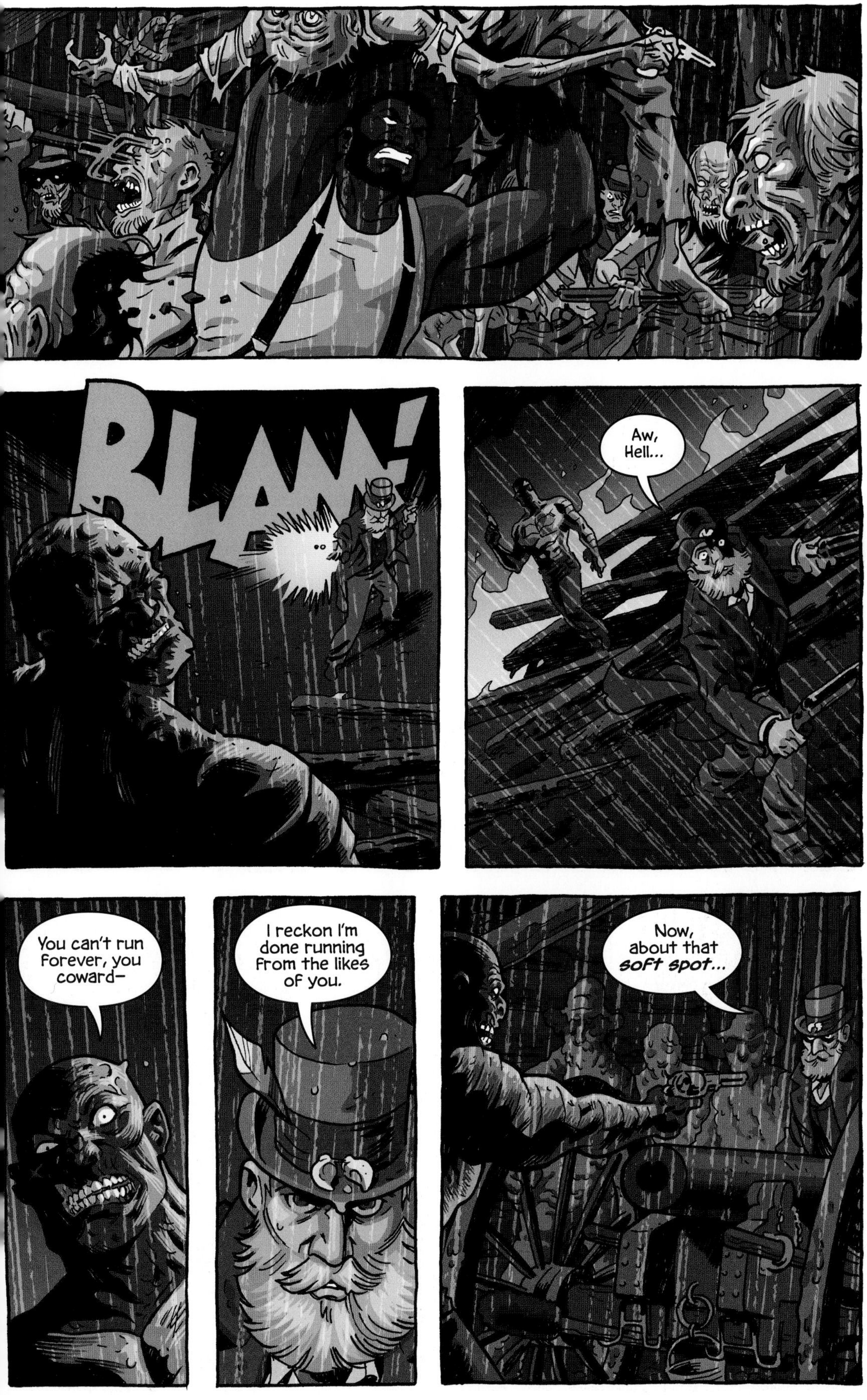
BLAM!
Aw, Hell...
You can't run forever, you coward–
I reckon I'm done running from the likes of you.
Now, about that *soft spot*...

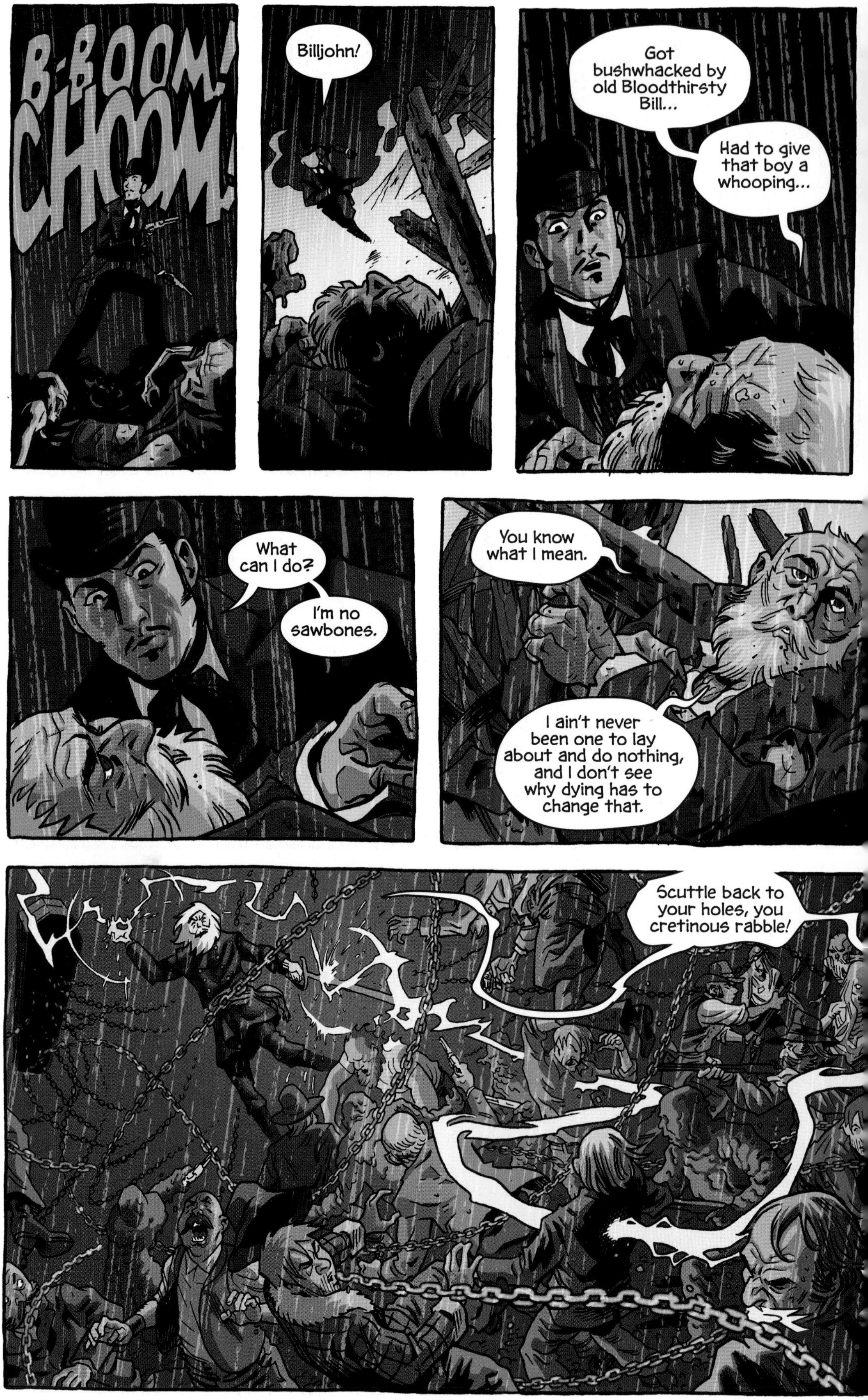
B-BOOM!
CHOOM!
Billjohn!
Got bushwhacked by old Bloodthirsty Bill...
Had to give that boy a whooping...
What can I do?
I'm no sawbones.
You know what I mean.
I ain't never been one to lay about and do nothing, and I don't see why dying has to change that.
Scuttle back to your holes, you cretinous rabble!

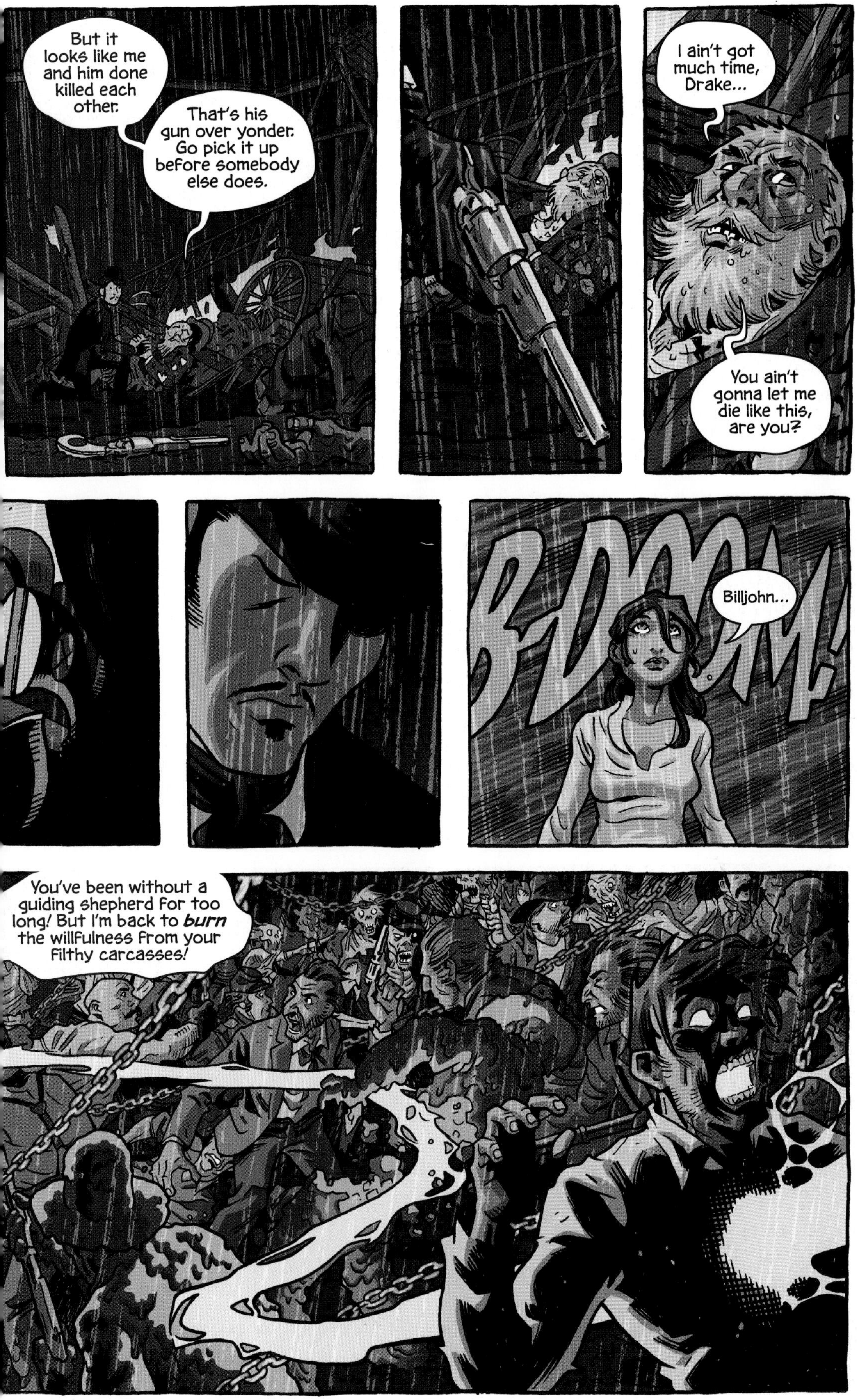
But it looks like me and him done killed each other.
That's his gun over yonder. Go pick it up before somebody else does.
I ain't got much time, Drake...
You ain't gonna let me die like this, are you?
BOOM!
Billjohn...
You've been without a guiding shepherd for too long! But I'm back to *burn* the willfulness from your filthy carcasses!

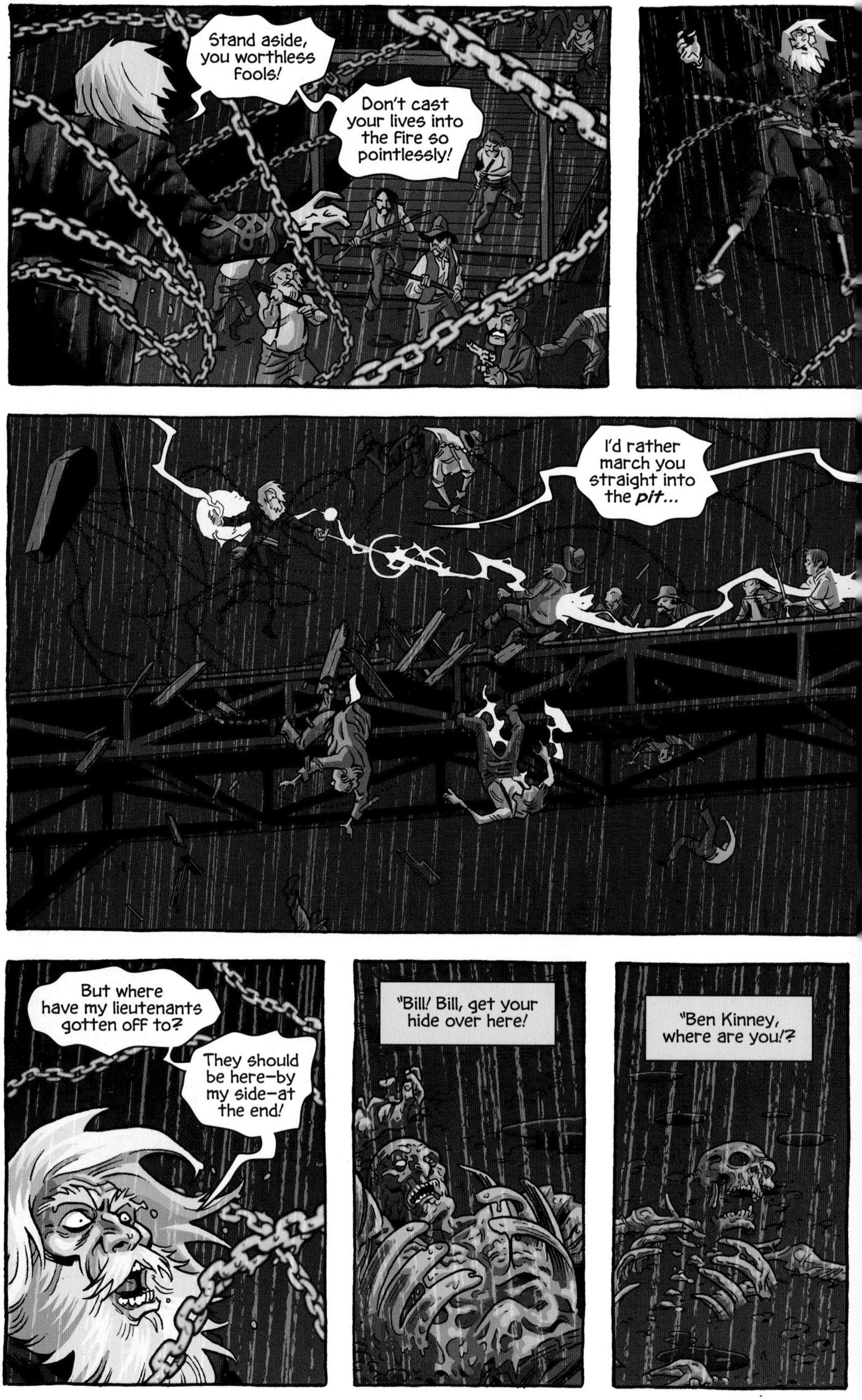
Stand aside, you worthless fools!
Don't cast your lives into the fire so pointlessly!
I'd rather march you straight into the *pit*...
But where have my lieutenants gotten off to?
They should be here—by my side—at the end!
"Bill! Bill, get your hide over here!
"Ben Kinney, where are you!?

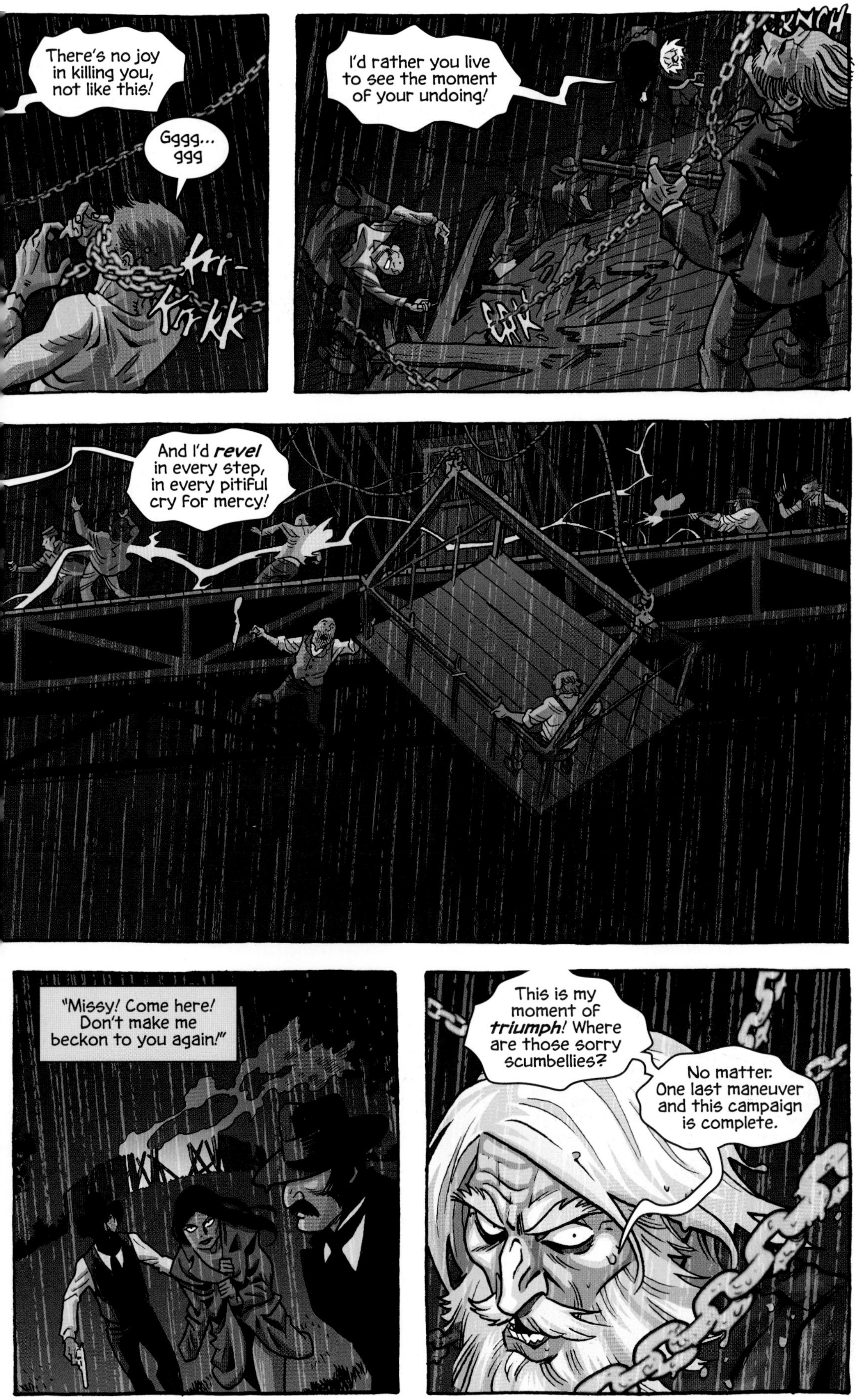
There's no joy in killing you, not like this!
Gggg... ggg
I'd rather you live to see the moment of your undoing!
And I'd ***revel*** in every step, in every pitiful cry for mercy!
"Missy! Come here! Don't make me beckon to you again!"
This is my moment of ***triumph***! Where are those sorry scumbellies?
No matter. One last maneuver and this campaign is complete.

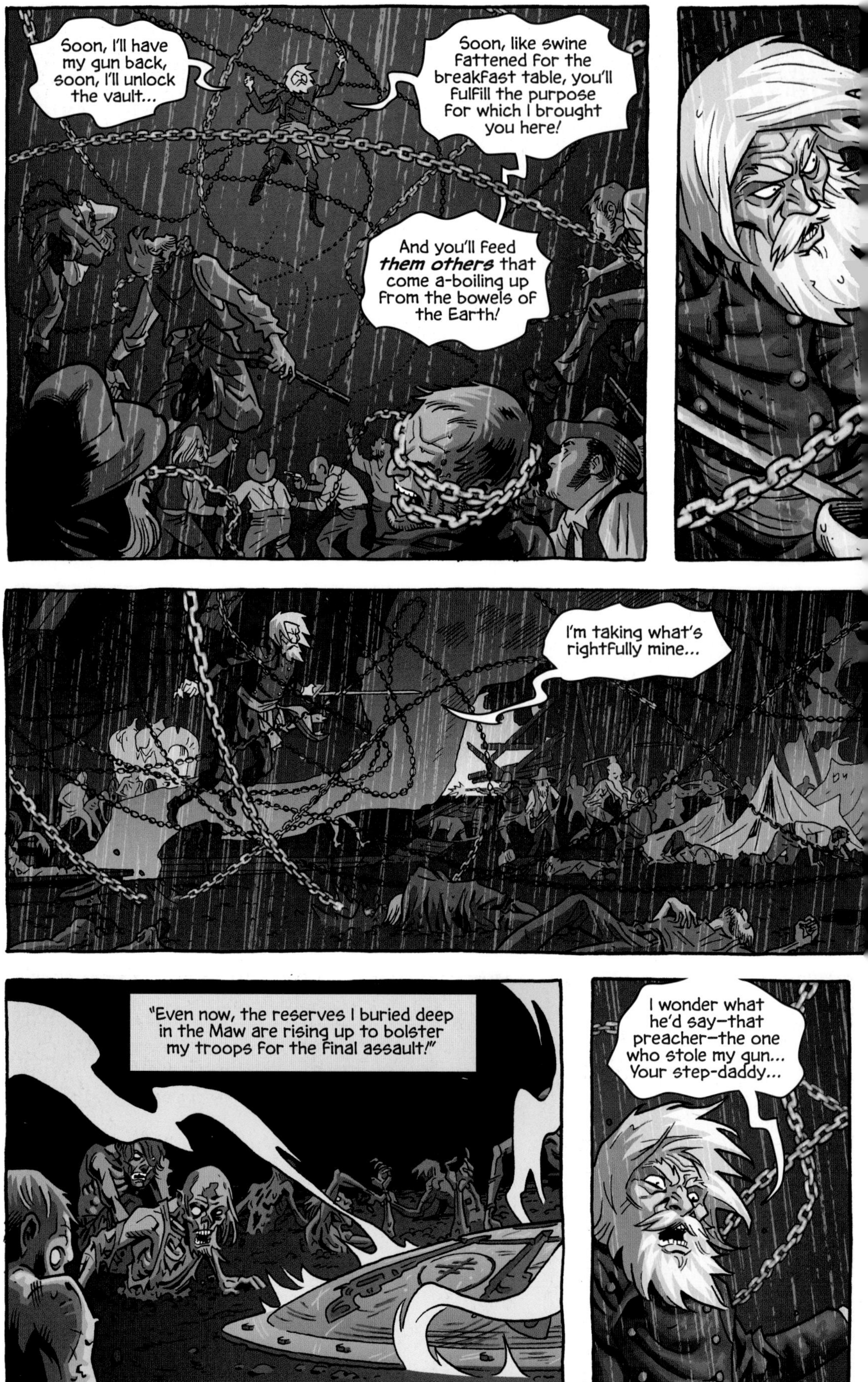
Soon, I'll have my gun back, soon, I'll unlock the vault...
Soon, like swine fattened for the breakfast table, you'll fulfill the purpose for which I brought you here!
And you'll feed *them others* that come a-boiling up from the bowels of the Earth!
I'm taking what's rightfully mine...
"Even now, the reserves I buried deep in the Maw are rising up to bolster my troops for the final assault!"
I wonder what he'd say—that preacher—the one who stole my gun... Your step-daddy...

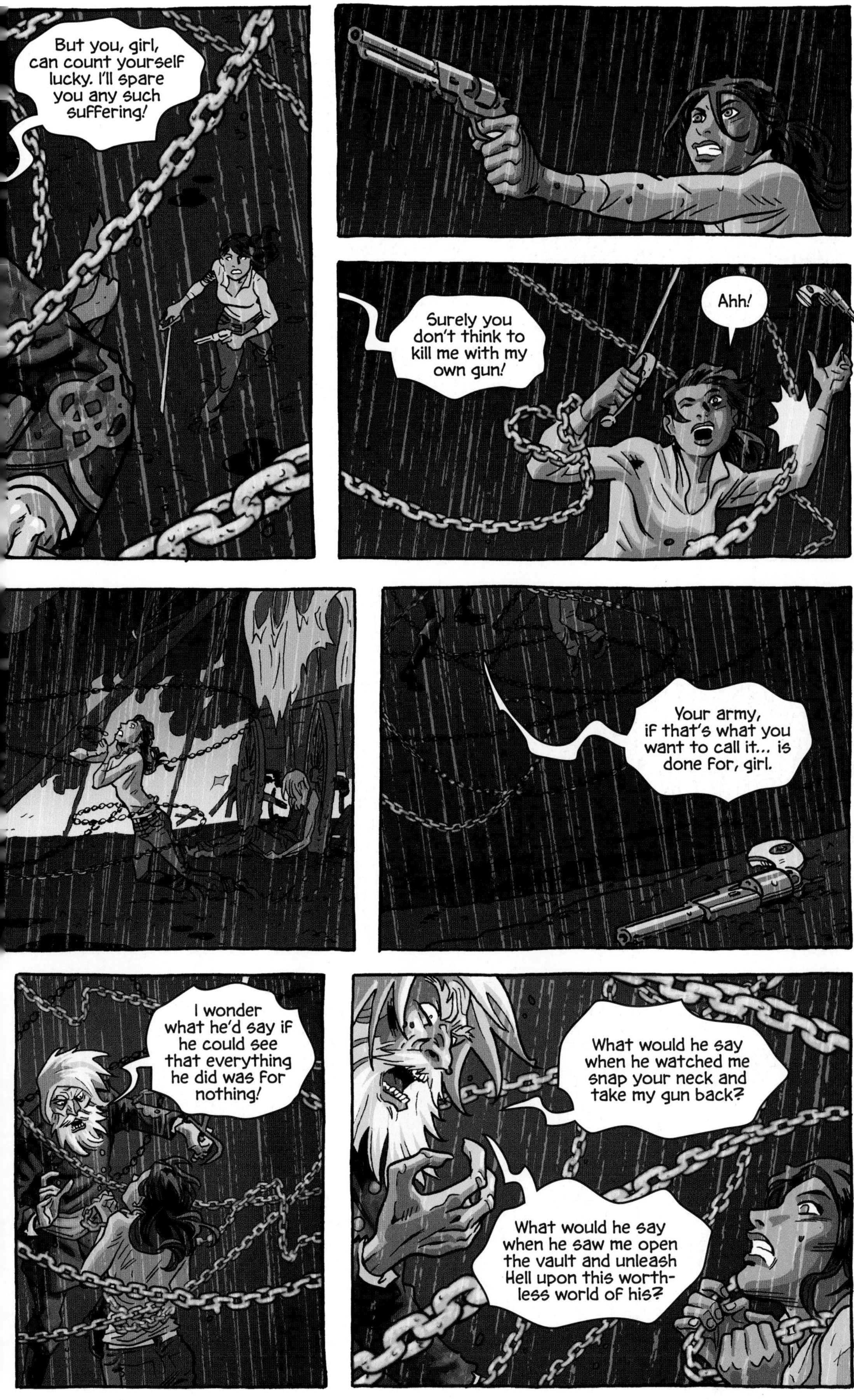
But you, girl, can count yourself lucky. I'll spare you any such suffering!
Surely you don't think to kill me with my own gun!
Ahh!
Your army, if that's what you want to call it... is done for, girl.
I wonder what he'd say if he could see that everything he did was for nothing!
What would he say when he watched me snap your neck and take my gun back?
What would he say when he saw me open the vault and unleash Hell upon this worth-less world of his?

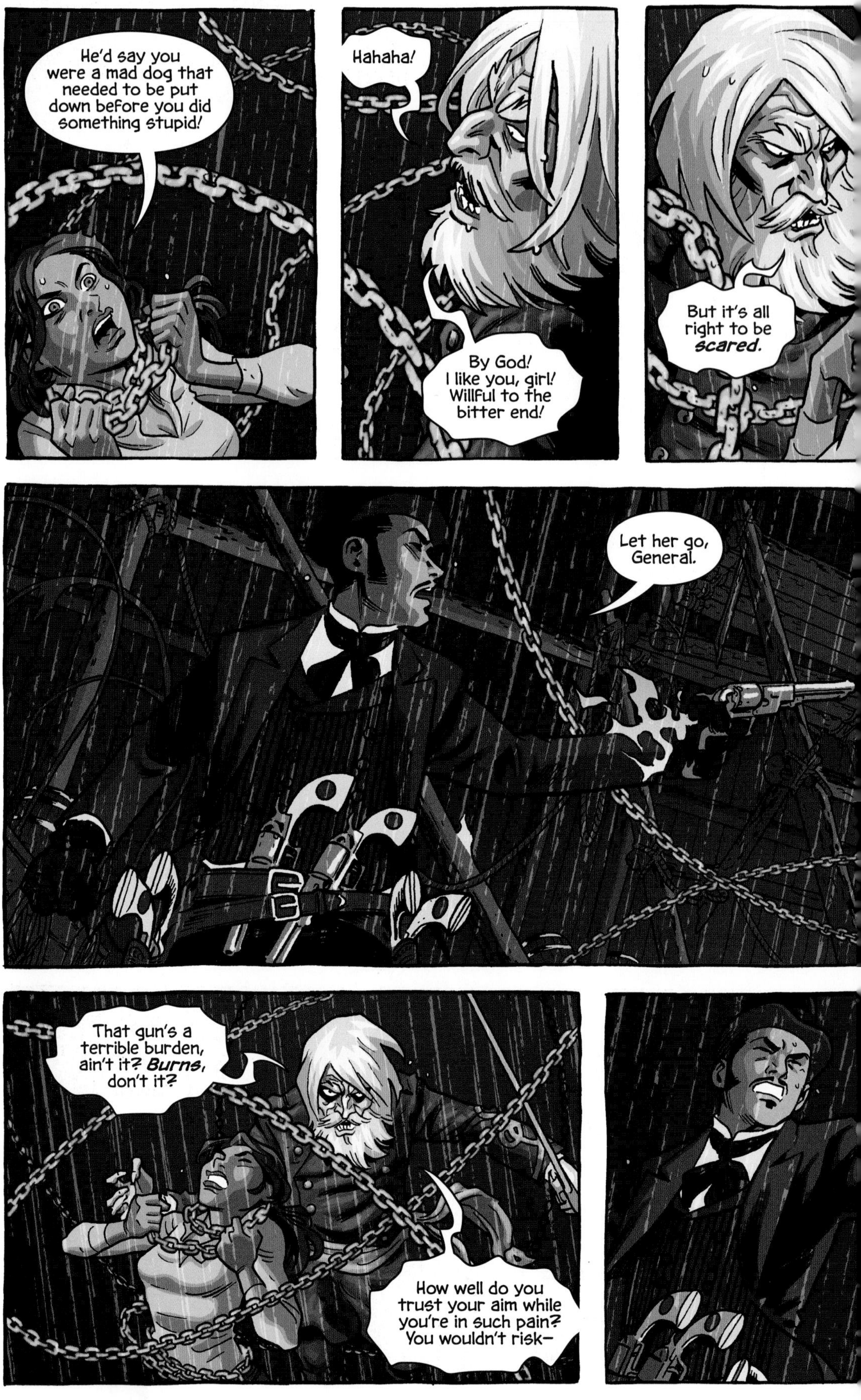

He'd say you were a mad dog that needed to be put down before you did something stupid!
Hahaha!
By God! I like you, girl! Willful to the bitter end!
But it's all right to be *scared.*
Let her go, General.
That gun's a terrible burden, ain't it? *Burns,* don't it?
How well do you trust your aim while you're in such pain? You wouldn't risk–

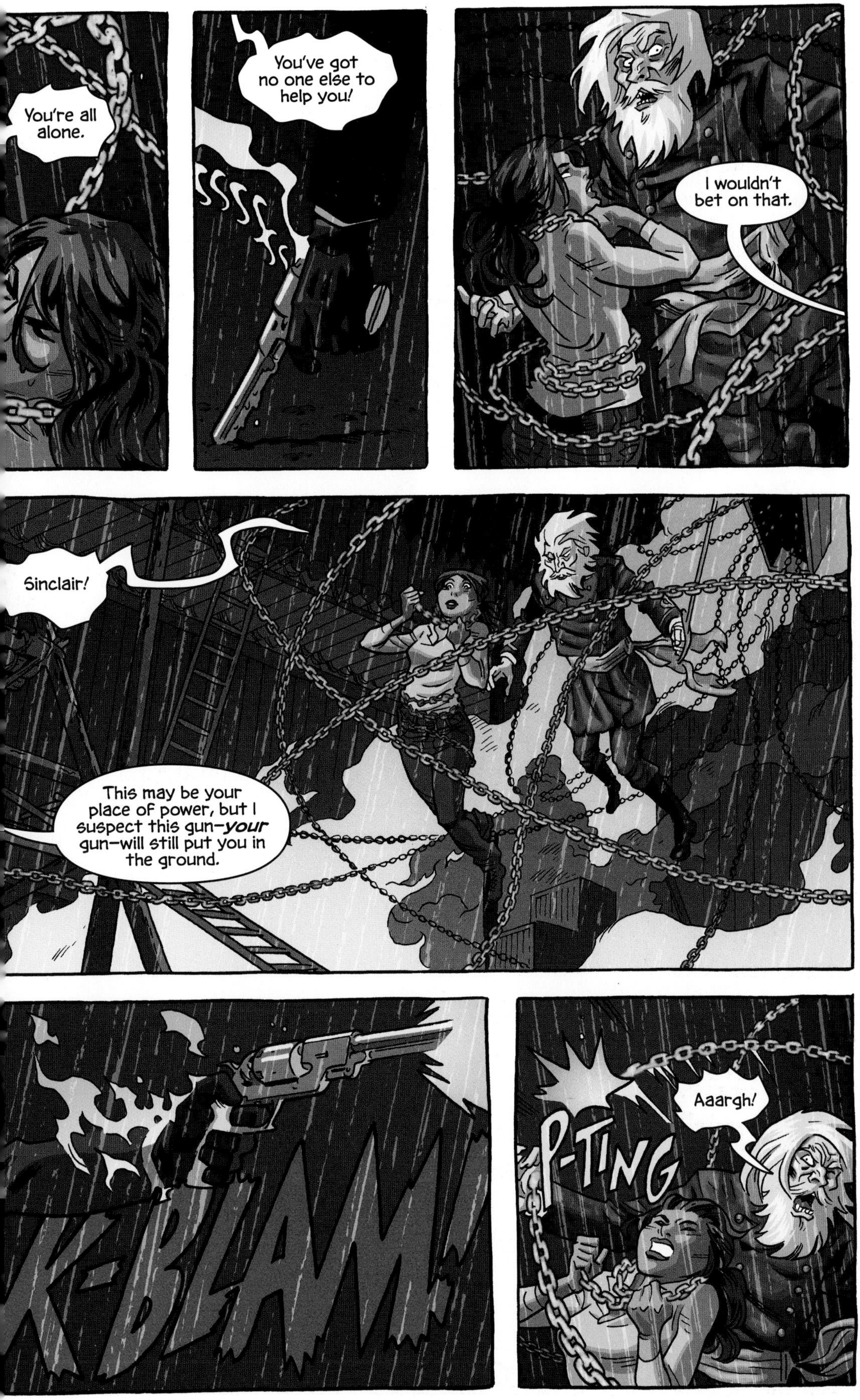

You're all alone.
You've got no one else to help you!
I wouldn't bet on that.
Sinclair!
This may be your place of power, but I suspect this gun—*your* gun—will still put you in the ground.
K-BLAM!
P-TING
Aaargh!

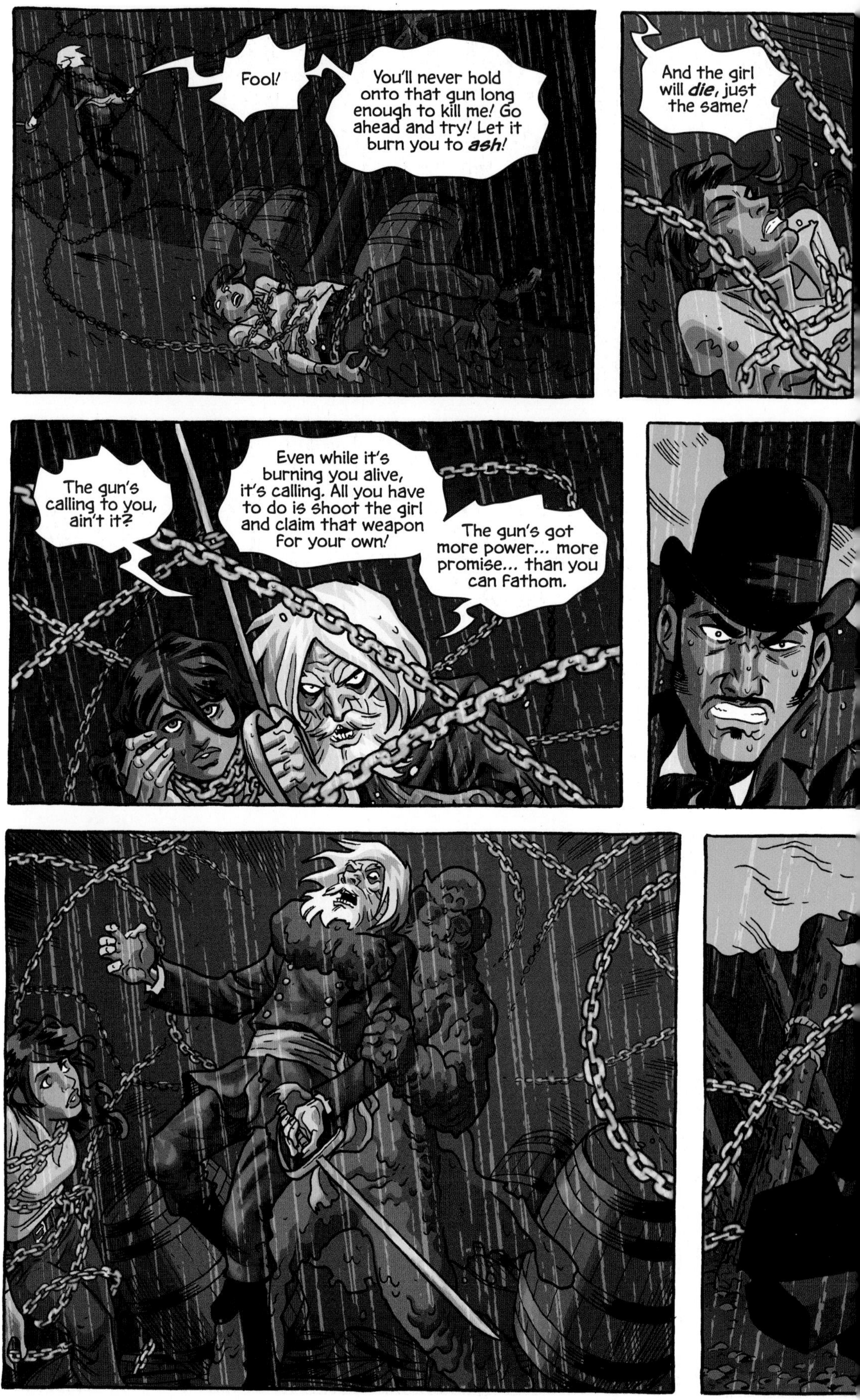
Fool!
You'll never hold onto that gun long enough to kill me! Go ahead and try! Let it burn you to *ash*!
And the girl will *die*, just the same!
The gun's calling to you, ain't it?
Even while it's burning you alive, it's calling. All you have to do is shoot the girl and claim that weapon for your own!
The gun's got more power... more promise... than you can fathom.

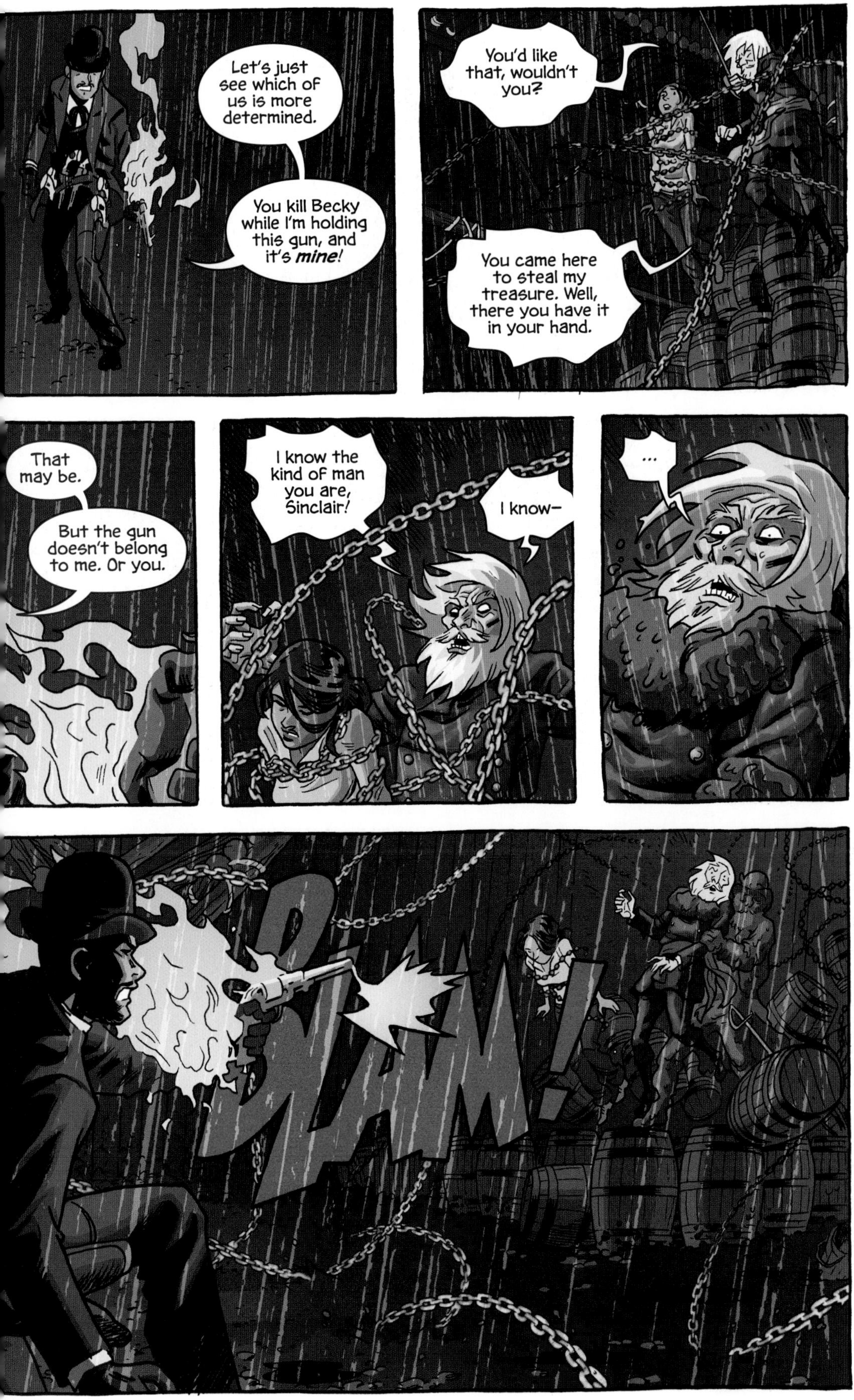

Let's just see which of us is more determined.
You kill Becky while I'm holding this gun, and it's *mine*!
You'd like that, wouldn't you?
You came here to steal my treasure. Well, there you have it in your hand.
That may be.
But the gun doesn't belong to me. Or you.
I know the kind of man you are, Sinclair!
I know—
...
BLAM!

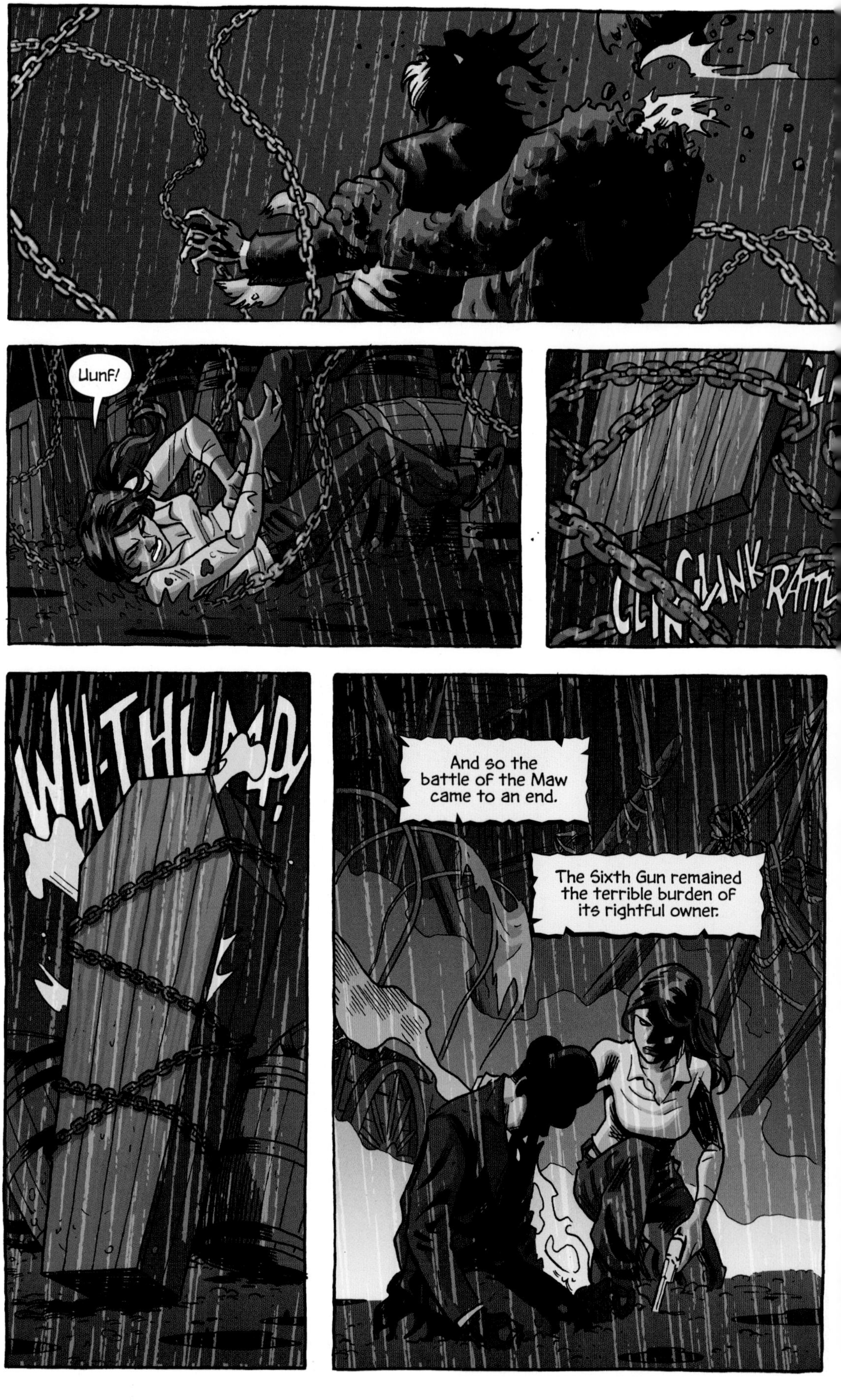
Uunf!
CLINK
CLANK
RATTL
WH-THUMP!
And so the battle of the Maw came to an end.
The Sixth Gun remained the terrible burden of its rightful owner.

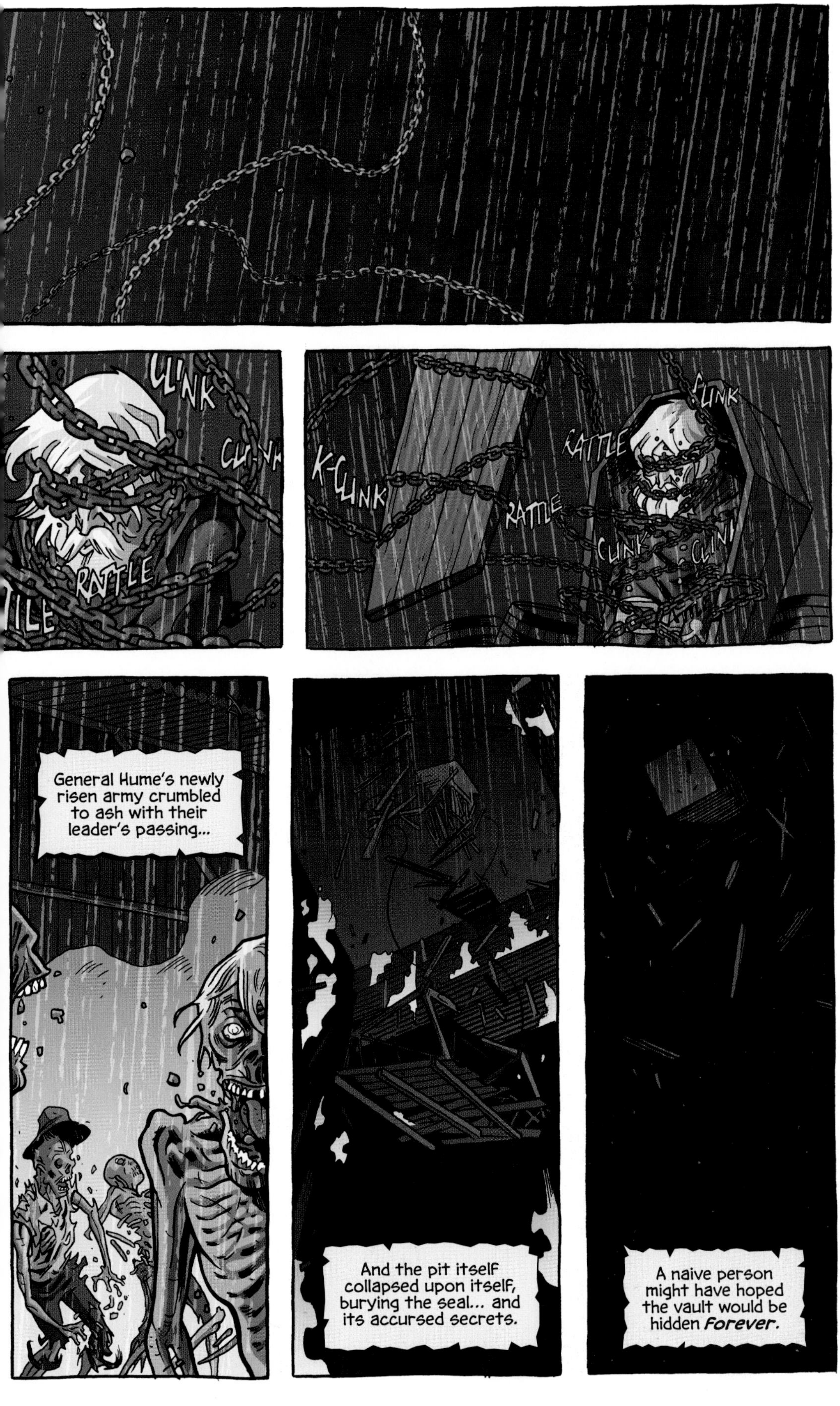

CLINK
CLINK
RATTLE
TTLE
K-CLINK
RATTLE
RATTLE
CLINK
CLINK
CLINK
General Hume's newly risen army crumbled to ash with their leader's passing...
And the pit itself collapsed upon itself, burying the seal... and its accursed secrets.
A naive person might have hoped the vault would be hidden *forever*.

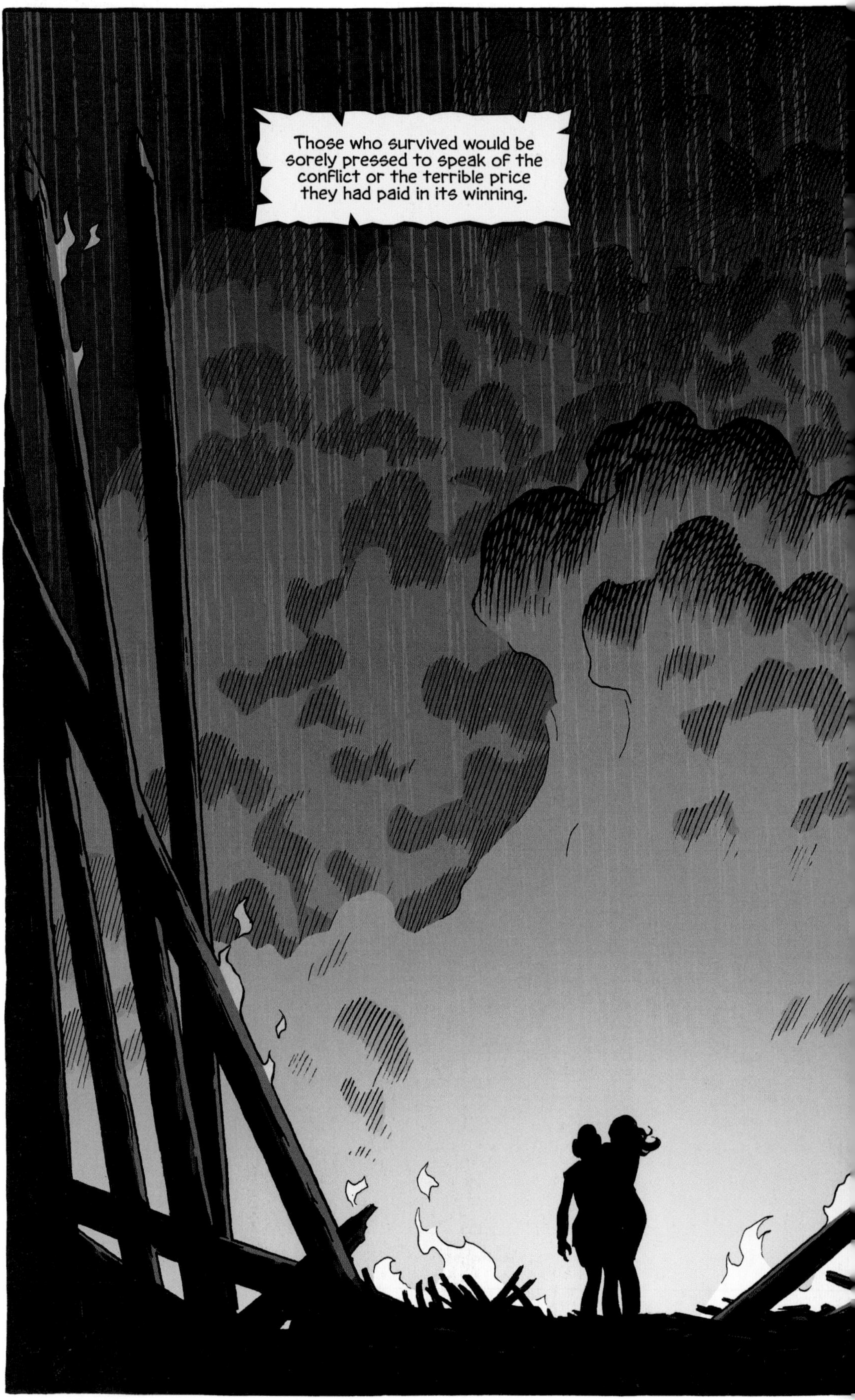
Those who survived would be sorely pressed to speak of the conflict or the terrible price they had paid in its winning.

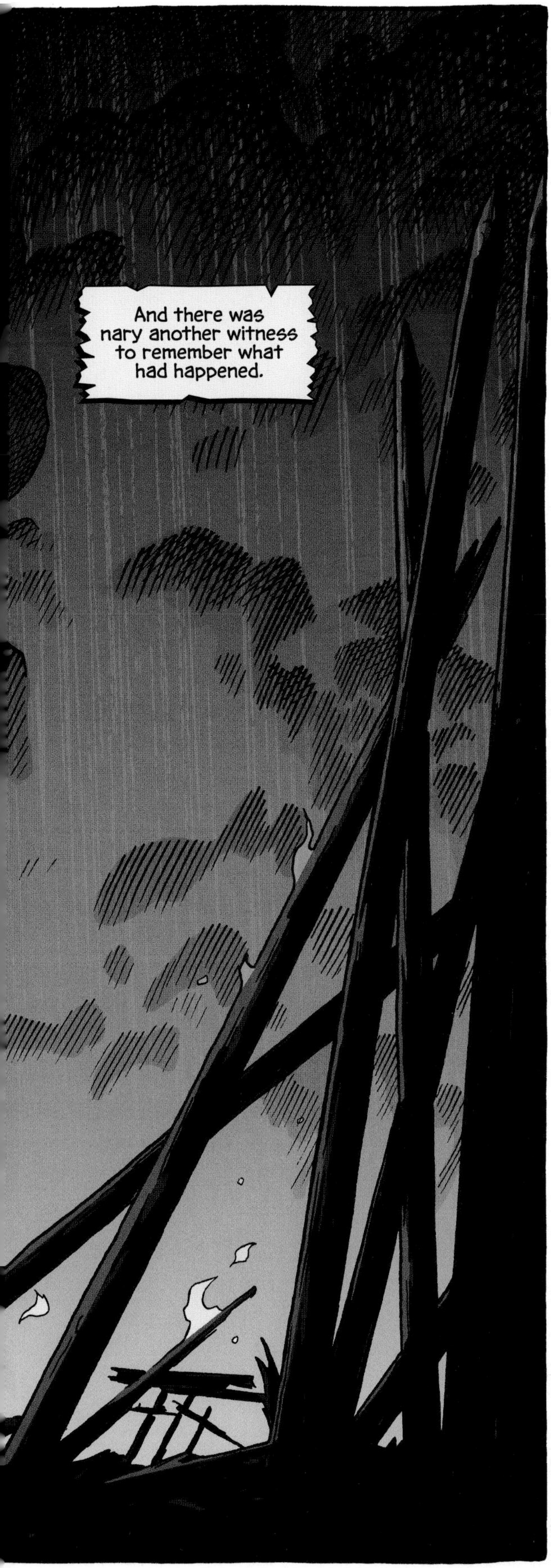
And there was nary another witness to remember what had happened.

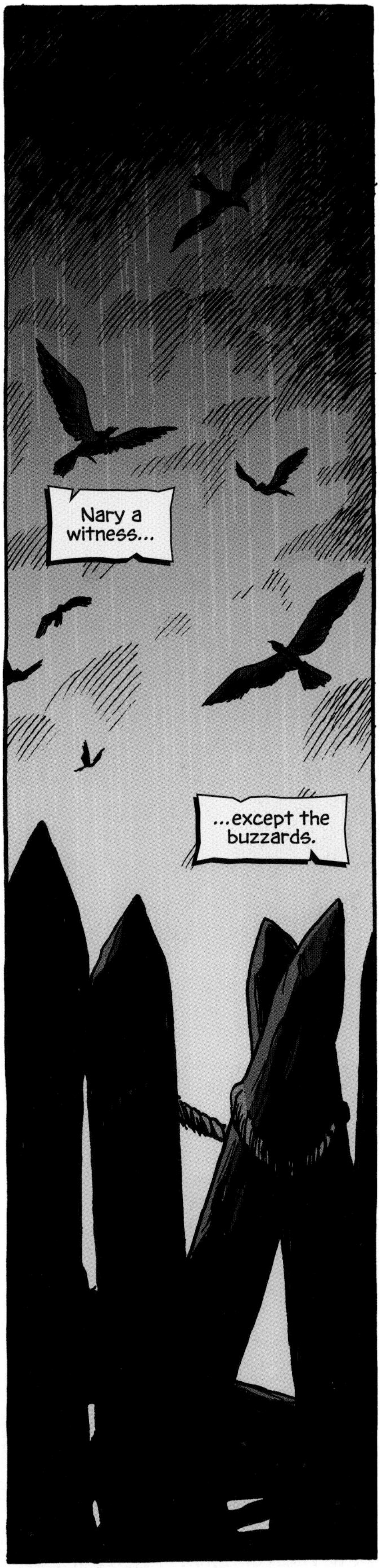
Nary a witness...
...except the buzzards.

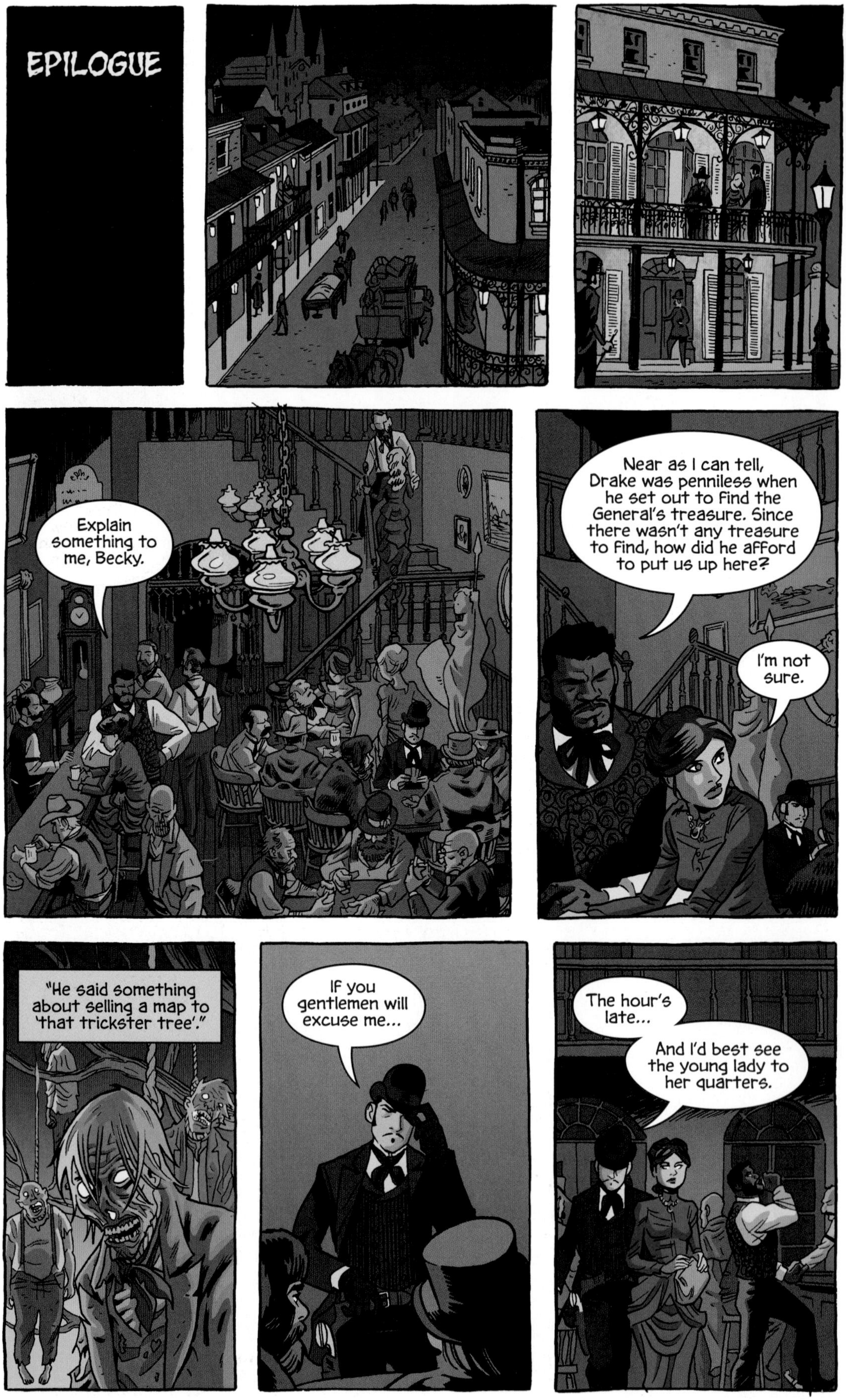
EPILOGUE
Explain something to me, Becky.
Near as I can tell, Drake was penniless when he set out to find the General's treasure. Since there wasn't any treasure to find, how did he afford to put us up here?
I'm not sure.
"He said something about selling a map to 'that trickster tree'."
If you gentlemen will excuse me...
The hour's late...
And I'd best see the young lady to her quarters.

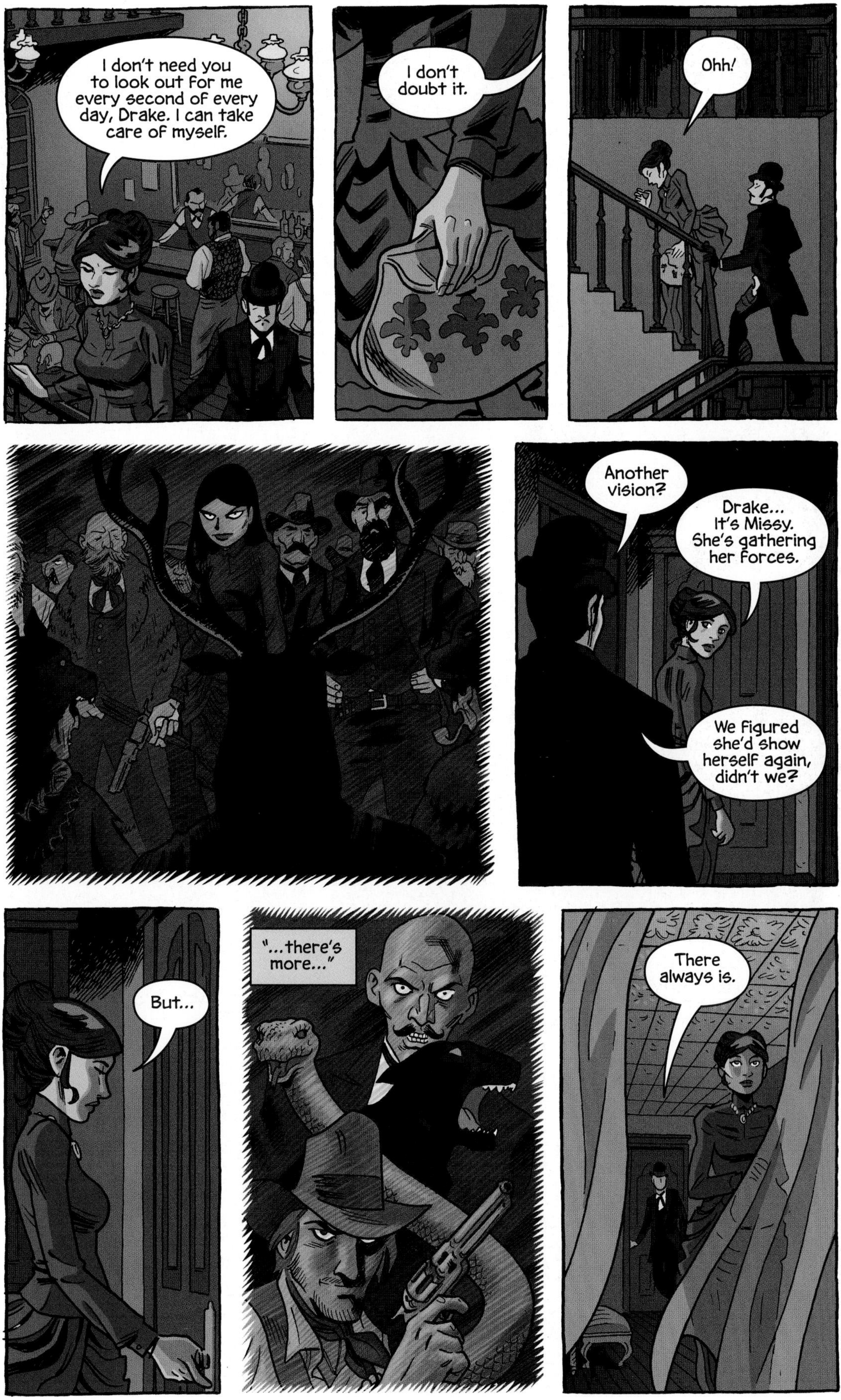
I don't need you to look out for me every second of every day, Drake. I can take care of myself.
I don't doubt it.
Ohh!
Another vision?
Drake... It's Missy. She's gathering her forces.
We figured she'd show herself again, didn't we?
But...
"...there's more..."
There always is.

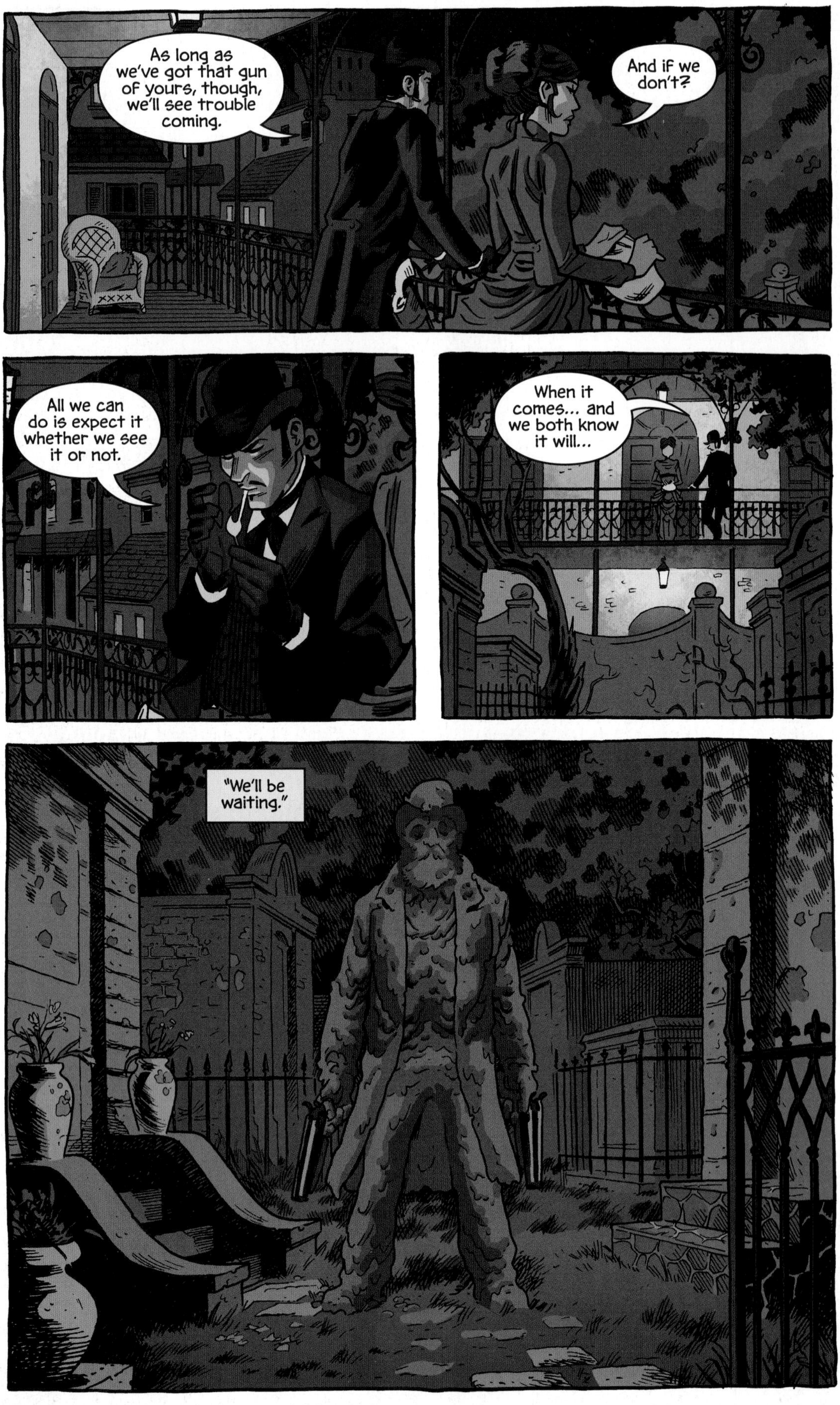
As long as we've got that gun of yours, though, we'll see trouble coming.
And if we don't?
All we can do is expect it whether we see it or not.
When it comes... and we both know it will...
"We'll be waiting."

# THE SIXTH GUN

ADVENTURE CONTINUES...

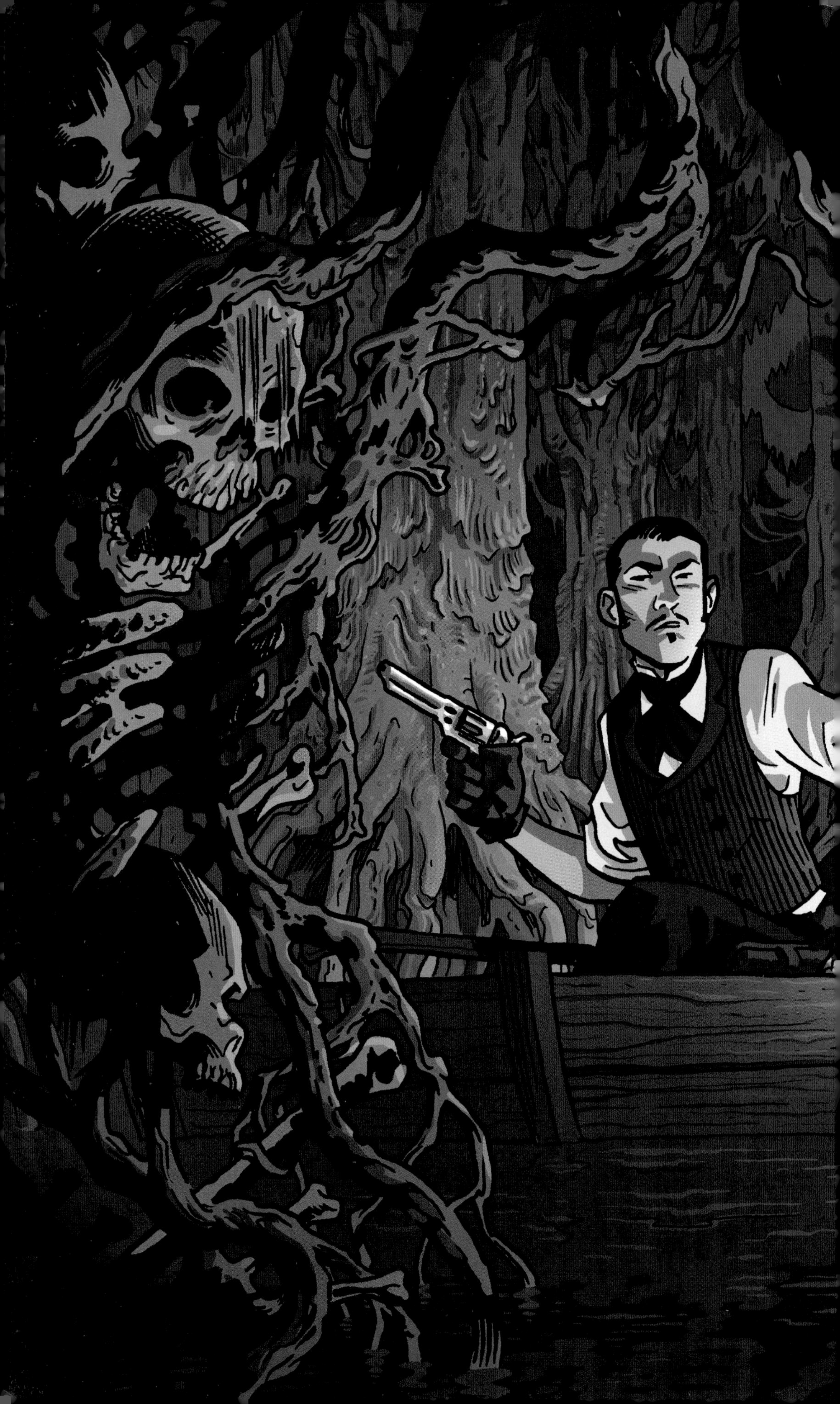

# THE ADVENTURE CONTINUES EVERY MONTH!

The Battle of the Maw is over, and Drake Sinclair and Becky Montcrief have claimed five of The Six. But old and new enemies alike are beginning to sense that the cursed weapons have resurfaced, and the true purpose of the cursed six-shooters remains unrevealed. The wheels of a war beyond anything imaginable are beginning to turn, and the dark forces in this world and the next are beginning to stir.

From the hustle and bustle of the Crescent City to the blackest heart of the Louisiana bog, Drake strives to uncover the secrets of The Six, and the mystery leads him into a web of voodoo, enraged spirits, shifty gunslingers, man-eating beasts, and a power that could very well end the world...

*Follow the continuing adventures of Drake Sinclair, Becky Montcrief, Gord Cantrell, Billjohn O'Henry, and The Six in the ongoing monthly series from Oni Press! Available at finer comic book shops everywhere!*

Cullen Bunn grew up in rural North Carolina, but now lives in the St. Louis area with his wife Cindy and Jackson, his son. His noir/horror comic (and first collaboration with Brian Hurtt), *The Damned*, was published in 2007 by Oni Press. The follow-up, *The Damned: Prodigal Sons*, was released in 2008. In addition to *The Sixth Gun*, his current projects include *The Tooth*, an original graphic novel from Oni Press; *Crooked Hills*, a middle reader horror prose series from Evileye Books; and various work for Marvel and DC. Somewhere along the way, Cullen founded Undaunted Press and edited the critically acclaimed small press horror magazine, *Whispers from the Shattered Forum*.

All writers must pay their dues, and Cullen has worked various odd jobs, including Alien Autopsy Specialist, Rodeo Clown, Professional Wrestler Manager, and Sasquatch Wrangler.

And, yes, he has fought for his life against mountain lions and he did perform on stage as the World's Youngest Hypnotist. Buy him a drink sometime, and he'll tell you all about it.

Visit his website at www.cullenbunn.com

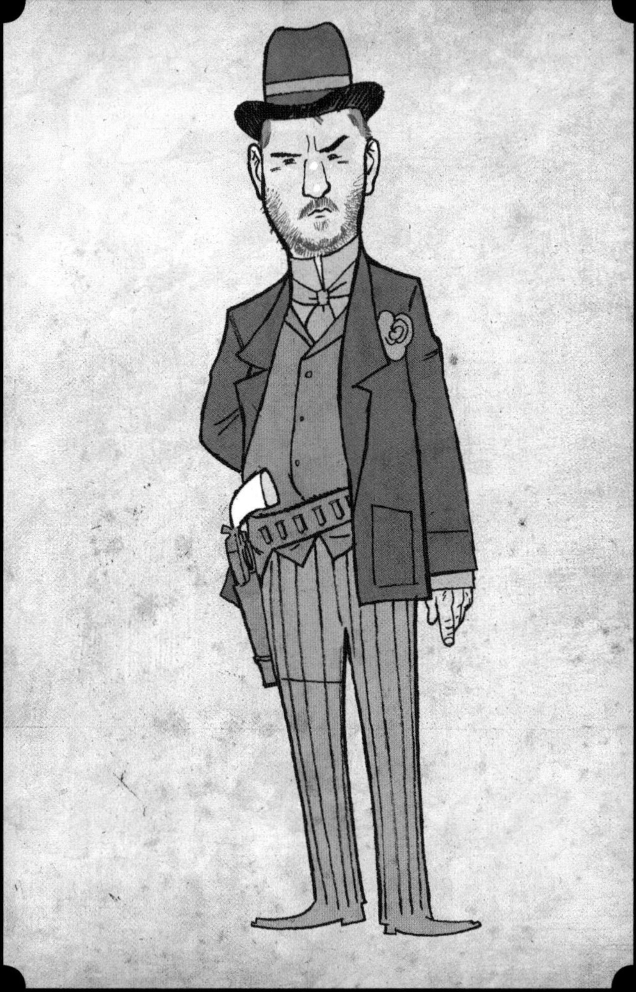

Author portrait illustrations by Jason Latour, jasonlatour.com

Brian Hurtt got his start in comics pencilling the second arc of Greg Rucka's *Queen & Country*. This was followed by art duties on several projects including *Queen & Country: Declassified*, *Three Strikes*, and Steve Gerber's critically acclaimed series *Hard Time*.

In 2006, Brian teamed with Cullen Bunn to create the Prohibition-era monster-noir sensation *The Damned*. The two found that their unique tastes and storytelling sensibilities were well-suited to one another and were eager to continue that relationship.

*The Sixth Gun* is their sophomore endeavor together and the next in what looks to be many years of creative collaboration.

Brian lives in St. Louis where the summers are too hot, the winters too cold, but the rent is just right.

*He can be found online at thebhurttlocker.blogspot.com.*

# From Cullen Bunn, Brian Hurtt & Oni Press...

THE SIXTH GUN
CULLEN BUNN
BRIAN HURTT
BILL CRABTREE

THE SIXTH GUN
CULLEN BUNN
BRIAN HURTT
TYLER CROOK
BILL CRABTREE

**THE SIXTH GUN, VOLUME 2: CROSSROADS**
By Cullen Bunn & Brian Hurtt
136 pages • Trade Paperback
Color • $19.99
ISBN 978-1-934964-67-5

**THE SIXTH GUN, VOLUME 3: BOUND**
By Cullen Bunn & Brian Hurtt
with Tyler Crook
136 pages • Trade Paperback
Color • $19.99
ISBN 978-1-934964-78-1

THE SIXTH GUN
CULLEN BUNN
BRIAN HURTT
A TOWN CALLED PENANCE
TYLER CROOK
BILL CRABTREE

DAMNED
VOLUME ONE
"THREE DAYS DEAD"

**THE SIXTH GUN, VOLUME 4: A TOWN CALLED PENANCE**
By Cullen Bunn & Brian Hurtt
168 pages • Trade Paperback
Color • $19.99
ISBN 978-1-934964-95-8

**THE DAMNED: VOLUME 1**
By Cullen Bunn & Brian Hurtt
160 pages • 6"x9" • Trade Paperback
Black and White • $14.99 US
ISBN 978-1-932664-6-38

the Tooth
A New Beginning!
The Tooth Unleashed!

PETROGRAD
PHILIP GELATT • TYLER CROOK

**THE TOOTH**
By Cullen Bunn, Shawn Lee, and Matt Kindt
184 pages • Hardcover
Color • $24.99
ISBN 978-1-934964-52-1

**PETROGRAD**
By Philp Gelatt & Tyler Crook
264 pages • 6"x9" Hardcover
2-Color • $29.99
ISBN 978-1-934964-44-6

GREG RUCKA
QUEEN & COUNTRY
DEFINITIVE EDITION
VOLUME 01

WASTELAND
ANTONY JOHNSTON
CHRISTOPHER MITTEN
BOOK 01
CITIES IN DUST

**QUEEN & COUNTRY DEFINITIVE EDITION: VOLUME 1**
By Greg Rucka with Steve Rolston, Brian Hurtt, and Leandro Fernandez
366 pages • 6"x9" • Trade Paperback
Black and White • $19.99
ISBN 978-1-932664-87-4

**WASTELAND: VOLUME 1**
By Antony Johnston & Christopher Mitten
160 pages • Trade Paperback
Black and White • $11.99
ISBN 978-1-932664-59-1

ONI PRESS
REVOLUTIONIZE COMICS
www.onipress.com

*For more information on these and other fine Oni Press comic books and graphic novels visit www.onipress.com. To find a comic specialty store in your area visit www.comicshops.us.*

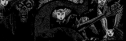

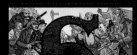